In my mind this was written
for all mums and daughters
especially those I hold dearest:

S. McE, S. S, F. McE & S. (Mc)S

In my heart it's all about Delilah.

allegra m^cevedy

Big Table BUSY kitchen

Quercus

contents

1 It Begins with Baking — 10

2 Broke & Bored — 44

3 The New Worker — 66

4 Impressing the Pants Off — 88

5 Just the Two of Us — 106

6 The Art of Entertaining PART 1 — 132

7 Soup: Theory & Practice — 158

8	Bun in the Oven	190
9	Family Favourites	208
10	Nursery Puddings	240
11	A Week of Sundays	262
12	The Art of Entertaining PART 2	288
13	Grown-up Puds & Small Sweet Treats	324

Appendices
Eggs, Spuds, Veg & the Final Few | 352

Index & Thanks | 375

When my sister and I were growing up, the most reached-for book on our mum's cookery book shelf was a rather tatty orange photo album, which contained all her favourite recipes. It was split into sections starting with hors d'oeuvres and hot starters going right through to cakes and rich puddings, each page with a stencil of a little blue flower at the top. Most recipes were cut out of newspapers or magazines, though some were copied out by hand. Often they had notes scribbled in her distinctive scrawl, notes that made me smile with familiarity after she'd died. She loved cooking, especially puddings, and was regarded by her friends as rather talented, in a homely way.

In our house, food and mealtimes were central to our lives. On Saturday mornings over a vat of coffee, Mama would write out the suppers and subsequent shopping list for the week to come before dispatching me and my dad to the local shops.

The only remaining page of my mum's recipe book

Later in the afternoon, after I had spent a good hour arranging the weekly fruit bowl (think 18th-century still life), my favourite activity was sitting at the kitchen table, turning to the cake section in that beloved orange recipe book and then making a mess of myself and the kitchen (some things never change).

Jump forward: I was a chef and had been for over 15 years; my mum had been dead for nearly 20 (she died when I was 17). The now supremely tatty photo album/recipe collection had become a deeply symbolic embodiment of my relationship with my mum. After all, this album represented all her favourite food, and I now cooked for a living. Cooking was a love that we shared and a link to one another, even though one of us was no longer here.

About this time I was working on a cookbook of my own. I turned to my mum's recipe book for inspiration and took it in to show my publisher. I nervously agreed to leave it behind, but only after explaining its exact meaning to me: quite simply, it was one of the three things I would grab if the house were on fire. Possibly the first.

The next day my mobile went: Mum's cookbook had gone. Forever. Not just gone, but it was halfway up the Thames on a barge heading for landfill. It had been put under a desk for safekeeping but the cleaners had come in the night and found Mum's cookbook in all its loved scruffiness, presumably in the vicinity of the bin, and had accidentally taken it away as rubbish. There was nothing to be done. Despite all apology, it was gone.

On that street in Shepherd's Bush where I'd answered my phone, I went through all the steps of grief: denial, anger, guilt and some others mostly based around screaming, crying and some fairly potent name-calling. And then, as with grief for a person, you just settle into getting used to not having this thing in your life any more. You learn to live with it, or rather, without it.

Seven years on, and I've had a daughter of my own. Delilah is many wonderful things, but a good sleeper she is not. One night she was in my bed, aged about 18 months. Even though I was nearly broken with exhaustion after she had drifted off, I lay awake at 4am. The strength of feeling for her at that moment was overwhelming. Just looking at her previously upset little body now sleeping peacefully and breathing steadily all cuddled up to me – her security – brought first my mum and then, randomly, Mum's recipe book into my mind. And there and then, in that special blue light of early dawn, I decided to write down my culinary legacy for my daughter, to ensure that when the day comes that I won't be here for her any more, my maternal love for her in recipe form always will be. And the best way I knew to make sure it didn't meet the same fate as my mum's cookbook was to get it published, to ensure there was more than one copy. Over the next few weeks, the more I thought about it, the more important the whole idea of a 'cookbook for life' seemed, not just for my own child, but for anybody who needs a bit of friendly guidance as their culinary needs evolve through each stage in their life. My daughter may or may not grow up to enjoy cooking, but if she does, this book will give her a bespoke and carefully deliberated starter pack of ideas … whether I'm around or not.

I feel hugely lucky that my current work life is based largely at home, cooking and inventing recipes. This means that my small daughter has spent a fair amount of time since birth sitting at first on, but now at, our kitchen table, watching me as I chop, sift, roll and fold. It may not be health and safety central but she's interested and I like having her there. Similarly, early memories of my young life are very much based around a big table in a busy kitchen. The recipes in this book are therefore understandably my family's legacy, and in turn my culinary advice to my daughter for her life in food. But really are we all so different? It doesn't matter who you talk to or where you are in the world, everybody has fond memories of magical foods cooked by mums or aunties, dads or grannies that live on long after the loved-one has gone. Tastes that are etched not only in our minds but in our hearts.

A good number of the recipes I've put in here come from stages of my life where I was a happy recipient at family meals, rather than the cook. Inevitably though, both in my work and personal life, I've come across some belters that I just HAD to pass on to my daughter: some recipes are from friends, others from restaurants I've worked in, a few I've picked up on my travels and some are meals-as-mum. Whether or not they were my ideas to start with, I've certainly made them mine, as what's most important to me is that my daughter knows that this is all food I've loved and worked on for her, with her future in mind; these are all bespoke from Mama ... except for those much-loved hand-me-downs which are sacrosanct to my chef's tweaking instinct.

Once I'd mentally committed to this 'cookbook for life' and was at the stage of space-staring and silent musing that I've come to understand is an important part of

Me, Mama and Floss

book-writing, the more I thought about it, the more there seemed to be only one natural way to structure it. So, it begins with baking, as that's where most toddlers start to get involved in the kitchen. The next big landmarks hold the reader's hand through leaving home, the first Serious Job, suppers to seduce, recipes I found useful in pregnancy, family favourites and so on, finishing with a climactic 'Huzzah' with those sometimes tricky but all-important celebration meals. The idea is that whatever life stage you're at (short of the puréed stuff that happens at the beginning and end of our lives, which I felt wouldn't make for joyful reading), this book will always be there for you, to support you and help you in much the same way that your mum, and indeed mine, might have.

The pudding you remember your gran making won't be the same as mine, but hopefully it will jog a few memories and get you thinking about those taste memories that mean so much to you, for whatever reason. So take the recipes in this book and scratch a few notes in the margin – or even better, write yours in too and begin your own family culinary legacy.

it Begins with Baking

BAKING is an almost universal first kitchen adventure, whether simply sitting at the kitchen table watching or helping with the stirring, sieving and pouring. Whenever I roll out pastry, the sound of my rings clacking on the rolling pin instantly takes me back to those times when I was a small child, watching my mum perform her magic; it's the same rolling pin too.

From experience, both in my own childhood and from cooking with lots and lots of kids, including my own daughter, first forays into baking are generally things like fairy cakes, jam tarts, cookies and gingerbread people. And because children love personalisation and ownership, these sort of bakes are ideal because kids can decorate and customise them to their hearts' content. Later on in childhood we upscale to whole cakes, and the joys of icing are magnified to a larger scale. My earliest successes in winning friends with food were based around a Never-fail Victoria Sponge recipe in my mum's cookbook, laden with cream and strawberries, which I used to make for my mates' birthdays. (It's on page 26, so your children can win friends with food too!)

A lot of baking involves flour, of course, and to children there's something intensely fun in all that farinaceousness. Not only does it make for legitimate messiness, but flour is the starting point for so many treats they know and love: bread, biscuits, scones, cake and beyond. And that really is magic. I clearly remember the day that my daughter and I had our first flour-fest. I was making empanada dough; she was making a mess. We were both intently immersed in our own worlds, me standing next to the kitchen table and her sitting on it. Two independently busy people, heads down, having fun, and I had one of those life-affirming 'it may not be perfect, but it's perfect for now' moments.

As a parent, I think the attraction for baking with my daughter is largely based around the low-level risk assessment: there aren't many heat/pan/fear factors involved in baking until the goodies disappear into the oven. You can also bet with almost absolute certainty that what emerges will be met with delight. For whatever reason, though, life in the kitchen generally begins with baking.

Apple Snow

As you'll see from this recipe, life in the kitchen technically begins with mixing, not baking. This and Peppermint Creams, over the page, were the first recipes I ever 'cooked'. Having not made apple snow for the best part of 40 years I was pleasantly surprised at how well it stood the test of time. It's light and frothy like syllabub and, as with all puds of this nature, is best eaten as soon as it's had time to settle – a scant half hour.

Makes enough for 4

5 Granny Smith apples, peeled,
    cored and each cut into 8
80g demerara sugar
2 egg whites
1 tbsp caster sugar

Put the apple pieces in a heavy-bottomed saucepan with the sugar and a few tablespoons of water. Stick a lid on and bring it all to a simmer, then take the lid off and stir occasionally as the liquid evaporates so you are left with an apple purée.

Depending on how much of a hurry you're in, either leave to cool in the pan or spread out to cool on a baking tray: whichever way, it needs to be completely cold before you go on or you'll cook your egg whites.

When your purée is cold, whisk the egg whites and once they form nice, soft peaks, sprinkle over the sugar and whisk a bit more until the peaks are firm and glossy. Stir in the apple purée in three goes: beat the first lot into the whites completely to soften them a bit. Fold in the second batch carefully and only fold the last lot once or twice so there are still streaks of apple.

Spoon into your vessels – we always used to have it in jam jars – or tuck straight into the bowl, though ideally chill in the fridge for 30 minutes or so first to firm up.

Peppermint Creams

Like After Eights for beginners, these are sticky, sugary fun for little ones, especially when clouds of icing sugar rise out of the bowl like an Icelandic volcano.

Makes about 20 of a smallish size (which is what I'd recommend as they're basically wall-to-wall sugar)

1 egg white
350g icing sugar, plus extra
    for rolling
2 tsp lemon juice
1 tsp peppermint essence
100g dark chocolate (optional
    but encouraged)

Whisk the egg white to soft peaks, then, tapping it through a sieve, add the icing sugar and use a wooden spoon to gently bring it all together.

Stir in the lemon juice and peppermint essence. You should now have a soft white ball. If it's very soft, stick it in the fridge for a few minutes, but if you are ready to roll, storm on by chucking quite a lot more icing sugar on a work surface.

Roll the mixture out to about 2cm thick, and use any cutter you have to make your shapes. Move them on to another tray, also dusted heavily with icing sugar, and this time stick them in the fridge as there's a bit of handling to be done at the next stage. Re-roll the off-cuts and use them to make more shapes.

Melt the chocolate in a heatproof bowl set over a saucepan of steaming water, making sure the bottom of the bowl doesn't touch the water (this is known as a bain marie). When ready, pick up the creams and dip either a part or the whole of them in the chocolate. Sit them on some greaseproof paper and leave to set somewhere cool, but not in the fridge.

Store in an airtight container, but in reality they won't need a whole lot of storing!

Cheese Columns (to make a Parthenon)

When I was a child, I once spent most of a summer making a model of the Parthenon out of plasticine. It may well have been my proudest moment, but when I took it in to school it wobbled, bent and ultimately collapsed some hours later in the heat of the classroom. I can't pinpoint exactly which part of my subconscious brought this back to mind as I contemplated cheese straws for this book, but in it flew, and the gauntlet was thrown down. The recipe here is for the cheese straws, but you can attempt any architecture you should wish.

Makes lots: about 25–30, but my how they fly

400g puff pastry
1 beaten egg
80g cheese, finely grated
(a combo works well:
Gruyère, Parmesan, Comté
and Mimolette, for colour)

Preheat the oven to 200°C/fan 180°C/Gas 6.

Roll your pastry out to a rectangle roughly 40 x 30cm and about 3mm thick. Brush all over with the beaten egg, then sprinkle over the grated cheese.

Run the rolling pin over it a couple of times to embed the cheese, then cut from the shorter edge into strips 1–2cm thick.

Pick the strips up one at a time and twist each, giving it a little tug to stretch it as you go. Lay it down on a baking tray and push both ends into the tray a bit to stick and secure. Bake 8 at a time – you only want to have one tray at a time in the oven on the top shelf. Meanwhile, get on with preparing the next tray.

Cook each batch for 12–15 minutes, until golden and the unmistakeable smell of cheese and pastry fills your kitchen. Leave to cool for a few minutes as they will then come off the tray more easily – they're fairly fragile fellows. Best eaten warm, unless you feel a Parthenon coming on …

Crunch-topped Banana Bread

This, and Dried Bananas (see page 374) are the best way I know to conquer the brown, spotty banana that is rife in fruit bowls up and down our land. It's more fun than most 'nana breads due to the sugar and spice topping, not to mention those naughty chocolate bits.

Makes 8–10 nice slices

100g butter, melted
180g plain flour
2 tsp baking powder
½ tsp salt
150g soft light brown sugar
2 eggs
3 large ripe Fairtrade bananas, roughly mashed
50g walnuts, chopped
40g chocolate buttons
1 tsp vanilla extract

For the topping:
2 tbsp demerara sugar
½ tsp ground cinnamon
¼ tsp ground/few scrapings nutmeg

Preheat the oven to 170°C/fan 150°C/Gas 3½, and grease and line a 900g loaf tin (about 23 x 13 x 7cm).

Put the melted butter in a big bowl. In a smaller bowl, mix the flour, baking powder and salt.

Stir the brown sugar into the butter, then beat in the eggs one at a time. Mix in the banana, walnuts, chocolate and vanilla, then in three stages add the dry ingredients, beating after each addition so that it's properly incorporated. Tip into the loaf tin.

For the topping, give your little bowl a quick wipe, then mix together the sugar with the spice (and all things nice) and sprinkle over the top.

Bake for 1 hour, then test by inserting a skewer into the centre; if the bread is done it should come out clean. If not, give it another 5–10 minutes and then test again. Leave to cool on a rack for 15 minutes before slicing.

Clockwise from top left:
Crunch-topped Banana Bread,
Samson & Delilah Flajacks,
Marshmallow Toffee Crispies

Marshmallow Toffee Crispies

The ingredients list says it all. Kids go absolutely nuts for these marshmallow crispies, and they're a marked improvement on the simple ones of my youth. All hail the crunch and chew. Oh, and the sugar.

Makes about 20 gorgeous piles of goo (see photo, page 18)

200g marshmallows
200g toffees
200g butter
175g Rice Krispies
50g milk chocolate, melted
    (if you fancy doing some
    patterns on top)

In a heatproof bowl set over a pan of steaming water (making sure the bottom of the bowl doesn't touch the water), melt the marshmallows, toffees and butter. There will be a really sticky moment when it looks like it's all split, but then it magically comes back together.

Stir in the Rice Krispies, then spoon into fairy-cake cases and leave to set – a matter of minutes. Drizzle with melted chockie if you fancy (see page 14 if you need help here).

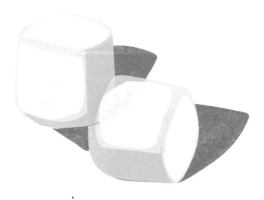

Samson & Delilah Flapjacks

Atora suet, Camp Coffee, Bird's Custard Powder, Lea & Perrins, Colman's Mustard and Lyle's Golden Syrup: all are graced with iconic British packaging, but it was that shiny gold and green syrup pot that was particularly intriguing to the young me, with its 'lion and bees' and its words from the Bible: 'Out of the strong came forth sweetness'. 'What does it mean again?', I'd ask our mum, and she would smile and once again tell the story of Samson and the Lion. Golden syrup is key to a good flapjack, so that's the Samson part. Delilah, well that's just for me ... or rather, for her.

Makes 12 chewy ones (see photo, page 18)

200g butter
3 tbsp demerara sugar
4 tbsp golden syrup
2 tbsp black treacle or molasses
a pinch of salt
300g rolled oats
150g dried fruit (such as dates, apricots, prunes), roughly chopped
zest of 1 large orange
50g whole almonds, skin on, VERY roughly chopped
a splash of sunflower or vegetable oil, to grease

Preheat the oven to 170°C/fan 150°C/Gas 3½. Lay your hands on a baking tray about 20 x 20cm and line it with lightly oiled greaseproof paper.

Put the butter, sugar, golden syrup, treacle and salt in a heavy-bottomed saucepan. Bring quickly to a simmer then take off the heat and stir in the oats, fruit, orange zest and nuts and give it all a proper roll around with a wooden spoon. Spoon the mix into the tray, then lightly press it down with the back of the spoon. Bake for 30 minutes on the middle shelf. When you take it out, leave it for a couple of minutes before cutting into squares while still in the tin.

Allow the flapjacks to cool pretty much completely before lifting out.

Gingerbread Families **for our Times**

I had to include a recipe for gingerbread. It's an absolute classic that has made children happy for decades, but in true feminist spirit, I made these equal-opportunity gingerbread people. So, this recipe goes out there to all and any minorities – you're all welcome on my bus. For your own multi-cultural crowd, split the recipe and make half with cocoa powder and half without.

Makes 25 adults of various sexual orientations OR 40 kids of multi-racial origins
OR 50 biscuits, some of which come from broken homes

350g plain flour
2 tsp ground ginger
½ tsp ground cinnamon
1 tsp bicarbonate of soda
2 tbsp cocoa powder (optional; for mixed-race families)
125g butter, cubed into roughly 20 pieces
100g soft light brown sugar
1 egg
6 tbsp golden syrup

For decoration:
Writing Icing squeezy tubes, sugar strands and stars, silver balls, Smarties

Preheat the oven to 180°C/fan 160°C/Gas 4.

In a big bowl, mix together the flour, spices and bicarb, add the cocoa powder if using, then rub in the butter until you have the consistency of breadcrumbs before stirring in the sugar.

In a separate bowl, beat the egg with the syrup and then mix into the dry ingredients using a wooden spoon until it just comes together. Tip out and press it until it comes together into a ball.

Lightly flour your work surface and roll out the dough to about 5mm thick (but not any thicker), then have fun with your cookie cutters. Ball up the off-cuts and roll them out again – it's a pretty forgiving dough.

Bake the biscuits for 6–8 minutes – they should still be soft and the lighter-skinned ones will go golden brown. Decorate as soon as they come out the oven, so they stick easily to the warm dough.

To make a bus and occupants like this ⇨ double all the quantities and buy plenty of royal icing and sweeties!

Lemon Curd Tarts ... and a Few Jammies

Little tarts are lovely, joyful and childish in the best possible way. Lemon curd has the edge for me, but for kiddies jam is the thing, so I tend to do a tray of each. Move over Mr Kipling.

Makes 12 tarts, or 250g lemon curd if that's all you're interested in

200g shortcrust pastry
(bought or see page 370)

For the lemon curd:
2 eggs, plus 1 yolk
100g caster sugar
zest and juice of 3 lemons
30g butter, softened

Or for jam tarts:
250–275g red jam (ideally
home-made, see page 371)

To make the curd, put the eggs, yolk, sugar, lemon zest and juice into a heatproof bowl and whisk them all together. Sit the bowl over a saucepan of steaming water, making sure the bowl doesn't touch the water. Whisk pretty regularly for the first 5 minutes, then as it starts to thicken, stir with a spatula.

After 10–15 minutes of constant attention, the mix should be smooth, thick and glossy. Check it's at setting consistency by holding up the spatula and dragging your finger through the curd: if it doesn't drip down through the track left behind, then it's ready.

Take the pan off the heat and stir in the butter in small knobs, then pass the curd through a sieve into a bowl and leave to cool to room temperature.

Preheat the oven to 180°C/fan 160°C/Gas 4 and grease the holes of a fairy cake tin. Lightly flour your work surface and roll out the shortcrust thinly, to just a couple of millimetres. Cut discs of pastry to fit into the holes in the tin – an 8cm cutter should be about right. Gently but firmly push a disc into each hole, then put the tray in the fridge to rest for 20 minutes.

Once rested, you need to blind bake the tart cases: prick the bottom of each case with a fork, sit a paper fairy cake case in each one and fill with baking beans (see page 370): the paper case makes it easier to lift out the beans. Bake for 12 minutes then take out the beans and paper cases and bake for another 5–7 minutes until the bases are golden and feel dry.

Leave to cool before filling with the lemon curd and/or jam. Pop just the jammy ones back in the oven for a minute or two for the jam to melt, level out and get a bit of a skin.

Lemon Curd Tarts and a Few Jammies

Never-fail Victoria Sponge

Butterfly Cakes

Squashed Fly Scones

Never-fail Victoria Sponge

This is a picture-perfect, light and tasty sponge, which as the name suggests is impossible to screw up. It is also the most important recipe in this book by a country mile. As I said in my introduction, the inspiration for this book comes from my mum's treasured recipe collection. To my devastation, Mama's book was lost a few years ago. But for some reason a couple of months earlier, I'd scanned in one batter-spattered page, which now hangs framed in my kitchen. On it was this recipe, which I'd turned to again and again as a youngster. That page is all that I have left of Mum's bespoke recipe collection, and although I still have a great many of her cookbooks, I'd swap them all like a shot for the rest of her lost book, because, as we all know, home-made is beyond price.

Makes a stunning 23cm cake; cuts into about 10 good slices (see photo, previous page)

6 eggs
3 tbsp whole milk
350g caster sugar
350g self-raising flour, sifted
3 tsp baking powder
a big pinch of salt
180g butter, melted, plus extra
    for greasing
170ml double cream
a few tbsp icing sugar, for filling
    and dusting
170g red jam (buy a decent
    one or use home-made,
    see page 371)

Grease and line two 23cm round cake tins with greaseproof paper and preheat the oven to 180°C/fan 160°C/Gas 4.

Either by hand or with a mixer, beat the eggs, milk and caster sugar until pale and fluffy. Sift together the flour, baking powder and salt and gently fold into the egg mixture. Stir in the melted butter, then divide between the prepared tins.

Bake for 22–25 minutes, until a skewer comes out clean and the cakes are slightly domed and golden on top. Leave to cool completely in the tin.

When you're ready to build, whip the cream to soft peaks with a tablespoon of icing sugar. Flip one cake over so the top is underneath and put it on a serving plate. Spread with jam, then cover with cream. Lay the second cake on top, domed-side up. Dust with copious icing sugar.

**To make
Butterfly Cakes**

Halve the quantities for about 15 cakes.

Spoon the mix into a muffin tin lined with paper fairy-cake cases and bake for 12–15 minutes. Once cool, cut off the tops, slice the off-cuts in half and flip over to make wings. Stick on with Vanilla Buttercream (see page 32) and decorate with sprinkles or silver balls.

Squashed Fly Scones

It's a bit of a jump from Italian hero of the Risorgimento to a rectangular brittle biscuit, but garibaldis – aka squashed fly biscuits – were an important part of this chef's young life. They're hard to replicate at home, so I've taken the most important part (the flies) and put them in a new carrier (the scone), though this means they're technically a bit less squashed now.

Makes 16–20 (see photo, page 25)

400g plain flour
1 tbsp baking powder
½ tsp bicarbonate of soda
a pinch of salt
3 tbsp caster sugar
100g cold butter, cubed into
    roughly 15–20 pieces
100g currants
1 egg
100ml whole milk, plus a splash
    more
50ml double cream
a splash of sunflower or
    vegetable oil, to grease

To serve:
red jam, ideally home-made
    (see page 371) or use a
    decent shop-bought one
clotted cream

Preheat the oven to 180°C/fan 160°C/Gas 4.

In a big bowl, stir the first five ingredients briefly together, then rub the butter in with your fingertips until it all looks like breadcrumbs. Now mix in the currants.

In a jug, whisk the egg with the milk and cream, then make a well in the middle of the dry ingredients and pour in the wet. Use a big fork to just combine them, adding a splash more milk if necessary – you're looking for a soft, almost sticky dough, and really you only want it to just come together (overmixing will really naff them up).

Flour your surface and pat the dough out to about 4cm thick. Use a 5–6cm fluted cutter to cut out the scones, remembering not to twist it, otherwise you'll muck up the ridges up the side, then flip them over and sit them about 3cm apart on a lightly greased baking tray.

Brush the tops (but NOT the sides) lightly with milk and bake for 18–20 minutes – don't worry about opening the door too much, these chaps aren't super-fussy.

Serve with the obligatory jam and clotted cream.

Liz at No. 24's Chinese Sausage Rolls

One of the most battered books on my mum's cookery shelf was Jane Grigson's *English Food*, which for some reason always fell open to a recipe for Chinese Yorkshire pudding. I don't remember my mum ever making it, but the rather odd concept lodged in my pre-pubescent head, only to emerge a quarter of a century later when my fabulous neighbour Liz handed me some of her Chinese-style sausage rolls through the garden trellis. It spurred me on to find Jane's recipe, which I was more than a little disappointed to discover was Chinese only by virtue of the chef, Mr Tin Sung Chan (who won the 1970 Great Yorkshire Pudding Competition in Leeds), and not because of his ingredients. He did include '½ tsp tai luk', but no such thing actually exists – it's a slang word for 'homeland'.

Liz's Sino-attack on a native classic is exactly the opposite: its English creator added some indisputably Far Eastern ingredients. My daughter excitedly says, 'little bit spicy' as she crams them into her mouth!

Makes about 25–30 cute little ones

400g lean sausage meat (ideally over 95% meat – if in sausage form, squeeze from the skins)

1–2 tsp chilli powder or flakes, depending on how hot you like it

1–2 tsp Chinese five spice (depending on taste)

3–4 garlic cloves, finely minced

⅔ tsp Chinese chilli oil (or add an extra ½ tsp chilli powder/flakes and ¼ tsp shrimp paste melted in a little warm sesame oil)

500g puff pastry (pre-rolled is fine)

1 egg, beaten with a splash of milk

a few sesame seeds

S & P

Preheat the oven to 200°C/fan 180°C/Gas 6. In a bowl, mix together the sausage meat, chilli powder, five spice, garlic, Chinese chilli oil (which contains shrimp paste, or use the shrimp paste option – either way, shrimp paste is essential to the taste here) and plenty of seasoning.

Roll out the pastry to about 5mm thick: you're aiming for a long rectangle 10cm across; it doesn't matter how long it is as you're going to cut it up. Put the meat in a line down the middle, to around the thickness of a chipolata, then brush the egg wash on to the pastry and fold it over. Make sure the join is sealed, and turn the roll over so the seam is underneath.

Cut your long sausage roll into little ones (Liz uses scissors for this and does cute baby ones about 4cm long), then score each one lightly on top about three times and move on to a baking tray.

Brush the outsides with the egg wash, then sprinkle over the sesame seeds. Bake for 17–22 minutes until they look golden brown and seriously desirable. Hold off eating them for a few minutes after they come out the oven, but definitely get in there while they're still warm.

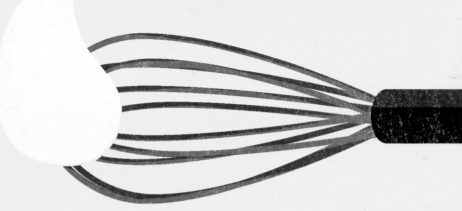

Chocolate Fudge Icing

Thick, soft, gooey and gorgeous; I've yet to meet a kid who doesn't think icing is the best ever entry point to cake world. A sugar thermometer is pretty useful here.

Enough to ice the top of a 23–25cm cake

150ml whole milk
50g dark chocolate (70%
    cocoa solids and Fairtrade
    if possible)
100g caster sugar
50g butter, softened

Top Tip
Chocolate can behave unpredictably, so if it starts to seize when you're incorporating the butter, add a tablespoon at a time of very hot water and beat like mad until smooth. Don't add more than 3 tablespoons, though, or the icing will be too loose.

Heat the milk in a pan over a medium heat, then stir in the chocolate and sugar. Once the chocolate has melted, crank up the heat until the mixture reaches the 'soft ball stage' – your thermometer will read 116°C (it'll whizz up to 100°C, then take a while to get to 110°C, then speed up again to hit 116°C). Or you can test it the old-fashioned way by scooping out a tiny bit of mixture with a teaspoon and dropping it into a small glass of cold water. If the mixture makes a ball, as opposed to splatting all over the water, pick it up and gently squeeze between your thumb and finger – if it squidges satisfyingly it's at the soft ball stage.

When you're happy your potion is ready, take it off the heat and rapidly beat in the butter, a teaspoonful or so at a time, with a wooden spoon, until thick and fudgy. Leave to cool for 10–15 minutes until the icing has thickened up a bit, but is not set solid.

MORE FAB ICINGS ON NEXT PAGE!

Clockwise from top left:
Chocolate Fudge Icing, Citrus Drizzle,
Cream Cheese Icing, Vanilla Buttercream,
Nougat Marshmallow Frosting

Cream Cheese Icing

This rich, creamy icing needs to be made with an electric mixer (either upright or hand-held) to make it fluffy and voluminous. Without the extra volume it won't ice a whole cake, or taste as special. It's particularly good with fruit or spiced cakes, such as ginger or carrot.

Enough to ice the top of a 23–25cm cake

100g butter, at room temperature
110g icing sugar, sifted
300g cream cheese

Beat the butter and icing sugar for a good 7 minutes (using the paddle attachment if you're doing it in an upright mixer) until white and fluffy, scraping down the sides every once in a while.

Tip in the cream cheese and beat for another 5 minutes until the icing is bigger, smoother and even fluffier.

Vanilla Buttercream

Sometimes, simple is best, and this classic is testimony to that – it's the mother of all icings. Like the Cream Cheese Icing above, this is another topping that needs to be made with an electric mixer for extra fluff/volume factor.

Enough to ice the top and sides of a 23–25cm cake

200g butter, at room temperature
100g icing sugar, sifted
1 vanilla pod, seeds scraped out
    (use the pod to make vanilla
    sugar – just bury it in a small
    jam jar of caster sugar)
5 tbsp milk

Using a hand-held or upright electric mixer, beat the butter with the icing sugar and vanilla seeds until pale and airy.

Add the milk a tablespoon at a time, until all incorporated. You need to use the buttercream more or less straight away (don't put it in the fridge or you'll have a hard time when it comes to spreading it).

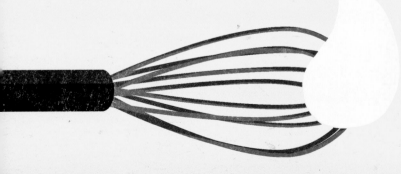

Citrus Drizzle

Tang-tasticly sharp and sweet – and pretty in a gentle way too.

Enough to drizzle over the top and sides of a single-layer 23–25cm cake

zest and juice of ½ lime
zest and juice of ½ lemon
zest and juice of ½ orange
175g icing sugar

Beat everything until smooth and away you go!

Nougat-marshmallow Frosting

There's a bit of a trend for American baking these days (see cookies, cupcakes and the onslaught of cinnamon in our lives), and this one is straight out of their songbook. Thick, shiny and glossy, it's totally fabulous in a slightly Betty Crocker way.

Enough to cover the top and sides of a double-layer 23–25cm cake

4 tbsp clear honey
200g caster sugar
2 egg whites
¼ tsp salt
¼ tsp cream of tartar
¼ tsp vanilla extract

Put the honey, sugar and 50ml water in a heavy-bottomed saucepan and bring to a rolling boil. Boil vigorously for 3–5 minutes until pale and frothy or at the 'soft ball stage' (116°C on a sugar thermometer or see the method for checking in Chocolate Fudge Icing, page 30).

As that's going on, whisk the egg whites with the salt and cream of tartar, either in an upright mixer, or in a large bowl using a hand-held electric mixer. Whisk until soft peaks form.

Turn the speed down and pour the contents of the saucepan into the egg whites in a slow, steady stream (be careful). Once it's all incorporated, turn the speed up again for another 5 minutes and whisk until the mixture is thick and glossy, and the outside of the bowl is almost at body temperature. Add the vanilla essence and whisk again briefly, then get icing. Yum!

Irish Kate's Oaty Soda Bread

Making soda breads requires none of the usual hanging around that is involved in making yeast-based breads – this one's out of the oven within an hour of your gathering the ingredients together. Soda bread works well for kids as they're geared towards immediate gratification, rather than being able to wait throughout the long, slow proving process; they tend to lose interest, get stuck into something else and forget all about the bread by the time it eventually goes into the oven.

This bread is so easy to make and so yummy. It's good for a day or two fresh and then toasts really well. Pile on the salted butter, says Dubliner Kate, my great friend and culinary sounding board.

Makes a lovely loaf of 10–12 slices, or 6–8 good chunks

300g wholemeal flour
300g plain flour
50g rolled oats, plus a few more
    for sprinkling on top
50g fine or ground oats
1 tsp bicarbonate of soda
1 tsp fine salt
300ml buttermilk (available in
    most supermarkets now, or
    just squeeze ½ lemon into
    300ml whole milk and leave
    for a minute)
100ml whole milk, plus a
    potential splash more
2 tbsp clear honey

Preheat the oven to 220°C/fan 200°C/Gas 7.

Mix both flours, both kinds of oats, the bicarb and salt in a big bowl. In a jug, whisk together the buttermilk, milk and honey.

Make a well in the dry ingredients and pour the wet ones into it. Set your hand as if you were pretending to be a scary monster (technically known as 'claw hand') and just bring the dough together, but don't overmix. This shouldn't be a wet dough, but add a splash more milk if it's too dry and not coming together.

Pat the dough into a round, slash the top with a big old 'X', sit it on a greased baking tray and sprinkle over a handful of oats.

Bake for 20 minutes, then turn the heat down to 200°C/fan 180°C/Gas 6, and cook for a further 20–25 minutes or until it sounds hollow when tapped on the bottom. Cool on a wire rack. This is one that tastes better totally cooled to room temperature, so be patient.

Dual Citizenship Pancakes

Although a traditionalist when it comes to pancakes, I believe that there's room for both the classic British flattie that we all grew up with, and the airier stackables that come from over the pond. Indeed, an enduring memory from my first trip to California aged about ten features a restaurant with the best name ever: IHOP – International House of Pancakes. Wowee!

Pancakes have a lot going for them as the perfect food for kids: easy ingredients, a bit of theatre, instant gratification and the sweet hit at the end with favourite fillings or toppings. Once a fortnight I make them for my daughter's breakfast, but they never taste as good as they do on Shrove Tuesday, which as the gods would have it, was the day my mum died.

American Pancakes

My American soulmate Jodi taught me how to make the absolute classic US-style fluffy puffy pancake. They're very much in vogue these days and a great stand-by for kids. The batter needs to be used pretty pronto as the mix doesn't sit, but you can cook and freeze them once cooled, which is useful when you need emergency pancakes – just pop them in the microwave for a minute.

Makes 8 nice-sized ones

150g plain flour
3 tbsp caster sugar
a pinch of salt
1 tsp baking powder
¼ tsp bicarbonate of soda
250ml buttermilk (or see
    ingredients, page 34)
1 egg
a knob of butter

To serve:
maple syrup
berries and/or crispy bacon
whatever else you fancy –
    blueberries, bananas,
    chocolate chips, whipped
    cream (naughty!)

In a big bowl, mix together the dry ingredients, and in a smaller bowl, whisk together the wet. Make a well in the middle of the dry, then pour the wet in and mix them together very briefly with a fork – you really are just barely combining them, the mix should still be a little lumpy.

Heat a heavy-bottomed pan or skillet until it's hot, then turn the heat down to the lowest temperature/ring setting.

Melt the butter, then blob in the pancake mix – make animal shapes if you're feeling good and creative. When you see bubbles appearing on the surface, after 2–3 minutes, flip over and cook for the same amount of time on the other side.

Eat straight away with whatever toppings you fancy: they're never better than they are right now.

BUT IF YOU'RE FEELING BRITISH, PTO...

British Pancakes

Unless you're very deft with your pans, don't try cooking more than one of these pancakes at a time. So either cook and fling them out as soon as they're ready (works fine for breakfast, as long as you're not in too much of a hurry) or keep them warm by popping on to a heatproof plate set over a pan of gently simmering water. As each pancake is done, stack them up on the plate, with a second, upside-down plate over the top to keep the heat in. This requires less energy than heating up a whole oven, and stops them drying out too.

Makes 10ish (see photo, page 36)

2 eggs
a pinch of salt
120g plain flour
400ml milk
50g butter, melted, plus a knob
    for frying

To serve:
lemon and sugar
Nutella and banana (nice with
    a few chopped hazelnuts
    on top too)

Chuck everything into a big bowl and whisk until smooth. Leave to sit for an hour with a tea towel draped over it.

Choose your pan wisely – it needs to be thin, shallow and hopefully have a bit of family history. Melt the butter over a medium heat and as it fizzles run it round the pan and up the sides. Ladle in just enough mixture to form a thin layer on the bottom as you are tipping the pan.

After a minute or two, when the pancake starts to brown around the edge, give it a shuffle to see if it's moving freely; if not, slide your best flippy thing underneath to loosen it.

Now flip away. Chances are you'll have to sacrifice the first one for a cook's snack – it usually works out that way, which is no bad thing. The pancake will need even less time on the second side so give it barely a minute, then tip it out and get on with the next one. There's no need to re-grease between pancakes.

When it comes to scoffing these, personally I'm a lemon and sugar girl, while Delilah prefers the Nutella and 'nana option.

Pizza Dough

I love a good pizza and have written quite a few recipes for pizza dough over the years. However, I'd now like to apologise and say please ignore them and use this one instead. I found this recipe last year and let's just say I'm never going to make my dough any other way again. Sorry!

Makes a 30cm square pizza (square makes more sense spatially in a domestic oven), enough for 6–8 kiddy slices, or 2 adults, or 1 pig-out with a slice left for breakfast

210g plain flour (though it's also good with Italian 'tipo 00' flour if you have any in the house)
1½ tsp (5–6g) fast-action yeast
125ml hot water
1 tbsp olive oil
1 tsp caster sugar
½ tsp salt
semolina, for dusting

Put 70g of the flour and the yeast into a food processor, then start it spinning as you slowly tip in the hot water. As soon as it's come together, turn it off and add the olive oil, sugar, salt and remaining flour, then set it going again. Once combined (this will take less than a minute), tip the dough on to a floured surface and knead for 5ish minutes until it's bouncy and feels like marshmallow.

Wrap in cling film and rest for half an hour for the yeast to kick in. Preheat the oven to 220°C/fan 200°C/Gas 7.

When you're ready to go, sprinkle semolina over the bottom of a square baking tray (35cm or thereabouts), then roll the dough out on a floured surface to 2–3mm thick.

At this stage you'll need to add your chosen toppings – the 15-minute Tomato Sauce on page 369 is an ideal base (you'll only need half a batch) topped by a bit of mozzarella and whatever else you fancy: mushrooms, salami, a cracked egg … and I always like a few rocket leaves on top once it comes out of the oven.

Bake for 10–12 minutes or until the edges are golden and crispy, and the underneath is firm and dry when you lift up a corner.

Peanutty Millionaire's Shortbread

This take on the classic may just be one of my finest baking inventions. Once the chocolate has been added and is cooling, be sure to keep it somewhere out of reach of small paws – I've come back to find little trench marks where someone just couldn't resist the allure of molten chockie.

Makes about 12 good-sized squares

For the base:
splash of sunflower or vegetable oil, for greasing
200g peanuts, roasted, salted and Fairtrade if possible
2 eggs, beaten
100g caster sugar
1 tsp bicarbonate of soda

For the middle:
200g caster sugar
130ml double cream

For the top:
250g milk chocolate

Preheat the oven to 170°C/fan 150°C/Gas 3½. Line a 27 x 22 x 5cm roasting tin or baking tray with lightly oiled greaseproof paper.

Blitz the peanuts in a food processor until they're ground to a combo of powder and little crunchy bits. Mix well with the other base ingredients, then press evenly into the bottom of the prepared tray and bake for 25–30 minutes until crispy and a bit darker. Take out of the oven and use a palette knife to briefly press and compact the dough before leaving to cool completely.

For the caramel middle, tip the sugar into a heavy-bottomed saucepan and mix in a couple of tablespoons of water. Put over a medium heat until the sugar slowly turns golden then a reddish-brown. This'll take around 10–15 minutes. Resist the urge to shake, move or stir the pan. Be ready with the cream as it nears the desired colour because the last bit happens quite fast. When the bubbles get smaller and the caramel becomes darker, turn off the heat and give it a brief swirl to even out the temperature. Quickly pour in the cream and whisk like mad for a minute before pouring on to the base. Leave to set at room temperature for about 30 minutes, or in the fridge for 15 if you're in a hurry.

Once the caramel is pretty much solid, gently melt the chocolate in a bowl over a pan of steaming water (don't let the bowl touch the water), and pour on to the caramel, evening it out with a palette knife. Leave to set at room temp. (Fridging chocolate is not a good idea – whitish marks appear on it, known as 'blooming'.)

When the chocolate is set, lift the whole bar out of the tray using the paper. Run a long knife under the hot tap for a minute, then wipe dry and cut the slab into squares. You may need to repeat the knife heating/wiping thing a couple of times.

Mysteries of the Baking Shelf Unfurled

It all started with cream of tartar ... Despite being a professional cook for over 20 years, until I started researching this section I had absolutely no idea what cream of tartar actually was and what it did. Say tartar to me, and I thought raw steak, Mongolian horse riders and a side for fish and chips, none of which have any connection to meringues. Then there was the question of how, why and with what do you cream it? So, I've rounded up the answers to this and a few other questions that I think about in the middle of the night. The ones to do with baking, anyway.

FLOURS

Plain or all-purpose flour is your best mate when baking – it's reliable and consistent, with a medium gluten content (the strands of protein that give a bake its structure). So, it can be used for pretty much anything from cakes to bread to pasta (though you'll get better results for bread and pasta with specialist flours – see below).

Self-raising flour is a fine plain flour with baking powder already in it, and is typically used for cakes and bakes. You can use it on its own or with more baking powder or bicarbonate of soda for extra rise. If your recipe calls for self-raising flour, you can substitute with plain flour and baking powder (about 1 tsp baking powder and a tiny pinch of salt to 125g flour).

Strong or bread flour has a higher gluten content than plain flour. Kneading it works the gluten strands into a huge web, which traps the carbon dioxide bubbles given off by the yeast. This is great when making bread, but don't use it for cakes or pastry as they will be too tough.

Italian 00 flour is white, very finely milled flour. The Italians grade their flour from 00 (finely ground) to 2 (more like wholemeal). Italian 00 flour is generally used for pasta or pizza doughs as it has less gluten and creates a less chewy result than a British flour would.

Gluten-free flours are now widely available for the growing number of people with gluten intolerance or allergies. Commercial versions are usually blends, often of rice, corn and potato flours, and are developed to behave as much like ordinary plain flour as possible.

WHITE POWDERS

Cream of tartar is an acidic by-product of the winemaking industry, and one of the two crucial components of baking powder (the other being bicarbonate of soda). Used alone, as in meringues, it acts as a stabiliser, helping to increase volume.

Bicarbonate of soda (baking soda in America): the alkaline component of baking powder is also used on its own as a raising agent in acidic batters (like those with yoghurt or lemon juice), or along with baking powder to give extra lift. Heat kick-starts its reaction, resulting in the release of carbon dioxide, helping things rise.

Baking powder is a mixture of the above two, plus inert starch (usually corn starch). The acid and alkaline react when water and/or heat come into play, making a mixture rise. Most modern baking powders are 'double-acting', meaning they start to react and release carbon dioxide as soon as they are wet, then have a secondary reaction when heated, producing two leavening phases. You can make your own baking powder with one part bicarbonate of soda to two parts cream of tartar.

YEAST

Fresh yeast is a living micro-organism that reacts with sugar and/or flour to produce carbon dioxide bubbles, which cause rising. You can get fresh yeast in specialist food shops, bakeries, online, or even from a good supermarket. It keeps for weeks (to a couple of months) in the fridge, wrapped loosely in damp cloth or paper, but don't seal as it needs to breathe. You can freeze it in small pieces to be defrosted as needed.

Dried yeast doesn't taste as good as fresh, but is the next best thing. It keeps for ages in a sealed container or can be frozen. Roughly speaking, if substituting fresh with dried, use half or a third of the quantity given in the recipe – dried yeast is more intense gram for gram.

Instant/quick/fast-action dried yeast is produced in smaller granules than ordinary dried yeast and tends to contain different strains of fast-acting yeast plus ascorbic acid to speed up the reaction. It's fantastically convenient as it's the most readily available and works fast, but for serious bakes, even of a domestic variety, it's a bit of a sorry second as it dies off quickly so isn't suitable for recipes needing a slow rise and a long prove.

VANILLA

Vanilla pods (aka beans) are the dried or semi-dried seedpods of the vanilla plant. They are expensive, so the smart move is to buy them in bulk from specialist online suppliers and store tightly wrapped in cling film in an airtight container (I keep mine in a tall bottle).

Vanilla extract is made from natural vanilla and is the next best thing to pods. It's more convenient as you don't have the hassle of scraping the seeds, so is useful when vanilla is only intended as a backup flavour, and a stronger taste isn't needed. Check the percentage of natural vanilla for the best quality.

Vanilla essence is the extract's rip-off cousin and usually doesn't contain any natural vanilla at all, with the 'flavour' coming from synthetic vanillin, often a by-product from papermaking. Avoid!

CHOCOLATE

Dark chocolate: for cooking use a chocolate with at least 70% cocoa solids, as the solids are predominantly responsible for flavour (while the cocoa butter dictates texture and melting consistency). You generally get what you pay for; better chocolates are more expensive.

Milk chocolate is cocoa solids mixed with milk (can be powdered, condensed or liquid) and sugar. To meet EU regs it must contain a minimum of 25% cocoa solids.

White chocolate does not contain any cocoa solids, just cocoa butter, usually mixed with milk solids, sugar and salt. Because of this, it doesn't really have a true chocolatey taste – just a sticky sweet one.

Cooking chocolate has a high cocoa content and often no sugar at all, thus giving more control over sweetness.

Compound chocolate or chocolate coating is NOT chocolate! It's a cheap blend of vegetable fats and flavourings; basically a chocolate-flavoured candy. It has a low melting point and is easier to handle than real chocolate, but tastes disgusting.

Cocoa powder: made from ground cocoa solids, this is natural and unsweetened, which makes it great for baking (and also yummy hot chocolate with sugar and milk). It's acidic, so reacts with bicarbonate of soda to create a rise. Try to use a good-quality cocoa.

Drinking chocolate tends to have a relatively low cocoa and high sugar content. It is better to use cocoa powder so that you can control the sweetness of the end result, whether for baking or drinking.

2

Broke & Bored

Student Days, Cereal Years

I'M the first to admit I'm no expert on this stage of life; I was one of only three girls in my year at school who didn't go to uni and the closest I got to further education was attending the Cordon Bleu at 21, which can't be judged as normal student life. My coursework and meals were centred around elaborate and largely ridiculous French dishes from a bygone era such as *lapin bonne femme* and *ballotines de volaille*; a far cry from my main point of reference for student eating at the time. Namely, *The Young Ones.*

The years following school can take many forms: college, apprenticeships, unemployment, work experience, menial jobs, soul-searching, navel-gazing, thumb-twiddling and other activities that involve small parts of one's anatomy. Interestingly though, in one respect it doesn't seem to matter which of these or any other paths you take: this is the time in your life when you have your first real, extended foray into self-catering and we take our initial stumbling steps into a world where mum and/or dad are no longer our principal providers.

By the age of 18, most of us have a finely honed repertoire of not many dishes, at least half of which are sweet. The idea of making supper for oneself on multiple occasions *within a single week* is pretty daunting, and as ever in the face of mild panic, people behave in different ways. At the far end of the scale there are the snackers – folks who just grab what they can from the fridge and use it to fill their bellies. Some opt for recreating their take-away favourites, and for them I've included simple noodles and spicy chicken wings. For others, as it was for me, this is a deeply political time of life, including one's food choices. At 19, I was both a member of the Revolutionary Communist Party *and* vegetarian, which naturally led to lentils, so I've included three of my favourite lentilly recipes in this chapter. Other people will instantly settle into a homemaker role. You'll find them at the stove cooking up big batches of comfort food for housemates to share, such as Melanzane Parmigiana on page 52.

Behavioural differences aside, there are limitations common to all as defined by age, dosh and inexperience. Therefore, almost universally, dishes that are cheap, quick and easy score highest. And if those really are the prize-winning criteria, then there really can only be one undisputed winner, so turn to pages 60–63 to see what I have to say on the subject of TOAST!

Egg-fried Rice with 'Everlasting' Veg

It's hard to think of a dish that is more universally loved than egg-fried rice; it's quick, easy, yummy, cheap and really does tick all the boxes, plus you get added nutritional points if you chuck in some veg too. After careful research, I've concluded that you get best results with fridge-cold leftover rice. No idea why, you just do. Of course, you can do this with fresh veg and cook rice from scratch, but I tend to see this as an emergency meal, so 'everlasting' veg from the freezer or a tin, plus leftover rice from the fridge, is more realistic.

Serves 2

1–2 tbsp groundnut oil
bit of sliced onion if you have it
    (spring onion is ideal but if
    not, any will do)
½ thumb (about 10g) fresh
    ginger, trimmed and grated
2 garlic cloves, grated
½ chilli, sliced (or just add a
    shot of chilli sauce at the end)
300g cooked, fridge-cold rice
    (long-grain ideally, but
    basmati is fine too)
couple of handfuls of everlasting
    veg (like frozen peas or
    broad beans, a drained tin of
    sweetcorn, or anything that's
    not too wet, such as spinach)
3 eggs
light soy sauce, to taste
black pepper

In a wide frying pan or wok, heat the oil till it's good and hot, then fry the onion, ginger, garlic and chilli (unless using sauce) until fragrant.

Chuck in the rice and veg and stir-fry until it's all hot. Make a hole in the middle, crack the eggs in and, after a few seconds, mix them into the rice and continue to stir and fry for up to 5 minutes more, until piping hot and starting to develop yummy crispy bits. Turn off the heat and season with soy sauce, pepper and more chilli sauce if you're in the mood. Nosh on!

Shown with:
Chinesey Chicken Wings

Chinesey Chicken Wings

Lip-smacking, finger-licking, palate-busting ... and the cheapest cut of chicken to boot. Winner, winner, chicken dinner!

Makes nibbles for a small crowd – about 15–20 wings (see photo, previous page)

4 big garlic cloves, chopped

1 tsp Chinese five spice

2–3 tsp chilli powder, depending on taste

1½ tbsp sesame oil

1½ tbsp dark soy sauce

2 tbsp sweet chilli sauce

2½ tbsp rice wine vinegar

1 tbsp fish sauce

½ tsp salt

1kg chicken wings

Preheat the oven to 210°C/fan 190°C/Gas 6½.

Put the garlic in a little bowl and stir in all the other ingredients except the chicken wings, which go into a big bowl.

Pour the sauce over the wings and mix to coat thoroughly (and ideally leave to marinate for anything from an hour to overnight). Then spread out on two baking trays, or do one load at a time. They need to be put on the top shelf of the oven and not too bunched up on the tray in order to cook properly.

Turn the wings over after around 15 minutes, once the tops are appealingly blackened. It will only be about another 12 minutes till they are good to go. Don't worry if the wing tips get a bit burnt – there's really no meat on them anyway and they make a good handle as you're gnawing.

Some motherly advice on dealing with a hangover

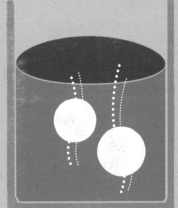

(from one who really knows)

This is the time of life when you will likely explore the wonderful world of alcohol to its fullest, and thus will also come up against tomorrow's hangover. This will continue well into mid-life, as I can assure you, so it seems only fair to give some advice on what to do when you feel like death.

First, **sink a pint of water and two painkillers** before you go to bed (or halfway through the night when you wake up as parched as the Gobi desert). If you were too far gone to act before morning, then do as above, but wash your meds down with Berocca. **Your next drink should be something sugary.** This is the only time I'll down a coke, but it must be full fat with lots of ice and half a lemon squeezed into it.

If you don't have the luxury of sleeping it off, then **have a short, strong coffee with two Fairtrade brown sugars**. This not only physically opens your eyes to the world, but may also make you ponder the injustices therein, and how, by comparison, your hangover is relatively inconsequential. **Have a shower** (baths lead to self-indulgence, and you did enough of that last night), or at least **put on clean clothes and brush your teeth twice**: once for you, and once for anyone you might be talking to in the near future.

However, in my experience a really brain-damaging hangover doesn't clear until three things have happened: 1) You've followed all the advice above. 2) You've eaten something – see next page. And 3) The clock strikes 4pm.

Hangover Eggs

Nothing helps a hangover like eating, and there are a few tried-and-tested cures. Raw oysters are one, believe it or not, but only if you happen to have a fantastic fishmonger or raw fish bar round the corner (and your student loan will stretch to it!). Otherwise, there are essentially two ways to go for the everyday hangover: zap (chilli) or stodge (carbs). For some reason, fried eggs help too. After decades of research, I've honed this recipe to perfectly combine all three: zap, stodge and eggs together on one plate.

Relief for 1 hurting soul

1 medium spud, peeled and
    roughly chopped
hefty splash of oil
1 small onion, sliced
½ tsp chilli flakes
handful of cherry tomatoes
1 egg
lots of chilli sauce
S & P

Put the spud chunks into a smallish frying pan, cover with water plus about 1cm, add a bit of salt, bring to the boil and simmer with the lid on for about 20 minutes until tender.

Drain, wipe the pan and pour in the oil. Fry the onion and chilli flakes for a few minutes until soft, then add the spuds and give them a bit of a squish with the back of the fork. Fry until they are approaching golden, with tempting crispy bits, then chuck in the toms and keep going for a few minutes until they've softened and are thinking about bursting. Season with salt and pepper.

Once you're happy with your spuds 'n' toms, clear a hole in the middle and crack in the egg. Cook until the white is set but the yolk is still runny and, depending on the severity of your post-boozing stupidity, top with more fresh chilli as well as copious amounts of chilli sauce. There's no need to plate this, just get stuck into the pan.

To kill that hangover, also try

- *fresh juices: kale and spinach/beet/carrot (they can be a tad hard to swallow, but are full of welcome vits and minerals; big in the penitence camp)*

- *raw seafood ... feels like brain food that re-engages the burnt-out synapses: oysters and clams*

- *more booze (hair of the dog) ... my friend and legendary St John chef Fergus Henderson swears by Fernet Branca in the morning, and, on occasion, I've known an ice-cold beer take the edge off*

Melanzane Parmigiana

A great dish for a house full of students: it uses accessible and affordable ingredients and it's vegetarian too, but more than that, it's soul-nourishing in a way that just tastes like home.

For 8

4–6 tbsp extra virgin olive oil
3 aubergines, sliced lengthways
   1cm thick
double batch of 15-minute
   Tomato Sauce (see page 369,
   but note the changes here)
3 mozzarella balls (each about
   125g), sliced quite thinly
150g Parmesan, finely grated
large bunch of basil (about 40g),
   leaves picked
S & P

Preheat the oven to 180°C/fan 160°C/Gas 4.

Get out a couple of baking trays and pour 2 tablespoons of olive oil on to each. Lay the aubergine slices on them in a single layer, then turn them over and give them a light seasoning with salt and pepper (you'll probably need to do this with a third tray if you have one – if not, cook them in batches). Bake for half an hour, turning halfway through.

Meanwhile, make up the double batch of 15-minute Tomato Sauce with a couple of amendments: ditch the ketchup, use only 2 bay leaves and cook the sauce down for a bit longer until rich and thick.

Choose a baking dish about 30 x 20 x 6cm and spread a handsome ladleful of sauce over the bottom. Then put in a layer of aubergines, followed by a few slices of mozzarella and cover this with a handful of grated Parmesan and some basil leaves. Season and repeat the layers until you run out of ingredients, making sure your top layer is tomato topped with cheese.

Drizzle on a touch more olive oil and bake for 30–40 minutes, until bubbling and beautiful. Let it sit for 5 minutes before tucking in. A simple salad on the side should suffice – it's richer than Croesus.

Not Pot Noodle

Ideal for combating the infamous 'freshers' flu'.

For 1 hard-working, hard-playing, hungry student

1 tbsp sesame seeds
500ml vegetable stock, chicken
 stock, or water mixed with
 1 tsp Bovril
1 chicken breast, cut into finger-
 thick strips (optional)
60g dried noodles (I tend to use
 udon, but any will do)
100g cabbage, sliced
1 carrot, peeled and sliced
 roughly 1cm thick
50g green veg, like mangetout,
 broccoli or French beans,
 cut into bite-sized pieces
juice of 1 lime
light soy sauce, to taste
chilli sauce (I recommend
 Sriracha), to taste

Put a saucepan big enough to hold all the ingredients over a medium heat and throw in the sesame seeds. Toast them for just a few minutes until golden, then tip them out on to a plate or bowl. Pour the stock into the hot pan, then drop in the chicken pieces one at a time so they don't all clump together.

Bring to the boil, skim off any scum with a spoon, then add the noodles, cabbage and carrot, followed a couple of minutes later by the green veg.

Simmer for just a couple more minutes, then turn the heat off and season with lime juice, soy sauce and the chilli sauce of your choice. Finish with a scattering of the toasted sesame seeds.

3 WAYS with LENTILS

Having lived through its dark hippy days, the lentil has rightly reclaimed its dignity and is now a 21st-century favourite. Lentils double up as a proteinous carb, they cook quickly, are so cheap they're practically free, and with just a little bit of set-dressing they're utterly delicious. They're the darling of the gastropub along with beetroot and ox cheeks. Here are my three top lentil recipes, each using a different kind to illustrate the breadth of their beauty.

Red Lentil Dhal

Main course for 2 (with some rice and a salad); or a side dish for 4

2 tbsp olive oil
3 garlic cloves, very finely
    chopped
1 tsp black onion (nigella) seeds
200g red lentils
1 x 400ml tin coconut milk
S & P

Heat the oil in a saucepan over a medium heat, and fry the garlic, stirring pretty constantly, until golden and sticky. Now tip in the onion seeds, give it all a good stir for about 30 seconds, just to get them to open up their flavour, then add the lentils.

Stir well again to coat the lentils in the garlicky oil, then pour in the coconut milk. Bring to a boil, then turn them down to a very relaxed simmer for 30–35 minutes, adding a couple of tablespoons of water if necessary towards the end of the cooking time if you don't think there's enough liquid left to get them beautifully soft. Season at the end – get happy with the salt and have a lighter hand with the pepper.

Clockwise from top left:
Puy Lentil & Herb Salad,
Red Lentil Dhal, Green/Brown
Lentil & Bacon Soup

Green/Brown Lentil & Bacon Soup

For 4–6 as a starter (see photo, previous page)

healthy splosh of olive oil, plus
    extra to serve
100g lardons or sliced streaky
    bacon
1 onion, chopped
2 garlic cloves, chopped
2 tbsp chopped rosemary
250g green or brown lentils
1.2 litres chicken stock
couple of handfuls of spinach,
    tough stalks ripped off
S & P
natural yoghurt, to serve
    (optional)

In a wide, heavy-bottomed pan, heat a splash of olive oil and then fry the bacon bits over a medium–high heat for 3–4 minutes, until browning and beginning to crisp. Chuck in the onion, garlic and rosemary and fry for a few minutes, then add the lentils. Give the lentils a good coating in the oil, then pour over the stock. Bring to a simmer and let it bubble gently for around 45 minutes, covered with a lid, until the lentils are tender but keeping their shape.

Ladle out a third and blitz in a blender or give it a quick whizz with a stick blender (not essential but it improves the texture), then tip back into the pan. Roughly chop the spinach and stir it in, along with a fair whack of seasoning – lentils love both salt and pepper. Cook for just a minute or two until the spinach has wilted, then serve with a blob of yoghurt if you fancy, and use a free hand with the olive oil.

Puy Lentil & Herb Salad

Enough for 1 hungry person, plus a bit of leftovers (see photo, page 57)

100g dried Puy lentils, or 1 x 400g tin, drained
½ red onion, very thinly sliced
2 tbsp sherry vinegar or red/white wine vinegar
lots of extra virgin olive oil
2 big handfuls of mixed herbs (like flat-leaf or curly parsley, basil, mint, chives, tarragon), roughly chopped
½ tsp Dijon mustard
½ garlic clove, finely chopped
50g ricotta
S & P

If using dried lentils, tip them into a pan, cover with plenty of cold water and bring to a simmer. Let them bubble for about half an hour until just cooked. Drain, run under cold water for a minute to cool, then allow them to dry in the residual heat.

Break up the onion slices, dropping the slivers into a bowl. Pour over the vinegar and leave to macerate for about 5 minutes.

Season the lentils with salt and pour over some olive oil, stirring to coat. Wash and chop the herbs.

When the onions have had their time in the vinegar, lift them out (reserving the liquid) and put in a mixing bowl with the drained lentils. Add the mustard and garlic to the vinegar and whisk in 3 tablespoons of the oil. Season the dressing with salt and pepper.

Toss the lentils with the chopped herbs and dressing and taste and season the whole lot for the last time. Spoon on to a flattish plate and finish by blobbing on the ricotta and giving it a twist of black pepper as well as a final shot of olive oil.

My Top 5 Toast Toppers

Toast has to be the best stand-by food ever. This is true for life, but for most, understanding its potential for greatness is something that fully dawns during further education. As a student, you'll discover within toast a world of opportunity. You know how you like it, but here are a few of my family faves ...

Tabernacle Mushrooms

Back in the closing years of the last century, I opened a café called The Good Cook in a much-loved community centre in Notting Hill called The Tabernacle. The aim was simply to provide decent food at an affordable price in a non-pretentious environment. In terms of business, the lunches were busy, the evenings less so (it was a slightly unforgiving space in the dark), but it was the weekend brekkies that went ballistic. This recipe went down very well with the vegetarians of Notting Hill. It's particularly good with scrambled eggs.

For 1

couple of handfuls of mushrooms
    (button, chestnut or whatever
    you have)
big knob of butter
1 garlic clove, chopped
a few sprigs of thyme, leaves
    picked, or ½ tsp dried thyme
couple of pieces of bread
2 tbsp crème fraîche, sour cream
    or double cream
couple of spring onions, sliced
squeeze of lemon juice
S & P

Briefly wash the mushrooms under running water and slice/tear them apart as you wish. In a frying pan, melt the butter over a medium–high heat and when foaming chuck in the mushrooms. Toss and stir for 3ish minutes until just beginning to soften, then throw in the garlic and thyme and stir to coat the mushrooms.

Start making your toast as the garlic is cooking, then turn the heat off under the 'shrooms and stir in the dairy, spring onions and a squeeze of lemon. Season to taste and pile up on the toast.

Pig Melba

Chicago Chilli
Tuna Melt

Tabernacle
Mushrooms

Pimped-up
Beans

Summer
Snack

Chicago Chilli Tuna Melt

All serve
1
Photo on previous page

The first time I went abroad on a parent-free holiday, my best mate Mudge and I went to Chicago to stay with some friends of my parents. It was the mid-1980s, and we had the best time ever, cruising the streets trying to look cool, smoking menthols and going to see *La Bamba* umpteen times. The lady we were staying with used to make us this for brunch before we went off exploring for the day, and although we were 15 at the time it feels to me like perfect student fodder.

couple of slices of bread
1 x 185g tin tuna (in spring water not brine), drained
bit of pepper (red looks good but any will do), finely diced
1–2 spring onions, sliced, or 1 onion, cut into small dice
¼ tsp cayenne pepper or chilli powder
3 tbsp mayo
handful of grated Cheddar
S & P

Preheat the grill and pop the bread in the toaster.

Mix the tuna, pepper, spring onions, chilli and mayo with a touch of salt and quite a lot of black pepper.

When the toast is ready, load on the tuna mix and cover the top with the Cheddar. Grill until the smell of bubbling cheese is irresistible.

Pig Melba

You call it cheese on toast – my family calls it pig melba, in honour of our porcine family talisman. To make this into **Swine Topping** you'll need half an avocado too.

couple of slices of bread
some cheese, usually Cheddar of a slightly dodgy origin
splash of Worcestershire sauce
½ an avocado (optional, see above)

Preheat the grill and pop the bread in the toaster.

Scatter the cheese on to the toast and place under the grill. When melty and bubbling, take it out and splash on some Worcestershire sauce. Top with sliced avocado for the definitive porcine experience.

Summer Snack

This cold topper is not one to eat when your student house is under-heated, but it's perfect in summer and carries some 'good for you' points thanks to the mackerel.

2 smoked mackerel fillets,
    peppered or not, as you like
couple of slices of bread
    (preferably wholegrain, rye
    or even pumpernickel)
60g cream cheese
squeeze of lemon juice
few slices of cucumber
S & P
Tabasco sauce, to serve
    (optional)

Flake the mackerel into a bowl, discarding the skin and any bones. Pop the bread in to toast.

Stir the cream cheese into the fish and beat well with a wooden spoon so they become one. Season with lemon, plenty of pepper and a little salt, to taste.

Load on to the toast, frisbee on the cuke and give it that Tabasco hit too. You know you want to.

Pimped-up Beans

splash of oil
few rashers of streaky bacon,
    sliced
couple of slices of bread
your usual serving of baked
    beans
handful of grated Cheddar
1 ripe tomato, chopped, or a few
    cherry toms, cut in half
1 spring onion, or bit of onion,
    diced
black pepper
a splash of chipotle ketchup
    really nails it, or Tabasco
    at a push

Heat the oil in a saucepan over a medium heat and fry the bacon in it until just crisping up, then take it out and give the pan a quick wipe with kitchen paper. Pop the bread in the toaster.

Warm the beans in the pan and stir in the bacon bits.

Beans on toast, cheese on beans, toms on cheese, onion on toms, pepper on top, and a little smokey ketchup or Tabasco alongside to really make these supreme beans.

Flat-pack Cooking the Mexican Way (aka Quesadillas)

Quesadillas are an excellent grazing snack: you don't need to eat them piping hot; they come in pizza-like slices so you can grab as you need; they're sustaining (it's a bean thing); and above all they're so yummy they make you feel happy. From personal experience I find a higher chilli level helps my concentration, it kind of keeps me 'in the room' and focused.

Makes a super-snacky supper for 1 starvaceous or 2 impoverished students

1 small red onion, half thinly
    sliced; half diced
2 limes
splash of oil
3 rashers streaky bacon, sliced
    (optional)
½ pepper (your choice of
    colour), roughly diced
2 garlic cloves, finely chopped
1 tsp ground cumin
1 tsp chilli powder
½ x 400g tin kidney beans,
    drained, rinsed and roughly
    mashed with a fork
2 flour tortillas (I use 25cm ones,
    but any size works as long as
    they're no bigger than your
    biggest frying pan)
handful of grated Cheddar
large handful of coriander, very
    roughly chopped
S & P

Put a wide frying pan over a medium heat (big enough so that a tortilla can sit pretty much flat in it). While it's heating, put the sliced onion in a bowl and squeeze over enough juice from one of the limes to coat generously. Stir, season, then leave aside.

Splash a little oil into the frying pan and fry the bacon and pepper until the meat is just browning, stirring frequently. Chuck in the diced onion and garlic, and fry for a few more minutes until the onion has started to soften. Stir in the spices and make sure all the ingredients are well coated before adding the mashed beans. Now do a bit of hardcore mixing to bring it all together, giving it a good season along the way.

While the mix is getting hot, lay a tortilla down on your counter or a board, then tip the mix on to it and spread it all over, leaving about 1cm and no more all around the edge. Press it down a bit with the back of a spoon, top with the grated cheese and rest the other tortilla on top.

Give the pan a quick wash, then put it back on a medium heat. Once it's dry and warming up, splash in a little oil and gently flop your tortilla sandwich into it. Fry for 2–3 minutes on this side, until the tortilla is crisp and lightly golden, then rest your hand on top, slip a spatula underneath and flip it over. Cook for the same amount of time on the other side, then slide on to a plate and cut into six. Finish by scattering the macerated onion and coriander on top and serve with lime pieces on the side.

THE NEW
WORKER

NOW we are grown-up ... or at least we think we are. We have our first proper job, do the commute, work hard, fix some things and fuck others up. After work we go to the pub with our new colleagues and sink a couple. We may or may not be in a relationship, but for most it's a bit soon to be living together anyway.

We are fledgling adults, approximate versions of the fully grown examples of the species we will become, and, by and large, we are happy. We care about the way we look, we go to the gym and we make better choices than our younger selves, including about what we eat. Eating is mostly a trifecta of going out, ready-meals and cooking, but when we cook, we give our recipes some proper attention compared to student days. We may know about seasonality and farmers' markets, but supermarkets are our reality, particularly the metro variety.

I like thinking back on my early twenties. After some dark times I fell into a career I really loved. I worked hard, played hard, had loads of energy and some money coming in to support the good times. I was really getting started on this business of Life and making a decent account of myself. Yes, I was still getting into scrapes, but generally they were of a less alarming nature. Being a chef, working double or split shifts, my nutritional intake at this time of my life was mainly fulfilled by staff meals or grabbing something crappy on my way home from work after midnight. One of the most paradoxical things about cooking in a fancy restaurant is the rubbish that pretty much all young chefs eat on their way home. Anyway, when I talk to my friends who don't work in the food industry about their foodie needs at this time of life, they overwhelmingly come back with, 'quick, simple suppers, but with better ingredients and a higher health factor than student days. Oh, and some simple packed lunches please.'

So in this chapter you'll find easy, yummy, nutritious dishes that one tired new worker can knock up for themselves after a long day at the coalface. And then some alchemy happens to the leftovers, because with just five or ten minutes extra input after dinner or before work the next day, they all transform into a very different-feeling, totally scrumptious packed lunch, ready to go. Magic!

THREE SIMPLE KEBAB SUPPERS
BECOME THREE FINE SARNIES

This does exactly what it says above: coming up you'll find three different kebabs for three different suppers (no, you don't eat them all together). Each is designed to be about a third more than you can eat in one go so that the next day you can make a thrilling sandwich with the leftovers. Thus, three tasty proteins = three good suppers (with rice and a salad) and the next day, three fine sarnies. Ta dah!

PRAWN KEBAB

BECOMES

CHICKEN KEBAB

LAMB KEBAB

CHICKEN BLT SUB

LAMB, YOGHURT & HERB PITTA

PRAWN & AVOCADO WRAP

CUMIN LAMB KEBAB

200g lamb, cut into
   3–4cm dice
1 tsp ground cumin
¼ tsp ground coriander
1 garlic clove, finely chopped
1 tbsp olive oil
S & P

Put the lamb in a bowl with all the other ingredients (except the salt) and leave to marinate for as long as possible – anything between 10 minutes and overnight.

Thread the lamb pieces on to a skewer and season with salt. Heat a griddle pan until blazing hot, then cook the skewers for 3 minutes on each side. Supper is two-thirds of the lamb, with rice and salad, so put the remaining third in the fridge for tomorrow's …

BECOMES

CHILLI CHICKEN KEBAB

200g skinless, boneless
   chicken thigh meat,
   cut into 3cm pieces
2 tbsp chilli sauce
juice of ½ lemon
S & P

Stick your griddle pan on to get bloody hot.

Mix the chicken pieces with the chilli sauce and lemon juice, season well and thread on to a kebab skewer. Cook the kebab for 4–5 minutes on each side, then take a third off for tomorrow's lunch before attacking the rest with rice or spuds and a salad.

BECOMES

LEMONGRASS PRAWN KEBAB

10 raw king prawns, heads off,
   peeled and deveined
juice of ½ lime
1 tsp sesame oil
1 tsp fish sauce
2 lemongrass stalks

Marinate the prawns in all the ingredients except the lemongrass for 15 minutes. Put your griddle pan on to get good and hot.

Use a sharp knife to cut the thin ends of the lemongrass into an arrow-like head, for ease of skewering, then thread the prawns on to the stalks.

Once the prawns are in place, cook the kebabs for 2 minutes per side, and serve with a salad, or rice, or whatever takes your fancy, but save 3–4 prawns for tomorrow's lunch …

BECOMES

LAMB, YOGHURT & HERB PITTA

1 pitta bread, cut in half
2 tbsp Greek or natural yoghurt
handful of salad leaves
a few slices of red onion
1 small tomato, sliced
yesterday's leftover grilled lamb
handful of mint leaves
squeeze of lemon juice
chilli sauce or pickled chilli
    (optional)

Spread the inside of the pitta with yoghurt, then load the salad leaves in first, followed by the onion, tomato, lamb and mint leaves. Give it a little hit of lemon and some chilli sauce or pickled chilli if you're brave.

All serve 1
Photos on previous pages

CHICKEN BLT SUB

simply build yesterday's grilled chicken with:
2–3 rashers streaky bacon, grilled or fried until crispy
slices of tomato
3–4 little gem lettuce leaves
mayo
S & P
...and load into a sub roll/small baguette

I cook my kebabs on a griddle because I like to keep an eye on my food as it cooks, which I can't do under the grill unless I whip it out every minute (although technically the grill is fine). I also prefer the flavour a griddle gives. If you don't own one, do get one next time you're feeling a bit flush – it's money well spent.

PRAWN & AVOCADO WRAP

1 flour tortilla
½ ripe avocado, sliced
½ red pepper, thinly sliced
yesterday's leftover prawns
handful of coriander
½ spring onion, sliced
squeeze of lime juice
2 tsp sweet chilli sauce

Lay down the tortilla and put the avocado and pepper slices in a line all the way across the middle.

Top that with the prawns, coriander, spring onion, a squeeze of lime juice and the chilli sauce. Lift the near side of the tortilla over the ingredients and give it a really firm squeeze with your fingertips, pulling it towards you, before you start to roll away from yourself. Cut in half and wrap tightly in foil and cling film – this is not one to chuck loose into a sandwich bag.

Five Feel-good Dinners

BECOME

Five Fun-packed Lunches

With a wave of your wand (and a little bit of chopping), this section continues the theme of turning last night's supper into tomorrow's packed lunch. But, as we don't always want to eat sarnies, these are a bit more substantial. The real beauty is that there's nothing leftoverish about them; sometimes they hardly look like they are related at all, let alone are direct offspring, and they certainly have very different flavour profiles. It's all a bit like culinary genetics.

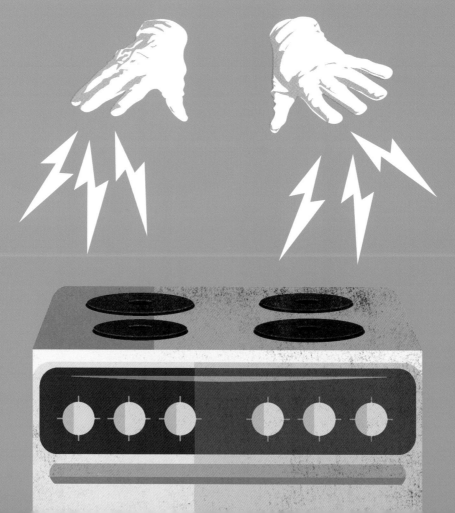

PERFECT CHICKEN BREAST with CHICKPEA PILAF

(including How to Cook a Chicken Breast)

These two recipes take a bit of stroll round the far side of the Med: the supper being more Turkish, as that is the origin of the pilaf recipe, whereas tomorrow's Lebanese salad was inspired by a dish I ate in the idyllic town of Batroun, just north of Beirut. Both dishes reflect the great cuisine of that neck of the woods: simple meats, excellent rice dishes and joyous, sun-filled salads.

BECOMES

Supper for 1 plus a different-feeling packed lunch for the next day (see photo, previous page)

For the chickpea pilaf:

50g flaked almonds
knob of butter
splash of extra virgin olive oil
½ onion, diced
1 x 400g tin chickpeas, drained
120g long-grain rice
400ml chicken stock
S & P
piece of lemon, to serve

For the chicken:

1 tbsp olive oil
2 small–medium skin-on chicken
   breasts or supremes (this
   means they have the little
   wing bone attached – nice
   but not essential)

Preheat the oven to 200°C/fan 180°C/Gas 6. As it's heating, put the almonds in to toast on a baking tray. Shuffle them after a few minutes and take out as soon as they're golden. Tip into a bowl.

In a saucepan, melt the butter into the olive oil and fry the onion until softened, then add the drained chickpeas. Pour in the rice, give it all a good roll around in the oil, then pour in the stock. Bring to the boil with a couple of pinches of salt, then stick a lid on and turn the heat down so it's at a steady simmer. Cook for 15–20 minutes until all the liquid has been absorbed; turn off the heat and resist the urge to stir at this stage.

Lift the lid, drape a tea towel over the pan, put the lid back on top and leave it like this for a further 15 minutes to absorb the extra moisture and really yum up. Meanwhile you need to cook your chicken breasts, and that's best done by following my sure-fire method opposite ⇨

While your chicken is resting and now that your pilaf has had its chill-out time, use a fork to fluff it, stirring in half the toasted almonds as you go and checking the seasoning.

Put one perfect chicken breast in the fridge and serve with most, but not all, of your perfect pilaf and some lemon. Go for a bit of salad too to round it off, maybe with a splodge of yoghurt and some pickled green chillies on the side. Put the almonds in a sealed jar and the leftover pilaf in the fridge for tomorrow's …

LEBANESE CHICKEN SALAD

the second chicken breast
handful of cherry toms or
    1 tomato
½ red onion
handful of flat-leaf parsley
the leftover pilaf
squeeze of lemon juice, plus a
    lemon wedge
1 tbsp pomegranate molasses, if
    you have any
the rest of the toasted almonds
S & P

Chop the cooked chicken breast into smallish pieces. Halve your cherry toms or chop your tomato, dice the red onion and chop the parsley. Mix them all with the leftover pilaf and add lemon juice and seasoning, to taste. Whack it into a container, drizzle on a little pomegranate molasses, if using, sprinkle over the almonds and chuck a wedge of lemon in there too.

The best way to cook chicken breasts …

Chicken breasts can be notoriously dry – I never order them when I eat out because I get the fear! There's nothing worse than a dry breast. At home, however, it's surprisingly easy to get it right every time with just a little bit of coaching.

Preheat the oven to 200°C/fan 180°C/Gas 6. Put a medium ovenproof frying pan over a high heat with the oil in it. As it gets itself to smoking hot, season the chicken on the skin side and gently lay the breasts in the pan skin-side down (you always do this with the meat flopping away from you to avoid being splashed with hot oil).

Now season the flesh side, and leave for 4–5 minutes on the highest heat for the skin to really crisp up before putting in the oven, still skin-side down. (The theory here is that chicken breast is essentially a lean meat, which means it has very little fat and therefore a tendency to dry out. By doing all the direct heat cooking via the skin, you provide a fatty, flavourful barrier so that your breast won't have any dry, chewy bits.)

After 8–12 minutes, depending on size, take them out, lift up the detachable bit of flesh you can see coming away (known as the filet mignon) and as long as you can't see any raw bits underneath it, take it out and give it a 3–4-minute rest, skin-side up. This lets the juices spread on down through the breasts, again keeping them moist, and ensures the skin stays crispy.

FULL-ON VEGGIE NOODLE STIR-FRY

Supper for 1, plus a different-feeling lunch for the next day

70-80g egg noodles
2 tbsp groundnut oil
2 garlic cloves, finely chopped
½–1 chilli, finely diced
1 carrot, peeled and sliced into
    half-moons
¼ head Chinese leaves, cut
    into 3cm-thick slices
1 courgette, thinly sliced
handful of mushrooms (shiitake,
    oyster, button or chestnut),
    sliced
handful of mangetout or French
    beans, cut in half (or whatever
    green veg you have to hand)
1½ tbsp light soy sauce, or to
    taste
1 tbsp oyster sauce
big squeeze of lime juice
2 spring onions, sliced diagonally
S & P

Cook the noodles as per the instructions on the packet.

Heat the groundnut oil in a wok or large, wide frying pan until it's bloody hot (smoking), and fry the garlic and chilli for a minute until the garlic is just going golden, then chuck in all the veg except the mangetout. Keep the veggies moving over a high heat until beginning to collapse but make sure you don't lose crunch. Scatter in the noodles then the mangetout, separating the noodles as they fall in, and fry a bit more until they're all hot.

Put aside enough for your lunch tomorrow and hit what's left in the pan with the soy and oyster sauce and a big squeeze of lime juice. Taste for seasoning and finish with the spring onions.

PEA & PEANUT NOODLE SALAD

handful of frozen peas
1½ tbsp sweet chilli sauce
1½ tbsp peanut butter (smooth
    or crunchy)
1 tsp light soy sauce
1 lime
1 tbsp warm water
yesterday's stir-fry leftovers
handful of peanuts

Run the peas under cold water to defrost.

In a bowl, whisk together the chilli sauce, peanut butter, soy sauce, a squeeze of lime juice and the tablespoon of warm water to make a creamy dressing. Toss yesterday's leftovers with the peas and dressing, whack into a container, chuck on the peanuts, stick half a lime on the side and there's something to look forward to for lunch.

GRILLED SALMON WITH COUSCOUS & COURGETTES

Supper for 1 plus a different-feeling packed lunch for the next day

90g couscous

few sploshes of extra virgin olive oil

big handful of frozen peas

1 x 250g piece salmon fillet, preferably not from the tail end, skin on

1 courgette, cut into bite-sized chunks

½ red onion, thinly sliced

1 small garlic clove, finely chopped

75g pistachios, shelled and roughly chopped

massive handful of mixed soft herbs (parsley is essential; top up with tarragon, mint, basil or whatever you fancy, but not hard ones like thyme, sage, rosemary)

zest and juice of ½ lemon, plus a piece of lemon to serve

S & P

Preheat the oven to 180°C/fan 160°C/Gas 4. Stick the kettle on.

Put the couscous in a bowl, splash in roughly a tablespoon of olive oil and mix it all with your fingers. Chuck in the peas straight from the freezer and a couple of pinches of salt. Pour over boiling water to cover, plus about 2cm. Cover tightly with cling film and leave somewhere warm.

Pour another splosh of olive oil into an ovenproof frying pan over a high heat and season the salmon on both sides. When the oil is hot, chuck in the courgette and red onion. Fry, stirring occasionally, until cooked but still with a bit of bite – about 5 minutes – then season. Tip them out, making sure no stray bits of onion are left in the pan, and pop the pan back on the heat.

Go in again with another slosh of olive oil and once it starts to smoke add the salmon, flesh-side down. Fry for about 3 minutes (don't move it) until it starts to go golden round the edge, then carefully lift up, turn over and chuck the pan in the oven. Depending on the thickness of your salmon it will be cooked in 5–7 minutes; use this time to finish your couscous.

Tip the chopped garlic into the couscous and use a fork to mix it through and fluff it up. Mix the courgette, onion and pistachios through too, and once it's cooled to around room temp, add the herbs, lemon zest and juice, plus another slosh of olive oil. Season, then taste and adjust with more seasoning or lemon juice as you fancy.

Nick about a third of it for your packed lunch, remembering to cut off about a third of the salmon too. Leave these bits to cool while you tuck into your yummy salmon and couscous dinner, then pop them in the fridge for tomorrow's ...

BECOMES

BECOMES

BEETROOT, SALMON & COUSCOUS SALAD

(See photo, previous page)

1 small raw beetroot, peeled and
grated using the big holes
1 head Little Gem lettuce,
shredded
yesterday's leftover couscous
(see previous page)
squeeze of lemon juice, plus a
lemon wedge
yesterday's piece of salmon,
flaked (see previous page)
a few more pistachios, shelled
and roughly chopped
S & P

Stir the grated beetroot and shredded lettuce through the couscous and give it a refresher course in zip: add more lemon juice and seasoning – it'll need them after a night in the fridge. Top with the flaked salmon and a sprinkling of pistachios. Chuck another piece of lemon in there too as it would be awful to be caught short at the office.

LEAF-FREE GRILLED TUNA NIÇOISE

Supper for 1, plus a different-feeling lunch for the next day

100g new potatoes
200g tuna steak (in one piece)
extra virgin olive oil
75g French beans, blanched
    (see page 366)
small handful of black olives
handful of cherry toms, halved
few slices of onion (red or shallot
    ideally, but white or spring
    also work)
S & P
House Dressing (see page 367),
    to serve

First get your spuds on to boil. Cover them with plenty of cold, salted water. Bring to the boil, with a lid on, then turn the heat down a bit, take the lid off and simmer until just cooked – good new potatoes should only take 10–12 minutes from boiling. When they're nearly there, put a griddle or heavy-bottomed pan on a high heat to get very hot.

Lightly brush both sides of the tuna with oil and season well. Depending on the thickness of your tuna and how seared you like it, cook for about 2–3 minutes per side. I like mine black and blue – charred on the outside and rare in the middle.

Drain the spuds and cut them in half or into quarters. Slice the tuna, putting a third in the fridge for lunch tomorrow, and toss the rest with the beans, spuds, olives, tomatoes and onion in some House Dressing. Check for seasoning – Niçoise loves a bit of pepper.

BECOMES

SPICY TUNA SALAD

yesterday's tuna, sliced
2 handfuls of whatever raw veg
    is knocking about (cabbage,
    mangetout, carrots, bok choy,
    courgettes, peppers, asparagus,
    cucumber), chopped into fine
    matchsticks
small handful of cherry toms,
    halved
small handful of nuts (cashews,
    pistachios, peanuts), roughly
    chopped
a lime or lemon wedge
around 4 tbsp Pan-Asian
    Dressing (see page 367)

This one is better tossed at lunchtime, so keep the bits separate. Wrap the tuna in cling film, pack the veg, toms and nuts into your container, keeping the lime or lemon wedge on the side, pour the dressing into a little jam jar and just bring it all together when the time is right.

PORK CHOP WITH LENTILS, PEARS & GINGER

Supper for 1, plus a slightly different-looking lunch for the next day

140g lentils (brown, green or Puy,
    just not red)
good knob of butter
1 ripe pear, of the short, fat juicy
    kind, not the hard, tall variety,
    cut into 8 pieces
2 tbsp stem ginger syrup, plus
    1 nugget of stem ginger, finely
    chopped
extra virgin olive oil
2 pork chops, 250–300g each
    (a couple of cms thick)
100ml red wine
good handful of basil leaves
2 tbsp red wine vinegar
S & P
English mustard, to serve

Put the lentils in a pan and cover with enough water to come about 4cm above the lentils. Pop a lid on and bring to the boil, then take off the lid and turn down to a simmer for about half an hour until they're cooked.

Melt the butter in a large frying pan and fry the pear slices for a couple of minutes until browning, then stir in the ginger syrup. The soft pears will become lovely and sticky. Tip into a bowl and cover with foil or cling film. You want the pears to be at room temperature or warm when it comes to serving up.

Give the pan a quick rinse and wipe, then put back on the heat to dry out. Pour in a good splash of olive oil and turn the heat up high. Season the pork chops on both sides, lay them in the hot oil and cook on one side for 5–6 minutes until golden brown, turning the heat down a touch if the colour deepens too fast.

Turn the chops over and turn the heat back up to high. Cook for just a couple of minutes until the colour matches the top, then turn the heat down a bit for as long as it takes for them to cook through – about 5–6 minutes, depending on thickness and size. The best way to test they're done is to stick a thin knife or skewer into the thickest part, right next to the bone, leave there for 5 seconds, then touch it to your top lip – it should feel hot but not piping. If it's cold or just warm, keep cooking for a bit longer and repeat the knife test.

Once your chops are cooked, turn off the heat, take them out of the pan and rest on a plate.

Pour the red wine into the pan and stir, scraping the porky bits up off the bottom as the wine reduces to a couple of tablespoons. If the pan is so hot that it bubbles dry, just add a splash of water.

CONTINUED

CONTINUED FROM
PREVIOUS PAGE

While the chops are resting, finish the lentils, which should be cooked by now. Drain them and put half aside for tomorrow's lunch. Mix the rest with the chopped stem ginger, basil, red wine reduction from the pan, red wine vinegar, a splash of good extra virgin olive oil and some seasoning.

When the pork has had at least 5 minutes of resting, pour the juices that have come out of it into the lentils too. Serve up one handsome pork chop with the lentils, sticky pear wedges and some English mustard, and put the other one in the fridge with the rest of the lentils for tomorrow's ...

BECOMES

(SLIGHTLY PORKY) LENTIL HERB SALAD

(See photo, previous page)

the leftover pork chop
the rest of the lentils
a few thin slices of onion (red
    or shallot are ideal)
1 tbsp sherry vinegar or red/
    white wine vinegar
1½ tbsp extra virgin olive oil
½ tsp Dijon mustard
2 big handfuls of chopped mixed
    herbs (such as flat-leaf /curly
    parsley, basil, mint, chives and
    just a little tarragon – it's quite
    strong stuff)
S & P

Cut the pork chop meat away from the bone, discarding all the fatty rind too (hot pig fat is a matter of personal choice, but unless cured, cold doesn't have a lot of fans).

Slice or roughly chop the meat and mix it with the leftover lentils, along with all the other ingredients.

ALL-DAY SPANISH TORTILLA

Even though this isn't a recipe that converts from supper to lunch, I'm throwing it in because a good Spanish tortilla can be enjoyed at breakfast, elevenses, lunch, tea, supper or as a late-night snack (even all on the same day). It happily lives out of the fridge for a day or two, and if there's still some left after that, then go and see a doctor as you're clearly not right.

Enough for 2 good meals and a couple of sneaky sliver snacks

1 large potato, peeled and cut into
    bite-sized chunks
2 tbsp light olive oil
1 large onion or 2 small, sliced
1 garlic clove, sliced
50g peas, defrosted
½ tsp paprika, plus a little extra
4 eggs, beaten with a little S & P
S & P

SERVING SUGGESTIONS

Supper: *eat half of it hot with some kind of veg or salad (nothing is yummier than the Slow-roast Tomato & Goats' Cheese Salad on page 363) and a large glass of Albariño.*

Brekkie: *have a sliver snack as you're packing up lunch (with ketchup).*

Lunch: *throw together a leafy salad with whatever bits you have and a sharp dressing. The tortilla can either be served hot or at room temperature depending on facilities at work; just avoid fridge-cold.*

Put the spud chunks into a pan with enough cold water to cover and a good pinch of salt. Pop a lid on as they come to the boil, then turn down to a simmer and cook for 15–20 minutes until you can stick a knife in, lift a piece up and it falls off. Drain.

Take a small, heavy-bottomed frying pan (18–20cm across) and stick it on a medium–high heat. Pour in the oil and when it's hot add the onions and garlic and fry until softened and golden – a good 5–7 minutes with regular stirring.

Chuck in the spuds, peas, paprika and seasoning, turn the heat up to high, and carry on frying and gently turning for a few minutes until they're all pretty much warmed through.

Preheat the grill to medium. Pour the beaten eggs into the pan and give it a gentle shifty to level the mixture. Cook over a low–medium heat for about 5 minutes until the egg is just setting at the edge, then sprinkle over a tad more paprika and finish it under the grill for about 5 minutes until only just set.

Let cool for another 5 minutes. Turn out and tuck in …

ALBARINO

LUNCH

BREAKFAST

SUPPER

4

Impressing
The Pants Off

WHETHER for a new love interest, a passing fancy or The One, the sure-fire way to the heart is through the stomach. It could be an impressive home-cooked meal or just a fabulous fry-up the morning after; either way, there's something about laying your heart and soul on a plate that tends to make the recipient, shall we say, more receptive?

This chapter contains two three-course menus for seduction, each building to a finale of fornication (the puddings, that is). What happens after that is out of my hands and hopefully in yours. The recipes I've chosen are those I think are damn sexy either by virtue of the ingredients, by the way you eat them or by the perceived love-input to make them: the trick is that they all seem much harder and more impressive to make than they really are.

In this chapter I'm essentially pre-empting a question that my daughter may or may not ever ask me: 'Mama, you know that person I really like? Well, I was thinking of asking them round for supper. What do you think I should cook?'

Bringing a food element into talking about sex with one's offspring makes it a bit less awkward. So far I've only experienced 'the talk' from the child's point of view (and my, *that* was a long time ago). I came home from a particularly busy New Year's Eve party aged 17, with a string of hickies on my neck. Mum was still awake and very gently started talking to me about my 'jewel above price'. She was lovely; I was mortified. Just six weeks later she died, and in hindsight I so admire that in the first hours of 1988 she chose to tackle The Chat with her somewhat wayward daughter. However embarrassed I was at the time, in the 25 years since that night, our awkward conversation has made me smile over and over, and think so very fondly of her.

Although it's still a long way off, once my daughter is through the cringing embarrassment of my writing recipes with her fledgling romantic life in mind, hopefully in time she too will be able to look back and smile.

All recipes feed two lovers – potential or current.

Menu 1

Steamy Asparagus,
Loving Hollandaise

*

Thai Seafood Curry

*

Horny
Chocolate & Chilli
Martinis

Steamy Asparagus, Loving Hollandaise

This is a double hitter of love and sex. Love, because making Hollandaise is an act of pure love, and sex because of the way you eat it. Not only is all that dip, suck and chew a fairly sensual experience, but there's something about mainlining a proper Hollandaise that jump-starts the libido. Please only make this with English asparagus: the season kicks off around May 1st, depending on the weather, and goes pretty much through the summer.

(See photo, previous page)

60ml white wine vinegar
1 shallot, sliced
about 10 black peppercorns
1 bay leaf
½ a pat (125g) salted butter
2 egg yolks
1 bunch of asparagus (about
    12 spears)
salt

First pour the vinegar into the smallest saucepan in the house and drop in the shallot, peppercorns and bay leaf. Bring slowly to a simmer and then turn the heat right down so that it infuses as it reduces down to just less than a tablespoon.

Either in another pan or in the microwave, melt the butter gently – not bubbling wildly, just so that the milk solids separate out and the rest is pure liquid gold.

Next find a round-bottomed bowl that sits snugly on a saucepan. Put about 5cm water in the saucepan and put it on a medium heat, with the egg yolks and a tablespoon of water in the bowl above. Lightly whisk the eggs as the water below comes to a simmer – don't let it boil furiously, you want the steam to gently cook the eggs as you whisk.

Don't leave the eggs for a moment – keep whisking until they become thick and ribbony – the whisk will leave drag marks in the mixture that last for a couple of seconds (for the food techies out there this is known as a *sabayon*).

Take the bowl off the heat and slowly dribble in half the butter, whisking all the time. Avoid adding too much of the milk solids (the white stuff) as this will upset the consistency (just a little bit is okay).

Now take your vinegar reduction and strain it through a sieve into the egg mix, really pressing down on the shallot to squeeze out every last drop. Give it a good whisk.

Back to the butter – keep whisking as you pour the rest of it in, again avoiding too much of the white stuff. Season with salt (around ½ teaspoon) and on this occasion I tend not to add pepper – it spoils the look somewhat.

Keep your Hollandaise in a warm place, like by the stove – not so hot that it splits, and not so cold that it solidifies (and then splits). Place a piece of cling film directly on the sauce to prevent a skin forming.

Put a pan of water on for the asparagus and trim just a couple of millimetres off the woody ends. (You probably won't be able to eat right down to the bottom but in this case it becomes a good, chewy vessel to mop up more of your excellent sauce.)

Salt the water well and then drop the spears in (if you're a real pro you'll do them in a tall pot, loosely tied together so that the tougher ends are submerged and the tender tips just steam, but I've never been too bothered with that). They'll only take 3 minutes or so – certainly no more than 4, then drain well and run under cold water for just 10 seconds to refresh the colour and stop them cooking further: this favourite starter of mine is all about the warm, not the hot.

That really is all you need. The seduction is on.

Top Tip

To turn your Hollandaise into Béarnaise (which is most excellent with steak, see page 121) all you need is 2 or 3 stalks of tarragon: pick the leaves from the stalks, and chop each separately. The chopped stalks go into the vinegar reduction and the chopped leaves into the finished sauce.

Thai Seafood Curry

Some time in the 90s, Thai green curries entered the great British culinary vernacular, born from a wave of immigrants (to whom I'm most grateful for breathing new life into pub food). The inevitable boom in its popularity led to Thai curry becoming supermarketed and ubiquitous. What was once a light, clean, aromatic bowl of transcendental deliciousness became claggy and insipid and overcooked. You can still get a good one in pubs or Thai restaurants, of course, but through so many pale imitations, we fell a little out of love with the Thai curry. So, this recipe is for falling in love, both with this very special dish and, as you inhale your bowls of fragrant freshness, with each other too.

(See photo, page 91)

For the sea bits:

70g cleaned squid

2 scallops, of a reasonable size (ask the fishmonger to remove the adductor muscle)

1 x 150g–250g sea bass fillet, skin on, cut into 4–6 pieces

4–6 raw king prawns (depending on size), heads off, peeled, deveined and split in half

200g mussels, cleaned (see page 100)

For the veg bits:

a few mushrooms (shiitake or button), sliced

1 bok choy, halved

½ red pepper, chopped into bite-sized pieces

handful of mangetout or sugar snap peas

handful of frozen peas, defrosted

First get your all your fish and veg prep out of the way so that everything is ready to go. Once opened out, a cleaned piece of squid has a rubbery side and a squidgy side. Lay your squid down so that the squidgy side is facing upwards, then score it in a cross-hatched pattern, as closely as possible, before cutting it into 2cm slices.

Put all the ingredients for the paste (see right) into an upright blender and pulse for a bit, then switch to a continuous blend, dribbling in just enough water to get it moving constantly (it should need around 4 tablespoons). Keep going until you have a smooth paste, which may require stopping and scraping down any bits splattered up the sides with a rubber spatula.

From here on the curry doesn't take long, so get your rice on now (cook it according to the timings on the packet).

Back to the curry: sit a wide, heavy-bottomed pan over a medium heat and scrape the contents of the blender into it. Stir with a wooden spoon for 2–3 minutes as the paste cooks, and don't let it brown at all. Shake the tin of coconut well then pour in half of it, giving it a good stir so that it's well mixed, then let it come to the boil with a lid on the pan.

Now throw in the mushrooms, bok choy and pepper, stick the lid back on and let it come back to the boil – just a minute or two.

For the paste:

1 lemongrass stalk, sliced
    thinish, tough end discarded
½ thumb (about 10g) unpeeled
    ginger or galangal, tough bits
    trimmed off, finely chopped
1 garlic clove, roughly chopped
20g coriander stalks (keep the
    leaves for serving), roughly
    chopped
1 spring onion, sliced
4 Kaffir lime leaves (found fresh
    in some supermarkets or in
    the freezer in Asian shops)
1–2 green chillies, deseeded
    (unless you're feeling tough)
    and chopped
1 tbsp fish sauce
2 tbsp groundnut oil

For the other bits:

150g jasmine rice
½ x 400ml tin coconut milk
fish sauce, to taste
light soy sauce, to taste
juice of 1–2 limes, plus an extra
    one to serve
salt, to taste
handful of beansprouts
    (optional)
coriander leaves, to serve (saved
    from above)

Add the fish in this order: scallops, sea bass, squid, prawns and finally the mussels (which don't need to be submerged) and pop the lid back on. Give it a couple of minutes to come back to the boil, then chuck in the mangetout or sugar snaps and peas, and give the pan a gentle shake.

Your curry will be cooked in just another couple of minutes – when the mussels are open (throw away any that are determined to stay closed), the prawns are pink and the squid is white (not opaque). Turn the heat off and have a taste: it'll need good splashes of fish sauce and soy sauce, and the juice of a lime (or two if they're dry). Once all that's in, taste again. I usually find it needs a pinch of salt too. The final seasoning of this dish is key, so keep going with gentle nudges of lime juice and salt until you're happy.

Serve it up with a pile of beansprouts on top (if using), a flourish of coriander leaves and half a lime on the side.

Horny Chocolate & Chilli Martinis

If you like chocolate, vodka, chilli and naughtiness of all kinds, this one's for you.

200ml whole milk
100ml single cream
1–2 tbsp caster sugar
some red chilli, very finely
　　chopped (any amount up to a
　　whole chilli, depending on how
　　hot you like it)
130g dark chocolate (70% cocoa
　　solids), broken up
80–100ml vodka
ice cubes

For the rimming:
1 tbsp vodka
1 tbsp demerara sugar
½ tsp cocoa
4 long red chillies

In a saucepan, gently heat the milk, cream, a tablespoon of the sugar and the chilli. Once steaming, add the chocolate pieces. Stir until melted and taste to see if the sweetness is to your liking. Sprinkle in a little more sugar if needed to hit the spot.

Leave to cool completely: you can do everything up to here ahead and leave it for a few hours somewhere cool, but don't fridge it.

For rimming the glasses, have two saucers ready: pour the vodka into the first and in the second mix the sugar with the cocoa. Dip the rim of each martini glass in the vodka, then run the rims all the way round the cocoa mix.

Cut the bottom off each chilli and make a small incision through the sides so that you can sit them on the rims of the glasses to look like little devils' horns. Cute.

Pour the cooled chocolatey mix into a cocktail shaker/thermos flask/really big jam jar along with the vodka, plus the bit from the saucer if you haven't necked it, and a small handful of ice. Give it your best mixologist moves: pros shake it over a shoulder, rather than in front of them, or underarm like a rugby ball. For girls, this move is all about the tit-sway, for boys it's more a cock-sure display of muscle. Either way there are only two aims: to look sexy and to shake up the drink. Each is as important as the other.

Pour into the glasses through a cocktail strainer, tea strainer or little sieve to ensure a satin texture. Drink in whatever manner comes to mind.

Shown with: Passionate Soufflés

M&NU 2

Moules Marinière

*

Hazelnut-crusted
Rack of Lamb
& F**k Me
Dauphinois

*

Passionate
Soufflés

Moules Marinière

As well as being a classic, belting bit of Frenchery, the best part isn't how quick, easy and fabulous a dish this is, or that it all happens in one pot. No, the best bit is how intrinsically rude these lovelies are.

(See photo, previous page)

1kg mussels, live and local
2 tbsp butter
3 banana shallots, or 5 regular
   ones, finely chopped
2 large garlic cloves, chopped
1 large glass (about 200ml)
   white wine
50ml double cream
handful of flat-leaf parsley,
   finely chopped
S & P
fresh baguette, to serve

The only time-consuming part of this recipe is cleaning the mussels, which can be done hours ahead. Gently tip them into a colander or straight into the sink. Keep a gentle flow of cold water over them as you work. One by one, have a quick look at each mussel: if it's closed, check if it still has a 'beard', which looks like a small frayed piece of sea string, sticking out of the side. This is how mussels attach themselves to the rope from which they were harvested. Remove any beards, which will come off with a sharp tug towards the pointy end.

Also check that they are still alive (which they must be in order to be tummy-safe). Throw out any that remain open when given a quick tap on the shell. Live ones will close up.

If you're doing this ahead of time, put all the cleaned mussels into a bowl and cover with wet newspaper – they like it dark and moist, so this is the most humane way to keep them, as well as the safest.

When you're about 10 minutes from suppertime, put a large, wide, lidded saucepan big enough to hold all the mussels over a medium heat and melt the butter. Gently fry the shallots and garlic for about 5 minutes with the lid on, stirring from time to time – you want them to soften and sweeten, but not brown at all.

Now tip the mussels in and stir well for a minute or so, then turn the heat up and pour in the wine. Immediately pop the lid back on, give the pan a little shake and leave it for about 3 minutes.

Ideally you want to serve the mussels in wide, shallow bowls. Now is the right time to warm them up.

Have a look in the pan – you want all the mussels to be open, so if some are still closed, stick the lid back on, give the pan another shake and check again in a minute or two ... no longer.

Chuck out any that haven't opened at this point (again, to be tummy-safe), turn off the heat and stir in the cream, parsley and some pepper. Taste for seasoning, you may need a bit more salt, but not much, and serve up. Use a slotted spoon to share the mussels between your bowls then ladle or spoon over the sauce and tear off a couple of chunks of baguette to soak up the yumminess. Couple of last tips: don't forget to put a big bowl on the table for the shells, and whatever you do don't fill up on bread. Your evening has just started ...

Top Tip

For the most luxurious mussel soup, cook the mussels as described but instead of serving up just let the whole thing go cold. Pick through the mussels, chucking the fleshy bits into the creamy base, then lob the shells in the bin and heat it up again. It doesn't take long and makes a couple of rather special bowlfuls. The quantities look small but it's so rich you're not left wanting in any way.

Hazelnut-crusted Rack of Lamb & F**k Me Dauphinois

There are some folks for whom the best way to their heart is a fabulous piece of meat (and purely as an observation over many years of cooking, they do tend mainly to be men). Combine meat with a spud dish that's dripping with sin, and you've an evening of fun ahead of you – as long as they don't keel over with a coronary.

This dish is so rich it definitely needs some kind of greens. Spinach, wilted in a pan with garlic and seasoned with salt, pepper and a touch of lemon juice, would be my plan for the colder months (see page 366), but a crisp salad of Little Gem lettuce, peas and mint leaves speaks to me for summer.

For an easy life, make the dauph and pre-crust the lamb ahead of time, just let them come up to room temp before you start cooking, else the timings won't work.

(See photo, page 99)

1 quantity of F**k Me Dauphinois (see page 356)
50g hazelnuts, shelled
1 x 7-bone rack of lamb, split into 2, French-trimmed (and check with your butcher that it's chined too, which it will be if it's a supermarket one)
olive oil
Dijon mustard, just enough for coating the lamb
1 batch of Garlic Sautéed Spinach (see page 366)
S & P

First get going on the dauph and preheat the oven to 200°C/fan 180°C/Gas 6. When hot, put your dauph on the middle shelf, then start the lamb.

Carefully pulse the hazelnuts in a food processor or chop them with a knife and then crush with the flat of the blade. You need to get the hazelnuts to a place where there are some bigger pieces and some fairly well ground bits to make a good coating.

Trim the outer layer of fat and some of the sinew from the lamb racks; you'll still have some areas of fat but good parts of the flesh will be showing below too.

Put an ovenproof frying pan big enough to hold both lamb racks on a high heat and pour a splash of oil into it. Season the racks well all over, and when the oil in the pan is smoking hot (extraction on/door open/window down/smoke-monitor manned), lay the racks in it, rounded flesh-side down. Fry quite aggressively for 3–5 minutes until the outside is well browned (don't do the ends), then turn the heat off and take the lamb out of the pan to cool.

So you don't smoke out the kitchen, tip out any excess fat from the pan and lightly rub it with kitchen paper. Brush the seared fleshy side of the racks with a fair amount of mustard, but not the ends. Put your chopped hazelnuts on to a plate and roll the mustardy part of the rack into it, so that you have a solid hazelnut crust. Sit the racks in the pan so that the bones point up in the air and interlock (see photo, page 99) to make sure they don't fall over … and they look loving too.

By this time, the dauphinois should have had about half an hour, so pop the lamb in to roast for 20 minutes on the shelf above, then take them both out and rest for 10 minutes with a piece of foil draped over them while you nail your greens.

This is a dish to serve at the table. Luscious lamb, seasonally appropriate greens and naughty dauph: impressive, tasty, rich and satisfying on every level … hopefully just like your date!

Menu 2
Passionate Soufflés

This is all about the air: once you start making it, you need to work fast, so have all your bowls, weights, trays, etc. sorted before your date turns up, but only start putting it together once you've finished eating your mains. It's amazingly straightforward, surprisingly fail-safe (it's never let me down yet), utterly impressive and ridiculously special.

(See photo, page 97)

3 tbsp caster sugar, plus 2 tsp
knob of butter, at room
    temperature
3 passion fruit (or enough so
    that you end up with 2 tbsp
    strained juice)
2 eggs, separated
a little icing sugar

Preheat the oven to 180°C/fan 160°C/Gas 4. Butter the insides of two soufflé dishes or large ramekins (about 8cm diameter and 6–7cm deep). Scatter a teaspoon of caster sugar into each one, tipping it all around the insides until completely sugared.

Empty the insides of the passion fruit into a sieve set over a bowl and push through the juice (you need about 2 tablespoons of juice). Keep the seeds for later.

Either by hand, or using an upright or hand-held electric mixer, whisk the egg yolks with 2 tablespoons of the caster sugar and the passion fruit juice.

In a separate bowl, whisk the whites until frothy, then add the remaining tablespoon of sugar and whisk again until just stiff and holding shape. Fold the whites into the yolks in three stages using gentle arcing motions – remember soufflés are all about the air, so keep it as light as you can in there.

Spoon the mix into the dishes to just below the rim, then run your thumb around the rim to totally clear it of any sugary butter or stray drops of mix, which would stop the soufflé rising. Pop the dishes on to a baking tray and bake for 12 minutes – *don't open the oven for a peek* or your work may be scuppered!

Meanwhile, get out the icing sugar, a sieve and the passion fruit seeds from earlier. When the soufflés are cooked they should be a good 4cm higher than the rim: check they're ready by lightly touching their tops – your finger should come away clean but they should still wobble in the middle. SERVE IMMEDIATELY.

5

Just
The
Two
Of Us

THIS is the magical time in your life when you're loved up and shacked up. You've upgraded from 'going out' to living together, and it's all very exciting, very grown-up, and rather electric.

You're probably renting, and you're certainly not talking about weddings yet (though you may be thinking about it). You have separate bank accounts but a shared bed. At this stage, nobody knows what lies ahead, it's all about the here and now.

Decisions that were previously taken on your own, with friends or with parental advice are now shared with your potential life partner (because why else would you be taking the plunge?). Where shall we live? What do we get Aunt Joan for Christmas? And of course most importantly, what are we having for supper? The key is 'we', and 'we' feels great. It's the next step up the Ladder of Life, and a big one at that.

So, this chapter is about the rookie co-habiting stage of life. The recipes have earned their place on two levels: first, I wanted them to be just a little bit flash, while still being straightforward and achievable enough to make after work. This is a time to show the one you love what you can do in the kitchen – a little bit of culinary primal chest-thumping if you like. The other criterion was simply that these recipes work best for two on the grounds that domestic kitchens don't usually have the benefit of a six-burner stove and the kind of oven which could house a sorority of suckling pigs that restaurants do.

In my mind, cooking a great steak sits perfectly at the intersection of these two sets: it's one of life's great skills and guaranteed to impress, which is why I've included my 10-Point Guide to Steak Heaven in here (see pages 118–9). Because the real truth of it is that lovers come and go, you can't control that, but the skill of how to cook a perfect medium-rare sirloin will never, ever leave you.

Steamed Bream
(al cartoccio/en papillotte/in the bag)

This is a beautiful, gentle and simple way to cook fish – quick to knock up too once you've got the hang of the bagging. You can use this method for any portion-sized piece of fillet, but I don't recommend cooking a whole fish this way because fiddling about with the bones jars with the simplicity and softness of the flesh. It's plain scrummy served with new potatoes, dressed with a little extra virgin olive oil and chopped parsley: a perfect summer lunch or light supper.

For 2

1 small fennel bulb, finely sliced
    (keep the feathery fronds)
½ small red onion, halved and
    finely sliced
1 chicory head, leaves separated,
    big ones halved lengthways
small handful of green olives,
    squashed and stoned
extra virgin olive oil
2 bream fillets, about 120g each,
    skin on, scaled and pin-boned
100ml vermouth
S & P
handful of flat-leaf parsley,
    roughly chopped, to serve
1 lemon, cut into wedges, to serve

Preheat the oven to 170°C/fan 150°C/Gas 3½.

Lay out two big sheets of foil, about 50cm square each, and put a piece of greaseproof or parchment paper roughly the same size on top. Make a pile of fennel, red onion and chicory in the middle of each one, then top with the olives. Splosh on a bit of extra virgin olive oil and seasoning, then season the flesh side of the fish too. Lay a fillet on each pile, skin-side up, and sprinkle with any fennel fronds.

Bring the near and far edges of the foil and parchment together to meet over the pile, then roll and scrunch them firmly together. Do the same with one of the ends, rolling it up tightly in stages until it hits the pile inside. Pour the vermouth into the open end, then close that end too – it's really crucial you get a good seal all round so the steam can't escape. (If you find that you've got a hole, just wrap the whole lot in another layer of foil).

Put the bags side by side on a baking tray and cook in the oven for 18–20 minutes. Have the chopped parsley and lemon wedges ready to chuck on there when you unfold the foil and open up the bags. Head down, breathe in.

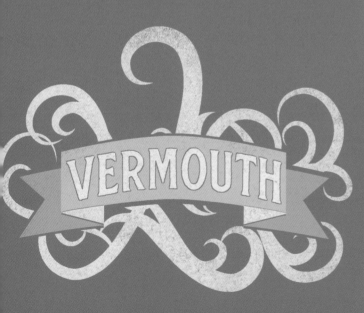

Veal/Pig Holstein

This feast of a dinner was named after a German count who was Bismarck's foreign minister, and it definitely feels rather grand in an old-school way. The reason it's best as a meal for two is down to the cooking – you're never going to find a pan that can hold more than two unless you ransack the kitchen at The Savoy. After careful testing and consideration I believe it is best as a two-pan operation: a massive one for the meat, and a smallish one for the potent butter that is both the making and the definition of this dish.

For 2

a scant handful of flour, seasoned
    well with salt and pepper
1 egg, beaten with 1 tbsp water
about 50g dry breadcrumbs
    (panko work well)
2 veal or pork escalopes
3 tbsp extra virgin olive oil
60g butter
3 fat anchovy fillets, chopped
    (but ditch these if you're going
    for pork)
1 tbsp capers, rinsed if salted,
    roughly chopped if massive
handful of flat-leaf parsley,
    finely chopped
2 eggs
S & P
½ lemon, cut in half, to serve

First breadcrumb your escalopes: get three flattish receptacles that are big enough to hold one of the escalopes at a time, as well as a big plate or small baking tray to put them on at the end. On the first one, spread out the seasoned flour; pour the egg mixture into the second and the breadcrumbs go into the third.

Lightly season the meat on both sides, then put one escalope into the flour, turn to coat all over, then tap off any excess. Move it into the egg and make sure all surfaces get covered. Next lay it in the breadcrumbs, turn it over and, once totally coated, put it on the end plate or tray. Do the same with the other one.

Now get all your other bits ready (butter weighed; anchovy fillets chopped, etc.) as once you get going this is a quick, busy cook. When you're all over the prep, put two frying pans on the hob – ideally one of them will be big enough to hold both the escalopes (though if you have to do them one after the other, it's no biggie – you'll just need to put in a bit more oil and butter for the second one), and the other need only be a small one. The big pan goes on a medium–high heat and the small one on a low–medium heat.

Pour 2 tablespoons of olive oil into the big pan, and melt a third of the butter into it. Once melted and starting to make a noise, lay the escalopes in the pan (either together or one at a time), and cook for 2–3 minutes each side, until golden and crispy.

CONTINUED

CONTINUED FROM
PREVIOUS PAGE

Meanwhile, in pan two (the little one), melt the rest of the butter save for a small knob, and once bubbling drop in the anchovies (if using), and capers. As it fizzles away, use the back of a spoon to squish the anchovy pieces so that they begin to melt into the butter, then turn the heat off and stir in the parsley. (And if you're not using the anchovies, just fry the capers for a minute or two before turning off the heat and stirring in the parsley.)

By now your escalopes should have been in and out, and as soon as the last one leaves the pan turn the heat right down and, if necessary, bravely wipe the pan out with kitchen roll to remove any burning/burnt breadcrumbs. Pour the last tablespoon of olive oil into the big pan and chuck in your last knob of butter. Crack in both the eggs, and fry them, basting them with the fats in the pan, until they're crisp on the bottom and soft on top.

Plate the escalopes, laying the eggs on top of them, and serve with the lemon wedges to the side and the punchy caper and parsley butter crowning it off – a truly magnificent feast.

Sea Bass, Lentils & Salsa Verde

Quite simply, this is a contender for my death row meal.

Handsome supper for 2

extra virgin olive oil
1 small onion, finely chopped
1 carrot, peeled and small diced
1 celery stick, split lengthways
    into 3, then sliced
150g Puy lentils, rinsed
2 bay leaves
½ small glass of red wine
½ quantity of Salsa Verde
    (see page 368)
2 sea bass fillets, 120–140g each,
    skin on, scaled and pin-boned
½ lemon, cut in half
S & P

Heat 2 tablespoons of olive oil in a wide, shallow pan and fry the onion, carrot and celery for a few minutes until softening, but don't let them pick up any colour. Add the lentils and bay leaves and give it all a good roll around.

Pour in the wine and let it bubble away completely for a minute or so, then add cold water to cover, plus about 2cm. Bring to the boil, then turn down the heat and simmer for 30–40 minutes until the lentils are cooked but still have bite (if it's a particularly obstinate batch, you may need to top up with more hot water from the kettle). Either way, don't drain them as you'll lose flavour and nutritional goodness.

While the lentils are working away, knock up the salsa verde and put your oven on to preheat to 180°C/fan 160°C/Gas 4.

Stick a heavy-bottomed, ovenproof frying pan on a high heat. Season the fish on the flesh side, pour a splash of olive oil into the pan and once it's smoking add the fillets, skin-side down. Flatten with a palette knife if they start to curl up. Turn down the heat to medium–high and cook until the skin is good and crispy. When the edge of the skin is golden brown and the flesh immediately above is going opaque, pop the pan in the oven for 6–8 minutes; the fish is cooked when it's white all over and not too soft when you gently poke the thickest part.

Check your lentils: by now they should be cooked and have nothing more than a coating of liquid left in the pan. Season them good and season them hard – pulses love a bit of salt and pepper, but not before they're cooked as the salt toughens their skins. Stir through a little extra virgin olive oil too.

To serve, it's lentils on the bottom, fish atop, with salsa verde and a supportive piece of lemon on the side. Perfection.

Seared Squid with Harissa

This is a cracking little bumptious plate of fun, full of surprises for the taste buds. Once the squid is prepped (which you can ask your fishmonger to do), you'll be in and out of the kitchen in 10 minutes. As written, it's a starter or even a light lunch. To make it a full-throttle supper, knock up a bowl of couscous or the Chickpea Pilaf on page 74.

Your starter for 2

1 large or 2 small squid,
    about 400g in total (ask
    your fishmonger to clean it)
1 garlic clove, thinly sliced
handful of flat-leaf parsley,
    finely chopped
1 lemon
couple of handfuls (about 30g)
    of rocket
3 tbsp extra virgin olive oil
1 tsp harissa paste
S & P

If your squid isn't in one flat piece, split the tube up the side and cut it into pieces about the size of the palm of your hand. Closely cross-hatch the inside of it with a sharp knife (the squidgier side, not the shiny, more rubbery one) and if the tentacles are fairly chunky then divide them into clumps of two or three.

Before you start cooking, do your prep (garlic, parsley) because once you start it's a fast one. Zest half of your lemon then cut it in half, and divide the rocket between two starter plates.

Once good to go, heat a large heavy-bottomed pan to explosively hot and season the squid with salt. Lay the tentacles into the dry pan first – they usually take a bit longer – followed just a minute later by the body, scored-side down. Don't fiddle with the squid and it will pick up some nice colour. After a couple of minutes you should see the tentacles curl up and the body just begin to brown: now turn them over. The squid is done when it has turned opaque and lost its slippery ivory look – this usually takes no more than 3 minutes. The body bit should be all curled up now, with the cross-hatching on the outside.

Lift the squid out, put it on a large plate and turn off the heat. There will be enough residual heat in the pan for the next part, as long as you keep a wiggle on. Immediately pour in the olive oil, swirl it around and scatter in the garlic slices and lemon zest. Once fizzling and turning golden, squeeze in the juice from the zested lemon half, then stir in the harissa and chopped parsley. This needs to come out of the pan sharp-ish before the parsley loses its colour, so spoon it over the squid and serve immediately with the other half of the lemon and a handful of rocket.

Steak Heaven

my 10 point guide

1 Once you get your meat home from the butcher or supermarket, take it off the polystyrene base or anything else that leaves it sitting in its own blood. This turns the meat grey, which is not a good look.

2 If your steak has been in the fridge for a while and you fear for its life, marinating will extend its fridge life for a few more days. My default quicko marinade is: enough extra virgin to coat, garlic, some tough herbs (like rosemary or thyme) and a tablespoon of peppercorns, all very roughly chopped and crushed together. (Once coated, cover the dish in cling film – at this point it's had enough communing with the air.) Wine also makes a good marinade, but remember to pat your steaks dry before cooking. Keep the marinade for the sauce, and for food safety be sure to heat it to boiling. You can use the pan the steak was cooked in to pick up a meaty flavour. Never salt your marinades – it draws moisture out of the meat.

3 If you like your meat rare or medium-rare, it MUST be at room temperature before cooking, or it will still be cold in the middle when the outside is done. Take it out of the fridge a good couple of hours before the event. (I'm not going to tell you how to cook a steak well done as it's truly unfair to the meat.)

4 Season your steak heavily on both sides just before you start to cook.

5 It doesn't matter how you cook your steak (frying pan, griddle or barbecue), always ensure the vessel is bloody hot before you lay the meat down – you only have one shot at that browning. (I never cook steak under the grill – you just don't get the impactful heat needed to sear it, and who wants to eat grey meat?)

6 Once the steak is down, don't touch it until you are ready to turn, unless you're griddling/barbecueing and totally wedded to the idea of some Steak House cross-hatching, in which case rotate them 90° after 2–4 minutes, depending on how you like your steak cooked.

7 Portion-sized steaks need about a third less time on the second side than they had on the first – most of the heat penetration is done on the first side. Cooking for the same amount of time on both sides is a fast route to overdone-ness.

8 Bigger hunks of meat, like onglet or chateaubriand, need an equal amount of time on the second side for the heat to reach the middle.

9 Always rest portion-sized steaks for at least 4 minutes after they have cooked. The texture of the meat is transformed as it settles. Leave small steaks uncovered, or they will carry on cooking too much in their retained heat. The bigger the cut of meat (especially cuts for two, like porterhouse, chateaubriand or a big old entrecote), the longer the resting time required, so leave larger hunks of steak for about 8 minutes with a piece of foil draped over them so they don't lose too much heat.

10 The juices that come out of the meat during resting time are pure gold – add them to your sauce or just spoon them back over the meat, even if serving with a non-stock-based sauce like béarnaise, salsa verde or garlic butter.

Griddled Sirloin
(classic, functional steak-eating at its finest)

The sirloin is a whacking piece of meat (over 60cm long) that runs along the middle back of the beast. It's a prime cut, and has an edge of solid fat on one side, which keeps it flavourful as it cooks.

For 2

2 sirloin steaks, 220–250g each
S & P
Home-made Chips (see page 358)
Béarnaise Sauce (see page 93)

Put a griddle over the highest heat and wait for it to become explosively hot. Season the steaks heavily on both sides.

If you like your steak rare or medium-rare, lay each steak in the pan slightly bunched up but still flat, rather than stretched out and elongated – it cooks better this way. Give it 3ish minutes on the first side and 2 minutes on the second for a very happy rare. To test for doneness, follow 'The Hand Game' on page 124.

Pan-seared Onglet
(a real steak experience)

Onglet is a relatively unknown cut that used to be known as 'butcher's steak' because they would keep it for themselves. It sits between the ribs and spine, and although not the most tender of cuts, has supreme flavour, colour and texture. It is a true steak experience.

For 2

Caesar Salad (see page 367)
½ batch of Rosemary Oven
    Crunchies (see page 357)
1 x 400g onglet steak, trimmed
    weight, at room temperature
olive oil
sea salt and pepper
watercress, to serve (optional)

First make your salad and crunchies, keeping the crunchies warm in a low oven. Now you can concentrate on the steak.

Put a small, heavy-bottomed frying pan (to fit the meat) over a high heat to get very hot. Rub a little olive oil over the meat and season on all sides with sea salt and pepper. When the pan is smoking, gently lay the meat in it and cook for 4 minutes, then turn over and cook for another 4 minutes. Now take it out to rest.

To carve, hold a sharp knife perpendicular to the meat's grain and slice though it obliquely, about 2cm apart. Serve with the Caesar salad, warm crunchies and some watercress if you like.

Chateaubriand with Red Wine Sauce (the lovers' cut)

This is the best of the best: not only is the meat from the fillet, itself the king of cuts, but it's from the thick end. Cook whole then slice and share, along with your favourite accompaniments (chips and a sharply dressed green salad do it for me). Tender, gentle and very, very special.

Supper for 2, plus sarnies in bed the next day

1 x 500g piece chateaubriand
S & P

For the red wine sauce:
80ml red wine
250ml beef stock (fresh or from concentrate is best – a cube is a poor third choice)
2 garlic cloves, unpeeled but smashed with the flat of a knife
about 10 sprigs of thyme
2 big knobs of butter, at room temperature
splash of sherry vinegar

Put a very large heavy-bottomed pan over a high heat. Measure out the wine and stock, and season the meat well on all sides.

As the pan becomes stupidly hot, do whatever necessary not to set off your smoke alarm (turn on full extraction, open windows, shut doors, alert the fire brigade, etc.). Once it's smoking, lay the meat in the dry pan on the side with the largest surface and cook for 2 minutes, then turn over and sear for another 2 minutes.

Now give it 1 minute on each small 'side', plus a minute on each end. You want it nicely browned all over, so the larger sides will need a bit more time. Now turn the heat right down to low, sit the meat back on its side and cook for another 8ish minutes in total, giving it a quarter-turn every couple of minutes. Transfer to a large plate, cover with foil and drape a tea towel over the top. After about 10 minutes' rest it will be perfectly rare and relaxed – just how you want this beauty.

For the sauce, turn the heat back up to medium–high and pour in the wine, which will bubble up. As it evaporates, chuck in the garlic and thyme. Once reduced by two-thirds, pour in the stock, and let that reduce by two-thirds as well. As it's bubbling, season with plenty of pepper and taste for salt – some stocks are salty already. When the sauce has become deep and rich but not sticky, turn off the heat and whisk in the butter in 4–6 goes. Taste again. I finish mine with a tiny wee splash of sherry vinegar.

Spoon the sauce directly over the steak, leaving behind the garlic. The thyme sprigs look pretty if you want to serve them up too.

Two easy ways to tell if your meat is cooked...

AS YOU LIKE IT

There is no better way to learn the ways of cooking meat than with practice. Some favour a meat probe (usually men), but I use more touchy-feely, low-tech methods to test for done-ness, which I call 'The Hand Game' (for steaks) and 'McEvedy's Lip Service' for bigger cuts.

TEST 1: The Hand Game

This is an approximate but useful guide to telling how cooked (as in rare/medium-rare/medium) a portion-sized steak is just by poking it. It's roughly equivalent to how the ball of flesh below your thumb (on your non-dominant hand) feels when you poke it, but not squeezing your thumb to your finger – just letting them touch.

Remember though: this is how the steak will feel as it's cooking – once rested, the meat will relax and feel much less tense, so it's an on-the-job game. I generally prefer to play it on my own, but you can also enjoy with friends at the risk of conversation ruining a good piece of meat.

How firm your steak will feel as it's cooking

Index finger to thumb = RARE

It should feel muscular but fleshy and with a fair amount of give.

Middle finger to thumb = MEDIUM-RARE TO MEDIUM

You can feel that the meat has tensed up a bit, with more resistance to pressure.

Ring finger to thumb = MEDIUM TO MEDIUM-WELL

There's now a relatively small amount of give - it's a pretty solid muscle.

Little finger to thumb = well, we're not going to go there.

TEST 2: McEvedy's Lip Service
Good for roasts, joints and other large hunks of meat (or fish).

While prodding is good for smaller pieces of protein, when you're talking about a big old joint (especially on the bone) or a whopper of a fish, then penetration is required to tell how it's getting on inside. After years of experience, this is my trusted method.

Find a sharp, thin, pointy thing, like a metal skewer or thin knife, and stick it into the thickest part of your beast. If your meat is on the bone, then be sure to push it pretty close to that. Leave your pointy thing in there for 5 seconds then pull it out and gingerly put it to your top lip – this is one goddam sensitive part of your accessible body and is as utterly reliable as a naked barometer.

What you ideally want to feel varies from case to case, but these rules generally apply:

COLD = not ready yet, so just keep cooking.

WARM = you're aware it's there but it's not painful to the touch –
your meat is ready, or rather, will be after a decent rest.

SCORCHIO = overcooked, i.e. dry – lesson learnt for next time.

Pork and poultry (and this goes for geese and turkeys too): aim for the hotter side of warm, but not as far as scorchio. Also, when you pull out the skewer/knife, look at the hole it's just exited: if clear juices seep out, then it's cooked.

Beef and lamb: I go for a solid warm. After a good foiled rest, that'll yield you rare in the middle and better done (all the way to well done) around the exterior. If it's a little too hot to keep the skewer comfortably on your lip, then you're looking at medium+, and if it burns you then you deserve it for ruining a good piece of meat.

Whole large fish: insert the skewer just behind the head and right up to the backbone. You want the skewer to feel on the hotter side of warm against your lip.

It's true that this method takes a little practice, but once you've got the hang of it, it NEVER lets you down: lips and learning, that's all it takes – no need to rely on gadgets when our bodies naturally have the perfect gauge.

Bistro Salad

The French know a thing or two about classic dishes, and this salad is right up there. You know how dogmatic the French are about their culinary rules, and I'm happy not to fiddle as it really is just perfect as is. For them it has to be made with French beans, lardons, croutons, soft-boiled eggs and frisée lettuce (the spiky one that's slightly hard work), all bound together with a mustardy dressing. Over this side of the channel it's hard to come across frisée on its own, rather than as part of a leaf mix, so get whatever lettuce you can that has a bit of volume, body, personality and (French) resistance to it.

Perfect main for 2 (or starter for 4 if you're double-dating)

House Dressing (see page 367; you need 2–3 tbsp)
140g French beans, tops trimmed, halved
2 eggs
150g lardons or pancetta, cut into 1cm dice
100g white bread (not of the sliced kind), crusts off and cut into rough 2cm chunks
splash of olive oil (optional)
about 150g of suitable interesting mixed leaves with volume OR 1 small head of frisée, torn up
couple of handfuls of chives, chopped as small as you can
S & P

First take a couple of minutes to knock up the dressing.

Next, bring a small pan of salted water to a rolling boil, drop in the beans and simmer for 3ish minutes, until just cooked with a bit of crunch. Lift them out with a slotted spoon, leaving the water boiling for the eggs. Run the beans under cold water until they've lost their heat, to keep them bright and stop them overcooking.

Now use the slotted spoon to gently drop the eggs into the boiling water. Check the clock and after 5–6 minutes tip them into the sink, cracking the shells as you go (makes them easier to peel). Run under cold water briefly and peel at your leisure.

Meanwhile, put a wide frying pan over a medium–high heat, chuck in the lardons and fry for a few minutes until golden and crispy. When done, use your trusty slotted spoon to transfer to kitchen roll for a brief degrease. Scatter the bread chunks into the pan and fry in the bacon fat for 4–5 minutes until golden and delicious, adding a splash of olive oil if needed (depending on how fatty your pig was), then turn off the heat and season.

Put the salad leaves or frisée into a serving bowl and chuck in the blanched beans, bacon bits, fried bread, chives, some seasoning and enough dressing to give it all a light coating. Toss well, then top with the halved eggs, each adorned with a little salt and pepper of their own.

Cardiac Carbonara

Carbonara = bacon and eggs. My version also has Parmesan-enriched double cream, and while there are lighter versions of this classic Italian sauce, I'm yet to taste one that beats this. I don't make it too often, for obvious reasons, but when it's carbonara time in our house I'm a little jittery with excitement all day. Soooooo worth it.

Mains for 2, in a gluttonous mood

150ml double cream
20g Parmesan, finely grated,
    plus a piece of the rind
    (the bigger, the better)
3 garlic cloves, peeled and
    smashed with the side
    of a knife
1 sprig of rosemary
olive oil
200g pasta (spaghetti or
    buccatini work best)
knob of butter
100g lardons or diced pancetta
2 egg yolks
S & P

Put the cream, Parmesan rind, garlic and rosemary sprig in a small pan on the lowest possible heat. Leave to infuse gently for about half an hour, stirring occasionally to make sure it doesn't catch on the bottom, until the garlic is soft and the sauce is thick.

Bring a big, lidded pan of salted water to the boil for the pasta. Once the cream infusion is ready, pick out the Parmesan rind and the rosemary sprig, scraping off any cream that's stuck to them before chucking them out. Fish the garlic cloves out too, chop up finely and stir them back in.

When the pasta water is boiling, slug in a big splash of olive oil (this helps stop the pasta from sticking to itself or to the pan when cooking), then add the pasta and give it a good stir. Put the lid on again till it comes back to the boil, then turn down to a busy simmer until cooked al dente.

Drain the pasta and put the empty pan back on a medium heat. Once it's dried out, pour in a tablespoon of olive oil and melt a knob of butter in it. When the butter starts to fizzle, chuck in the pig bits and fry for about 3 minutes, stirring, until they start to brown, then turn off the heat. Tip in the drained pasta and stir well so that it's all coated in the piggy oil, then pour in the cream, giving the pan a good scrape with a rubber spatula, and drop in the egg yolks. Stir, roll and coat.

Season with pepper, and taste for salt before adding any – cured pig is quite salty, as is Parmesan, and we don't want to work the old ticker more than we have to. Serve up with the finely grated Parmesan on top and a defibrillator on the side.

Shown with: Spag CPG

Spag CPG
(Spaghetti with Chilli, Parsley & Garlic)

This is one of those totally reliable recipes that everyone should know (forgive me if you already do). Quick and easy, delicious and cheap – it just performs on every level. I've been cooking this at work and home for decades, and like many old and trusted friends that's why it's ended up with a shorthand nickname. It's worth wheeling out your very best extra virgin olive oil for the final splashes, and seasoning makes sure it fulfils its potential.

For 2 (see photo, previous page)

250g spaghetti (the long stuff is more fun)
splash of regular olive oil
½–1 red chilli, deseeded and very finely diced
2–3 garlic cloves, finely chopped
big handful of flat-leaf parsley, finely chopped
about 2 tbsp (a good slosh) of your best extra virgin olive oil
S & P

Bring a big pan of water to a rolling boil with the lid on. When it's busy bubbling, pour in a little plain olive oil (this helps stop the pasta from sticking to itself or to the pan when cooking). Add the spaghetti and give it a good stir to prevent clumping, then cook for the allotted time on the packet.

Meanwhile, get on with your chopping – the amount of garlic and chilli varies depending on size and personal preference – but the key is to chop them pretty tiny.

When the spag is al dente, turn the heat off, drain and give it a little stir in the colander. Leave to drain for a minute then tip back into the pan and mix in the chilli, garlic, parsley and some salt and pepper. Pour in just enough of your best extra virgin to coat the pasta in a lip-smacking way, then lift a strand out and taste. Adjust the seasoning if necessary. Tongs work best to get a good pile-up on the plates. No need for Parmesan with this one – the joy is in its simplicity.

Spatchcock Poussins
with Sweet Chilli & Yoghurt Marinade

Roughly speaking, poussins are handy portion-sized young chickens, and although they're cute just roasted whole, flattening them out ('spatchcocking') allows more of the skin to get crispy ... and we all know how heavenly crispy chicken skin is. With the addition of this no-brainer marinade, it goes simply stratospheric.

For 2

3 tbsp Greek or natural yoghurt
3 tbsp sweet chilli sauce
2 poussins, spatchcocked (ask
    your butcher to do this)
S & P

Serve with:
long-grain rice (see page 358
    for how to cook perfect rice)
small bunch of coriander,
    chopped
2 limes, halved
green salad
Tabasco sauce (optional)

In a big bowl, stir together the yoghurt and sweet chilli sauce with some seasoning. Drop in the birds and use your hands to give them a thorough coating all over.

Cling film the bowl and put in the fridge for 15 minutes to 1 hour.

Preheat the oven to 210°C/fan 190°C/Gas 6½ and get your rice going. Lay the birds, skin-side up, on an oiled baking or roasting tray. Use the palm of your hand to press down on them so they are as flat as possible. Give them another light season with salt and pepper and roast for 25–30 minutes until they are deliciously golden and the juices run clear when you insert a knife into the base of the thigh joint.

When the rice is cooked, stir through most of the coriander, along with a squeeze of lime juice. Serve up with a green salad, halved limes, a scattering of the remaining corry on top and Tabasco on the table.

The Art of Entertaining

6

Part **1**

A Liability in the Kitchen

HAVING friends and family over for a meal is one of my top five pleasures in life. It's the perfect combination of relaxed chat, being at home and making those you care about happy. But as any reasonably experienced host knows, and no one tells you when you're a novice party-thrower, there's a basic rule of entertaining, which I call McEvedy's Pleasure Principle.

This covers everything from the menu, shopping, tidying up and hoovering (only if really necessary), checking you have enough knives/chairs/glasses/soufflé dishes, remembering to take the cheese out of the fridge, having your wine at the appropriate temperature (not still in the boot of the car), doing a bit of low-level food prep and, most crucially of all, making sure that all the dirty dishes are done when your guests arrive.

This chapter contains recipes and instructions that are Really Useful to Know: how to master a risotto; an easy and impressive pâté; some helpful, timeless canapés, and a small lesson in quiche, because everybody loves a tart. I've also given a few cracking dinner party stand-bys that I felt compelled to share with the group. They are all achievable and useful to have in your back pocket (or wherever you keep your recipe book) and will hopefully save you from flailing on the periphery of your culinary ability, because when you first start having folks round there is a definite but irrational tendency to overextend yourself. My sister, who missed out on the culinary gene (but got the drawing one so it

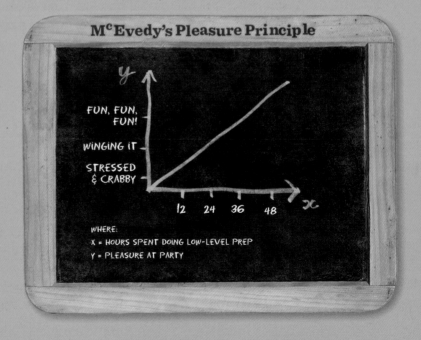

all evens out), was absolutely unstoppable in the late eighties, whenever our dad had friends round, in reaching for her Escoffier cookbook. This resulted in some totally hilarious suppers chez McEvedy.

Think 19th-century French crossed with nouvelle cuisine as interpreted by my sister's misplaced confidence in the kitchen. Pa's poor friends inevitably left gastronomically bewildered, not to mention still hungry.

The fondness my sister and I have for entertaining goes back to our early days. Once every couple of months our parents threw a major dinner party and we would sit at the top of the stairs listening to the chatter and laughter. In the morning we'd inspect the scenes of debauched debris in the dining room: Mama's best plates scraped clean of her trademark rich chocolate cake (see page 332); a ridiculous quantity of dirty glasses for the number of guests, some still partially full; scrunched-up napkins chucked aside. But above all I remember the after-party smell: I used to breathe it in greedily when we opened the dining room door. It was a bit like unlocking Tutankhamun's tomb: snuffed out candles; red wine; stale smoke from Mama's little café crème cigarillos she toyed with on such occasions, stubbed out on side plates; and just a whiff of that famous chocolate cake too. Those are my earliest memories of entertaining: food, friends, laughter and a lingering atmosphere of a good time had, which really, when it comes down to it, is what it's all about.

1 SEARED CHORIZO WITH QUAIL'S EGGS

Quail's eggs were just made for canapés and here they are teamed up with one of the egg's best friends – cured pig. The eggs can be cooked in advance and served at room temperature. To get really ahead of the game you can fry the chorizo and pepper pieces, sit the pepper on top of the meat, pop them all on a baking tray and just blast in the oven for a couple of minutes when your guests arrive.

Three quick and timeless party nibbles ...

Makes 12 (see photo, overleaf)

6 quail's eggs
2 chorizo sausages (raw ones, not the cooked, pre-sliced variety)
½ red pepper, cut into bite-sized pieces
sea salt, or even better, celery salt if you can find it
couple of pinches of ground cumin
couple of pinches of smoked paprika

Bring a small pan of water to the boil and gently lower the eggs in as quickly as you can. After 3 minutes tip the eggs into the sink and run the cold tap over them while you give them a slightly aggressive roll around to make sure that you crack the shells well all over.

Turn the tap off and peel – the trick with peeling quail's eggs is to break through the membrane just under the shell – it's much tougher than in hens' eggs and if you don't get through that, your eggies will look a bit of a mess. Cut the eggs in half lengthways.

Put a biggish frying pan on a medium heat and slice the chorizo into pieces 1–2cm thick (remember canapés are supposed to be dainty so don't make them too fat). Arrange them in the pan in a single layer and fry without oil for a couple of minutes each side until nicely browned, then set aside on kitchen paper as you fry the pepper pieces for just a couple of minutes to soften them up.

In a little dish, mix together some sea or celery salt with the cumin and smoked paprika.

Now build: chorizo on the bottom, then a piece of pepper, then half an egg, yolk facing up. Secure with a cocktail stick and sprinkle generously with your salty spice dust.

2 AVOCADO & BLACK BEAN SALSA TORTILLAS

I've driven tens of thousands of kilometres through plains and mountains all over Mexico, taking in its vibrant colours, warm people, mezcal and music. And I never tire of their food – it just tastes like the party people they are: fun, uplifting and full o' beans.

Makes about 25

handful vine-ripened cherry toms
½ tin (200g) black beans, rinsed
2 spring onions, sliced
½ red chilli, finely chopped
handful coriander, chopped
zest and juice of 1 lime
little slosh of olive oil
1 ripe avocado, chopped small
small bag of corn tortilla chips
S & P

A bit ahead of time (so that you've got less to worry about later), quarter the tomatoes and mix with the black beans, spring onions, chilli, coriander and lime zest and juice. Pour in just enough olive oil to coat and make glossy and stick in the fridge until needed.

When it's party time, stir the diced avocado into the mix, season with salt and pepper, then taste (it may need more lime juice and salt), and spoon on to the tortilla chips.

3 DRESSED CRAB ON CUKE

As always, the better the ingredients, the less you have to do to them, so use the best and freshest crab you can get. If you've time on your hands, then it's cheapest to buy a whole crab and pick it yourself (true, frozen or pasteurised is cheaper, but just won't work for this). It really does need to be freshly picked, either by your hand or somebody else's, to make your guests feel the love.

Makes around 20

120g fresh, picked white crabmeat
¼ red chilli, diced
small handful of chives or a
    spring onion, finely chopped
zest of ½ lemon
1 tbsp mayo
a few stalks of dill, chopped
100g fresh brown crabmeat
about ½ thick cucumber
S & P

Have a quick sift through the white meat for shell then put it in a bowl with the chilli, chives, lemon zest, mayo, most of the dill and some seasoning.

Slice the cuke on a slight angle to make little carriers for the crab, and spread a little dollop of brown crab meat on each piece.

Top with a teaspoon of the sprcued-up white meat and finish with a tiny sprig of dill.

CEVICHE COCKTAIL

Ceviche is a classic Central/South American dish of raw fish and/or seafood cured with lime juice. It just sings of sunshine: warm oceans, tropical fruit and fiery chilli are its natural surroundings, which is why it's best in summertime, made with only the freshest fish. Ceviches are quick to make, but don't let that fool you into thinking it isn't spectacular both to the eye and, more importantly, for the taste-buds. In fact, the first time I made it and ate it my exact words were, 'F**k yeah!' Says it all really. The fish should meet the lime juice only shortly before serving, so that it is just lightly cured and still very tender.

For 6

½ mango, peeled
½ ripe avocado, peeled
handful of cherry toms, quartered
2 spring onions, thinly sliced
2–3 limes
small handful of coriander, chopped
1–2 chillies, deseeded and finely chopped
2 tsp sea salt
6 regular scallops, with the adductor muscle removed (ask your fishmonger to do this)
1 sea bass fillet, about 250g, skinned and pin-boned

Slice the mango, and cut it into long matchsticks, then into small dice. Do the same with the avo, then put them both into a mixing bowl with the cherry toms, spring onions and a good squeeze of lime juice. Give it a gentle stir and leave to macerate.

Put the coriander into a non-metallic bowl with as much chilli as you like – heat is an important factor in this dish but don't get all macho and start blowing people's heads off. Squeeze over enough lime juice to make a drizzle-able consistency, then stir in the sea salt and put this aside too.

Separate the coral (roe) from the scallops and slice the scallops into thin discs – you'll probably get about four good slices from each one, then chop anything left over into small chunks.

Using a very sharp knife, dice the sea bass into pieces about 1cm big and do something similar with the coral. When you are just 5–10 minutes away from serving, mix the fishy bits into the lime-chilli-coriander bowl, and stir so it's all well coated.

Divide the mango-avo mix between six glasses. Spoon the marinated fish on top, and finish each glass with a few discs of wonderfully translucent scallop and a final splash of the reserved chilli-lime juice.

PEAR, PARMA HAM & PECORINO SALAD

This looks, sounds and tastes restaurant-posh, but is actually pretty simple. The pears and ham can both be done a bit ahead of time, but should be reheated to warm before serving. It's got a multi-level textural thing going on that's out of this world.

For 4 as a lunch, 6 as a starter

8–10 thin slices of Parma ham
big knob of butter
4 juicy pears (the shorter, fatter kind) washed, cut into 8 wedges and cored
400g mixed leaves (any mix of rocket/radicchio/Italian leaves works well)
2 tbsp white balsamic or white wine vinegar
3 tbsp extra virgin olive oil, plus a splash more
80–100g pecorino (the aged one), thinly sliced or shaved
S & P

Put a wide frying pan over a medium–high heat and fry the slices of Parma ham on each side (in two batches) until crispy and smelling scrummy. When the first lot is done, take it out and drain on kitchen paper while you get the next lot in.

When all the ham is crisped, melt the butter in the pan and chuck in all the pear wedges. Once they have warmed through, turn the heat down a bit and cook for about 5 minutes with a grinding of pepper, until the pears are sweet and softening around the edges, but not falling apart.

Put the leaves into a big mixing bowl, and dress with the vinegar, extra virgin olive oil and some seasoning. Chuck in most of the pecorino and all of the pears along with their juices and give it a good fumble with your paws.

Share this between the number of plates/people you have, then top each one with some crispy ham, broken up a bit, and the last of the pecorino.

PERFECTLY PINK PARFAIT & PORT JELLY

In posh French restaurants in the old days, when we were all naughty and ate foie gras, the sommelier usually recommended a glass of something sweetish to complement the rich liver. This is a more humanitarian reinterpretation of that combo. It's sublime, impressive and surprisingly straightforward.

Makes 6–10, depending on your vessel
(I usually do mine in 10 ovenproof espresso cups, which looks fun, but it also works in 6–8 ramekins)

200g chicken livers, with the
    stringy sinew trimmed
2 eggs, plus 3 yolks
160ml double cream
2 garlic cloves, finely chopped
2 tbsp brandy
2 tbsp port
1½ tsp salt
few cracks of pepper
toast, to serve

For the port jelly:
3 gelatine leaves
125ml port (nothing too
    expensive)

Preheat the oven to 150°C/fan 130°C/Gas 2. In a food processor, blitz the livers to a runny goop, then scrape into a mixing bowl using a rubber spatula. Beat the eggs with the yolks and whisk into the liver purée, then add the cream, garlic, both kinds of booze, salt and some pepper, and whisk again for a minute or so until it's come together. Stick the kettle on with plenty of water.

Put your vessels (see above) into a roasting tin, quite closely packed, and share the mix between them using a ladle or jug – try to keep their edges clean. Tip a mug of cold water into the bottom of the tray, then pour in boiling water from the kettle to come up to the level of the parfait mix. Cover the whole tray tightly in foil and put in the oven for 20–23 minutes for espresso cups, and 25–27 minutes for ramekins, until set around the edges but still a bit wobbly in the middle. Lift them out of the water and let stand until completely cool, then put in the fridge.

Only start the exciting jelly once the parfaits have been in the fridge for about half an hour. Slip the gelatine leaves into a jug or bowl of cold water and leave for a few minutes to soften. Gently warm the port with 75ml water in a small pan until just beginning to steam, then turn the heat right down.

One by one, pick the gelatine leaves out of the water and gently squeeze before whisking them into the port. Once totally dissolved, turn off the heat and leave to cool for 10–15 minutes to room temperature. Carefully pour the jelly on to the parfaits, to a depth of 5mm, then put back in the fridge. They should be set in an hour. Most pleasing all round.

SPRING PRAWN DUMPLINGS & CHILLI DIPPING SAUCE

These cute prawn parcels are an absolute doddle to make and pack a lot of flavour into a very small space. You do need to make them with dumpling wrappers rather than wonton ones though, to get the see-through thing that makes these so pretty, with the pink of the prawns alluringly veiled.

Makes about 20, which is a light elegant starter for 6 (3 each plus a chef's snack)

130g raw king prawns, heads off, peeled, deveined and finely chopped
1–2 spring onions, green part only, finely chopped
1 garlic clove, finely chopped
zest of 1 lime
½ red chilli, deseeded and finely chopped
handful of coriander, finely chopped
1 tbsp light soy sauce, plus an extra dash for the prawns
1 pack of dumpling wrappers
3 bok choy heads, quartered through the root
1 tbsp sesame oil
2 tbsp sesame seeds

For the all-important dipping sauce:
3 tbsp rice wine vinegar
1–2 tsp caster sugar (to taste)
½–1 red chilli, deseeded and finely chopped

First make the filling: mix the prawns with the spring onions, garlic, lime zest, chilli and coriander. Season with a dash of soy and mix well. Stir together the ingredients for the dipping sauce, which can just sit quietly infusing on the side.

Now make the dumplings: lay down five wrappers and dampen all around the edges with water. Put a teaspoon of the prawn mix into the middle of each one, then pick them up one at a time and bring the edge of the wrapper up and around the filling to make a little money-sack. Give the joining seams a bit of a squeeze then put them on a tray lined with greaseproof paper and cover lightly with a damp tea towel while you make the rest.

Fill a big wide pan with about 10cm of water and bring to a busy boil with a couple of good pinches of salt. Drop in the bok choy and cook for about 2 minutes until just blanched, then lift out with a slotted spoon and transfer to a sieve to drain thoroughly.

Bring the water back to the boil, then, working quickly, drop in the dumplings one by one: in 3–4 minutes the wrappers will be translucent and the prawn beneath will be pink.

Meanwhile, toss the bok choy in a bowl with the sesame oil, soy sauce and sesame seeds before laying on each plate.

When the dumplings are ready, use the slotted spoon to lift them on to greaseproof paper to drain briefly – don't tip into a colander – they're too fragile. Share them between the plates and serve with little dishes of the dipping sauce.

POACHED TROUT WITH WARM POTATO SALAD & ARTICHOKE CRISPS

You wouldn't necessarily think it, but this is a true heritage dish. With the exception of chilli, all the ingredients are either indigenous or centuries-old imports, like wine and lemons. But while this recipe could have been written 500 years ago, what's extraordinary is how timeless it is, and it's easier than trying to get four-and-twenty blackbirds into a pie, that's for sure.

For 4

4 trout, about 200g each, cleaned
    and gills removed
handful of fresh herbs like dill,
    parsley or thyme
1 onion, sliced
2 celery sticks, sliced
1 garlic clove, chopped
2 bay leaves
75ml white wine
S & P
2 lemons, quartered (optional)
1 batch Artichoke Crisps (see
    page 361), to serve

For the salad:
800g large new potatoes, halved
½ tsp fennel seeds
¼ tsp chilli flakes
50ml white wine vinegar
1 tbsp sugar
1 cucumber, peeled, deseeded
    and sliced into 1cm
    crescent-moons
3 tbsp extra virgin olive oil
big handful of dill, chopped
2 spring onions, sliced

Preheat the oven to 190°C/fan 170°C/Gas 5. Put the spuds in a large pan of cold, salted water with a lid on, bring to the boil, then turn the heat down a bit, take off the lid and simmer for 10–12 minutes until just cooked.

Meanwhile, put a saucepan on a medium heat and dry-fry the fennel seeds and chilli flakes for just a few minutes until you can smell them. Pour in the vinegar and 2 tablespoons of water, then stir in the sugar and season as you bring to the boil.

Chuck in the cucumber, turn the heat down to a simmer and pop a lid on. Stir, and after a couple of minutes, when the cuke colour has become muted, take off the lid and simmer for a further 5ish minutes: you want it to keep a bit of bite and the liquor to reduce to 2–3 tablespoons, then turn off the heat.

Meanwhile, season inside the fish and stuff with the herbs. Scatter the onion, celery, garlic and bay leaves over the bottom of a roasting tray and lay the fish on top. Pour in the wine and an equal amount of water then cover with foil and bake for 15–17 minutes until the fishies are cooked. To check, follow the instructions for McEvedy's Lip Service on page 125.

While the fish cook, halve or quarter the spuds and stir into the pickled cucumber and remaining cooking liquor along with the olive oil, dill and spring onions. Mix well, taste for seasoning and pop a lid on so it stays warm. Gently move the fish to a warmed serving dish and spoon over the juices from the roasting tin. Serve with the spuds on the side, lemon quarters if you like, and the artichoke crisps on top.

1 CRAB & CHILLI RISOTTO

Once you get the hang of them, risotti are pretty easy yet impressive. The basic principles apply across the board: use a decent stock; don't rush; feed and starve; be sensitive with the seasoning; and make sure that the rice has the right texture at the end – rich and creamy with a distant but discernable bite.

For 6 as a starter, 4 as a main

3 tbsp extra virgin olive oil, plus an extra splash
1 small leek, halved lengthways, thinly sliced and well washed
3 celery sticks, halved lengthways then thinly sliced crossways
2 garlic cloves, chopped
1 courgette, diced
about 1.5 litres mild stock, either veg, fish or very light chicken (if not home-made, dilute it to half the strength)
1–2 red chillies (depending on how hot you like it), deseeded and finely diced
300g risotto rice
200ml white wine
20g butter, at room temperature
big handful of flat-leaf parsley, finely chopped
zest of 1 lemon
300g picked white crab meat (fresh not frozen)
S & P

Heat the oil in a wide, heavy-bottomed pan and fry the leek, celery, courgette and garlic for 5–7 minutes until they have brightened and are beginning to soften. Meanwhile, warm the stock in a separate pan until just steaming.

Stir half the chilli into the veg pan and fry for a minute before adding the rice. It's important to give the rice a proper fry for a few minutes until it gets pretty noisy, clamouring for liquid, and in protest starts to stick to the bottom. Only then give it some relief in the form of the wine. Stir gently as it bubbles gratefully and drinks up the booze, and keep stirring till it gets sticky again. It's this feed-then-starve process that makes a good risotto. Add a large ladleful of warm stock (about 250ml), and let it gently bubble away. Hold off on the next ladleful until the rice is desperate, then kindly scratch the itch. Sadomasochism in a pan.

After 30–40 minutes – when pretty much all the stock has been sucked up – your rice will have developed into a beautiful risotto. Turn off the heat while some liquid is still pooling, or if all absorbed, then add a half ladle of stock. Reward the risotto's hard work by dotting the top with soft butter and giving it a rest.

Your risotto now needs something frisky to wear on top: mix the parsley, lemon zest, remaining chilli and the crab with a touch of seasoning and a splash of extra virgin. When the risotto's had 5 minutes to pull itself together, stir in half the chilli-crab mix and taste for seasoning. Serve sexy spoonfuls of perfectly wet, creamy risotto with masterful pleasure – the texture should be pert with a gentle wobble. Top each bowl with its share of the remaining crab mix, and whatever you do, don't ruin it with Parmesan.

Top: Risotto Primavera
Bottom: Crab & Chilli Risotto

2 RISOTTO PRIMAVERA

This is all about the light, green, spring feel to it. It doesn't really matter what greens you have as long as you've a fair representation of seasonal freshness and you keep a degree of crunch to the whole thing. No one will know (or care) if your peas and broad beans are fresh or frozen if you include some obvious fresh spring signposts like asparagus and mint.

For 6 as a starter, 4 as a main (see photo, page 148)

a knob of butter
2 tbsp olive oil
1 small onion, finely chopped
1 garlic clove, finely chopped
1.5 litres veg stock
250g risotto rice
small glass (125ml) white wine
100g French beans, sliced into
    2cm batons
50g mangetout or sugar snaps,
    very roughly chopped
big handful (about 50g) frozen
    peas
150g asparagus, tough end
    discarded, stems chopped into
    1cm batons; tips kept whole
handful of basil, chopped
handful of mint, chopped
zest of ½ lemon
80g pecorino, finely grated
S & P
couple of handfuls of rocket,
    very roughly chopped, to serve
extra virgin olive oil, to serve

In a wide, heavy-bottomed saucepan melt the butter in the oil until it starts to fizzle, then tip in the onion and garlic. Fry them over a medium–high heat, stirring regularly for about 7 minutes until they are starting to soften, but don't let them brown at all.

Meanwhile, put the stock in a separate saucepan and heat it gently until steaming, then hold it there.

Once the onion is looking a bit softened, stir the rice in, give it a good roll in the onion and oil for a few minutes until it starts to stick to the bottom, then pour in the wine and keep stirring as it reduces away entirely.

When the rice starts to stick again, add a big ladleful of the stock (about 250ml) and keep repeating this process (see notes on feeding and starving in the previous recipe), until the rice is just cooked with a little bit of bite.

Now tip in all of the veg and another ladle of stock and keep on the heat for 5ish minutes until the asparagus is just cooked, then turn the heat off. Stir in the herbs, lemon zest, a handful of the pecorino and season with salt and pepper. Taste.

Serve up and finish each bowl/plate with a little handful of rocket, some more pecorino and a decent splash of your best extra virgin.

BUTTERNUT, RED ONION & GOATS' CHEESE TART

During my eleventh summer a book was published, accompanied by a lot of noise that both intrigued and confused me, called *Real Men Don't Eat Quiche*. Why not? What was wrong with quiche? I liked quiche (and I was already something of a tomboy, averse to all things girlie). The book itself neither troubled nor interested me, but the statement of that title hung around in the back of my mind. Fast-forward about 15 years and the gastropub had arrived, espousing all things Great and British and suddenly there were savoury tarts aplenty. We had reclaimed the right to fill a pastry case with whatever we wanted and to bind it with eggs and cream. They were bold, they were beautiful, and most crucially they were not gender specific – because everybody loves a tart. This and the one on page 154 are two of my favourites.

Everybody Loves a Tart

For 8–10, made in a 28cm fluted loose-bottomed tart tin (see photo, overleaf)

500g shortcrust pastry (bought, or see page 370 – use half the recipe and freeze the rest)

1 butternut squash (about 1.5kg), peeled and cut into 3cm cubes

good splash of extra virgin olive oil

2 red onions, not peeled but halved through the root

15 garlic cloves, unpeeled

1 egg white

small handful of sage leaves, chopped

½ tsp chilli flakes

3 eggs, beaten

200ml double cream

125g goats' cheese

handful of grated Parmesan, for the top

S & P

First the pastry: if making, follow the recipe up to lining your 28cm tin and resting it in the fridge or freezer. If using bought pastry, simply follow the same instructions for rolling, lining and resting. Preheat the oven to 180°C/fan 160°C/Gas 4.

Put the butternut chunks in a large roasting tin, pour on a splosh of olive oil and season well. Roll around until well coated, then push to the edges. Fit the onion halves, cut-side down, and unpeeled garlic cloves into the middle.

When the tart case is rested, prick the base all over with a fork, cover with a big scrunched-up piece of greaseproof paper and fill with baking beans (see page 370). Put the squash tray in the oven on the top shelf, and slip the tart case on to the shelf below. Roast the veg for 45–55 minutes in total, but after 20 minutes take out the garlic, turn all of the squash pieces and flip the onions over. Meanwhile, the tart case gets baked for about 25 minutes, then carefully lift out the greaseproof and beans and bake for a further 5–7 minutes until golden brown.

CONTINUED

CONTINUED FROM
PREVIOUS PAGE

Lightly whisk the egg white until just frothy, brush all over the tart case and pop back in the oven for a final 3–5 minutes until the white is hard and shiny, which will stop your pastry from going soggy once filled.

Once the veg is well cooked (soft, and the butternut has some nicely browning edges) take it out and turn the oven down to 170°C/fan 150°C/Gas 3½.

Pop the garlic cloves out of their skin and very roughly chop them along with the cooked onion (peel it now). Tip into a big mixing bowl along with the butternut, sage, chilli, beaten eggs, cream and some seasoning. Stir well but gently with a wooden spoon so as not to break up the butternut. Last in goes the goats' cheese, crumbled into rough chunks. Give it the briefest of mixes and gently ladle the whole lot into the cooked and glazed tart case.

Sprinkle the top with Parmesan and bake for 30–35 minutes, until the tart is cooked with the faintest of wobbles in the middle. If you'd like your tart to be a tad more golden, then whack the temperature up to 200°C/fan 180°C/Gas 6 and blast it for a few minutes; just be careful not to muller your pride and joy. Let it sit for 10 minutes to settle down a bit before tucking in.

BACON & EGG TART

Formerly known as 'Quiche Lorraine', I hereby reclaim this crowd-pleaser for the nation.

Serves 4–6 'real men' as a main with salad, or 6–8 as part of a picnic
(made in a 22cm loose-bottomed tart tin, fluted or straight-sided)

350g shortcrust pastry (bought
    or use a third of the recipe on
    page 370 and freeze the rest)
1 egg white
175g pancetta or lardons, cut into
    rough 1 cm cubes
50g Gruyère cheese
3 eggs
300ml double cream
1 tbsp thyme leaves, chopped
pepper

Preheat the oven to 180°C/fan 160°C/Gas 4.

First, prepare your pastry case, following the method on page 370 for rolling, blind baking and glazing. Once your glazed tart case is out of the oven, turn the heat down to 160°C/fan 140°C/Gas 3.

Scatter the pancetta on to the base of the tart case. Cut two-thirds of the Gruyère into cubes and scatter them over the base too.

Whisk the eggs with the cream, thyme and some pepper (no salt required, and the French would add a scraping of nutmeg too but I'm not bothered) and pour into the pastry case.

Grate the remaining cheese and scatter over the top, then bake in the oven for 20–25 minutes until just set and golden brown around the edges – if you want more colour then just whack the heat up to 200°C/fan 180°C/Gas 6 for a few minutes. Leave to cool for about 5 minutes as this tart is best when not piping hot. In fact, it's excellent cold too.

SUSI'S FENNELLY SAUSAGE PASTA

Susi is my closest friend, Delilah's other mother and my ex-wife. She didn't really cook at all when we met, so, apart from our beautiful daughter, I like to think that the great positive from our time together is illustrated by this recipe, which she invented. I'm as proud of it as if it were my own.

For 4–6 (4 blokes or 6 girls. That's just the way this dish goes down – simply an observation)

5–6 sausages (any kind you like, as long as they're thick – not chipolatas)
1½ tbsp fennel seeds
good splash of olive oil
4 shallots, diced
2 garlic cloves, chopped
small glass (125ml) red wine
250ml chicken stock
1 tbsp tomato purée
1–2 tsp harissa paste
1 x 400g tin chopped tomatoes
500g big shell pasta (conchiglie grande)
few squeezes of lemon juice
handful of finely grated Parmesan
handful of flat-leaf parsley, chopped
S & P

Bring a saucepan of water to the boil, drop in the sausages and cook for 5 minutes. Drain and leave to cool.

Heat a big wide saucepan over a medium heat and dry-toast the fennel seeds for 2–3 minutes until releasing their distinctive aroma and beginning to brown. Tip into a bowl and put the pan back on the heat. Pour in a small glug of the olive oil and fry the shallots and garlic for a few minutes to soften and sweeten.

Peel the skins off the cooled sausages and break the meat into chunks. Throw into the pan, add the fennel seeds and cook on a low–medium heat for 5 minutes, stirring occasionally, for the fennel to flavour the sausages. Season with salt and pepper, and when the mixture starts to stick to the bottom of the pan, pour in the red wine. As it reduces, scrape off any bits stuck to the bottom with a wooden spoon. Once the liquid has pretty much gone, pour in the stock, give it a jolly good stir and bring to a simmer. Add the tomato purée, harissa paste and chopped tomatoes. Mix well and simmer with a lid on for 10 minutes, then another 10 with the lid off, stirring occasionally.

Get your pasta water boiling, adding a splash of oil and a hefty pinch of salt. Tip in the pasta and cook according to the packet.

Check your sauce: it should be loose enough to coat the pasta but not sloppy. When ready, take it off the heat, add a good squeeze of lemon juice and stir in most of the Parmesan. Drain the pasta, tip it back into the pan and ladle on the sauce. Stir until two become one, cooking for a further 5 minutes or so over a very low heat. Give it a supportive squeeze of lemon, and stir in the parsley. Have a last taste for seasoning, then serve up with more Parmesan on top, just to be sure. Yum, says Susi.

soup

Theory & Practice

WHEN I was eight, my mum and her cousin opened a wine bar in Shepherd's Bush. Not only did this make me a latch-key child (a freedom I rather enjoyed), it was also my first lesson in soups. The wine bar mainly served for after-work boozing by BBC employees, but it also offered a small menu, cooked by my mum. The lunchtime best-seller was always her daily soup. 'The food of today is the soup of tomorrow,' I remember her telling me, and many a time I'd trot round there after school, stand in the small galley kitchen and watch her give leftover chicken, a tray of roasted veg or a pot of lentils a whole new lease of life.

The irony is I didn't like soup then. To prevent my sister and me from becoming fussy eaters, our mum allowed us each a list of five things we didn't like. If what she put in front of us for supper wasn't on our list, then we had to eat it (we could amend the list after the meal, but not before). Soup sat at number one on my list for years, but I've absolutely no memory why – I thought it was maybe a kiddy thing but my toddler daughter absolutely hoofs my soups down, seemingly amused by its unique place between food and drink. Anyway, soup now does it on every level for me: it's homely, cheap to make, healthy, warming, a great way of recycling leftovers, soothing and filling.

The soups I've chosen to arm you with are my absolute unmissables and hands-down winners: the ones I can't live without. There are veg-centric soups, pulse-based soups, stocky soups, dairy-led soups, meaty and fishy soups, and of course there are all the intersections where two or more overlap.

A bowl of home-made soup is so much more than just a source of nourishment – there's magical healing properties in there too, which you can tangibly feel spreading the love throughout your body. And that's why I've also included some top tips for the poorly in this chapter. Because once you have the theory of soup in your bag of tricks, you really will find it useful for life.

Pages 163–165

The Yin & Yang of Pulse Soups

Anything from the House of Pulse lends itself easily to souping. The two recipes I've given here are opposites not only in colour, but also in character. The bold one is black and hearty, the lighter one calmer and more sublime. Consider these the alpha and omega, and fill in the rest with whatever bean takes your fancy.

Dairy-based Soups

In the seventies, 'cream of' soups were all the rage. These days they are a little out of fashion but there's still a whole world of dairy-based products out there that play a vital role in making soups yummy.

Pages 166–171

Veg Soups

Pretty much every soup relies on vegetables to give a fully rounded flavour: boiled stock just isn't that interesting without the support that veg gives. The soups that follow let veg play far more than just a supporting role so it can bask in the glory of being centre stage.

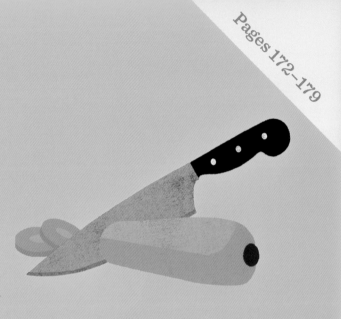

Italians Broth Better

I love broth-based soups: they're healthy, warming, cheap and, if you get them right, have a taste that will remind you of that wonderful lunch you had in Italy all those years ago. Broths are a good reason why you should always have home-made chicken stock in the freezer – you'll get a fabulous supper in half an hour.

Black Bean & Bacon Soup
(of a Central American leaning)

This soup is at least halfway towards a big beany casserole with all its warming, comforting attributes. As a nod to the zippy nosh from that part of the world, the toppers complement the cuddle-factor with a feisty pinch on the bum.

Filling starter for 4 (see photo, overleaf)

80g smoked streaky bacon or pancetta, cut smallish
splash of olive oil
1 large red onion, finely chopped
2 garlic cloves, chopped
½ chilli, deseeded and finely chopped
1 tsp smoked paprika
½ tsp ground cumin
1 tsp dried oregano
1 tbsp tomato purée
2 x 400g tins black beans
S & P

For the toppers:
juice of 1–2 limes
½ red onion, sliced as thinly as possible
sour cream or crème fraîche, for blobbing
big handful of coriander, leaves picked

In a wide saucepan over a medium–high heat, fry the bacon in the olive oil until golden brown and beginning to get crispy edges, then chuck in the onion, garlic and chilli. Stir occasionally for the 5ish minutes it will take the onion to soften, then lob in the spices and oregano and give it all a thorough roll and coat. Squeeze in the tomato purée and give it another good stir so that everything is well combined. Tip in the beans, plus any liquid in the tins, then fill both tins up with water and tip that in too.

Bring to a boil, then turn down the heat and leave it on a ticking-over simmer for 15–20 minutes, until it's looking thick and rich (know anyone like that?).

Meanwhile, prepare your toppers. Squeeze lime juice all over the onion and give it a stir until well coated, to give it a quick pickle. It's key that all surfaces of the onion are in contact with the lime juice. Leave it on the side, giving it a poke and a stir from time to time. After 20 minutes the onions will have gone a really charming pink.

Finish the soup by gently blitzing about a third of it in a blender or food processor (or use a stick blender), but don't make it totally smooth; it should be a chunky purée. Tip back into the pan, if necessary, to reheat. Taste and season with salt and pepper.

Tip away the excess lime juice from the onions and stir in a little salt. Serve the soup with a blob of your chosen dairy, a spoonful of the onions and some sprigs of coriander.

White Bean & Rosemary Soup

This soup contrasts very well with the black bean one on the previous page in terms of flavour, colour and sophistication. It's got a gentle, soothing romantic soul, rather than the Latin American party next door. If making this for guests I take a few minutes to knock up some pesto (see page 368) and blob or stir a little into the bowls at the end.

For 4 as a starter

3 tbsp olive oil
4 garlic cloves, sliced
2 tbsp finely chopped rosemary
2 x 400g tins white beans (ideally cannellini, but haricot also work; they're just a bit less creamy), drained
1.5 litres light stock, either chicken or veg (chicken is my preferred, but if using a cube or concentrate go for half strength)
handful of flat-leaf parsley, chopped
S & P
extra virgin olive oil, to serve

Heat the oil and fry the garlic over a medium heat, stirring all the time with a wooden spoon until it's golden all over and beginning to go sticky. Chuck in the rosemary and stir for another minute until it aromatises, then tip in the beans.

Turn the heat up and give it a good mix so that the beans are well coated in the garlicky oil, then pour in the stock and pop a lid on. Bring to the boil, then take the lid off, turn the heat down to a gentle, steady simmer and cook for another 30 minutes.

Ladle half the soup into a blender or food processor (or use a stick blender) and semi-blitz it until pretty much smooth but still retaining plenty of texture. Tip back into the pan, if necessary, to reheat. Season well, then stir through the chopped parsley and serve with a good crack of black pepper and a slosh of extra virgin on top.

Top: White Bean & Rosemary Soup
Bottom: Black Bean & Bacon Soup

Turkish Yoghurt Soup

In Britain, we stumble back from the pub and grab a kebab. In Turkey, they eat this soup after a big night out. I guarantee it's unlike any other soup you've ever tried, both in texture and flavour (unless you've ever been on the raz in Istanbul).

For 4 as a starter

40g long-grain rice
1 litre chicken stock
1 egg
2 tbsp plain flour
350g strained yoghurt (don't
　　call it Greek or you'll upset
　　the Turks – it's thought
　　they invented it first!)
40g butter
2 garlic cloves, finely chopped
1 tbsp dried mint
juice of ½ lemon
S & P

Put the rice in a medium pan and pour in the chicken stock, then pop a lid on and bring to the boil. Once boiling, turn down to a simmer, leave the lid on and simmer for about 10 minutes until the rice is soft.

In a separate biggish pan, off the heat, gently mix together the egg, flour and yoghurt until smooth.

When the rice is cooked, put that pan aside but don't drain. Sit the yoghurt pan over a low heat for a few minutes, then pour the entire contents of the rice pan (liquid and all) on to the yoghurt base and whisk till smooth. Season with salt and pepper as you increase to a medium heat and bring to a simmer. Let it bubble away for about 10 minutes as it all comes together.

Give the empty rice pan a quick rinse and put it back on the hob to dry out. Melt the butter in it, then gently fry the garlic and mint until the garlic is just going golden and the mint smells gorgeous. Add a squeeze of lemon juice to the soup to taste, and have a final seasoning check – it'll probably like a bit more salt now. Serve up with a swirl of the garlicky, minty butter on top.

Shown with: Saracen Stuffed Peppers, p363

Chow-down Clam Chowder

Manhattan vs New England = red or white? I prefer the creamy white New England version, as I think the deep tomato of the Manhattan variety masks the delicate taste of the clams, but I've tweaked the traditional recipe a bit by adding wine. Also, a true New Englander would be thickened with flour then finished with cream, so I've written into the recipe where the flour and cream go if you're after a trad version, but I think my lighter take is a bit more attuned to European palates.

For 4 as a pretty substantial starter or light lunch

1kg live clams (palourdes are ideal)
175ml white wine
25g butter
1 leek, sliced into small dice and well washed
½ chilli, deseeded and finely chopped
2 celery sticks, halved lengthways then sliced to make rough dice
2 garlic cloves, chopped
2 medium spuds (about 400g in total), peeled and cut into 1–2cm dice
1–2 tbsp plain flour (optional)
1 corn cob, husked
150g green cabbage (hispi, sweetheart or Savoy), finely shredded
200ml whole milk, or half milk and half single cream
S & P

Slap a big saucepan over a medium heat to warm up. Run the clams under cold water in a colander, giving them a good shuffle. Throw out any open ones for tummy safety, and wash any dirt off the outside of the shells. Tip them into the pan and immediately pour on the wine and 300ml cold water. Pop a lid on, give the pan a brief shake and leave for 3–5 minutes, until they've all opened (throw out any that haven't), then strain through a colander into a bowl, keeping both the clams and the liquid.

Put the pan back on the heat to dry out, then melt the butter in it. Add the leek and gently fry over a medium heat along with the chilli, celery, garlic and spuds for 10–15 minutes with a lid on but stirring regularly to make sure the veg doesn't brown.

Meanwhile, pick most of the clams out of their shells, leaving just a handful still in to look pretty when you serve. Throw the empties away. If you like a thick soup, rather than a broth, chuck the flour into the veg pan now and stir for a minute or two to coat.

Next, pour in the clam cooking liquid, bring to the boil with a pinch of salt, and simmer for 7–10 minutes until the spuds are just cooked but not falling apart.

Stand the corn cob on its end and slice down the length with a sharp knife so the kernels fall away. When the spuds are just about there, stir the corn, cabbage and milk (and cream if you fancy) into the soup, whack the heat up and bring it swiftly back to a simmer. Turn the heat off and chuck the clams back in for just a couple of minutes to warm through before serving: use this time to taste and adjust the seasoning.

Mushroom Soup with Meaning

If you're wedded to tinned mushroom soups, look away now. If, like me, you find them a bit floury and gloopy with only the faintest whiff of mushrooms (and cheap ones at that), then this will work for you. You'll find lots of deep, foresty fungal flavour, with the edges smoothed by a bit of cream and a tipple of booze. This soup is only for grown-ups as the alcohol doesn't really burn off.

For 4 as a starter or non-sexist ladies' lunch

300g mixed mushrooms (mostly chestnut backed up by oyster, or shiitake or even button – avoid Portobello or flat as they make the soup very grey)
20g dried mushrooms (best with porcini but whatever's going)
1 litre boiling water
splash of olive oil
knob of butter
1 onion, finely diced
1 leek, finely sliced and well washed
2 garlic cloves, chopped
small bunch of thyme sprigs, tied together with string
3 tbsp plain flour
100ml double cream
3 tbsp dry sherry or Madeira
S & P

Pull all the stalks off the fresh mushrooms, give them a good wash and put them in a mixing bowl with the dried mushrooms. Pour over the boiling water to make a stock, then thinly slice the mushroom tops and set aside.

Heat the olive oil and butter in a pan until the butter is fizzling, then fry the onion, leek, garlic and thyme for 5–8 minutes over a medium heat until nicely softened. Chuck in two-thirds of the sliced mushrooms (putting a third aside for later), give them a good stir and continue to cook until they begin to brown and start to stick to the bottom of the pan – about another 5 minutes.

Scatter in the flour, and keep stirring as you gently coat everything for a minute or two, then strain in the mushroom stock. (Keep the dried mushrooms but chuck out the stalks.) Give it another good stir, bring to the boil, then turn the soup down to a steady bubbling for 10 minutes.

Chop the rehydrated dried mushrooms up small and chuck them in too, then lift out the sprigs of thyme and blitz the soup in a blender or food processor (or use a stick blender) until pretty much smooth. Tip back into the pan, throw in the fresh mushrooms you set aside earlier and bring the soup back to a simmer. Add the cream and booze, as you let it cook for a final few minutes, then have a last taste for seasoning.

Slow-cooked Fennel Soup

Fennel is one of my all-time favourite veg, though many people still regard it with a degree of uncertainty. Its culinary role is usually as a background flavour, often for fish or pork, but here it really stands out. Slow cooking reveals a sweetness that usually remains hidden and knocks out that full-on potency that makes it quite divisive. This soup is sophisticated but simple to make, with gentle but deep flavours and a texture that is sexy, silky and so sublime as she goes down.

For 4 as a starter or lovely lunch with a salad

2 fennel bulbs (about 650g)
2 tbsp olive oil
1 onion, chopped
2 celery sticks, thinly sliced
2 garlic cloves, chopped
½ tsp fennel seeds, roughly
   chopped
1 litre veg or light chicken stock
   (half-strength if using a cube)
S & P

Halve the fennel bulbs through the root, then cut the root out and do the best you can to roughly chop the rest (including stalks and fronds) into smallish pieces. They don't need to be pretty.

In a wide, heavy-bottomed pan, heat the olive oil and gently fry the onion, celery, garlic, fennel seeds and chopped fennel over a medium heat. Once they begin to soften pop a lid on, lower the heat and keep stirring every now and then – you want it all to get very soft, mushy and sweet, but without browning at all. After 30 minutes of very gentle cooking, pour in the stock and bring to a simmer. Give it a good stir and a bit of a season, then blitz to a smooth, creamy purée in a blender or food processor (or use a stick blender). Tip back into the pan, if necessary, to reheat.

Taste again before serving. Some little croutons go down well in this for a bit of textural contrast (see page 367 for how to make them).

Clockwise from top left:
*Roast Tomato Soup; Very Green Spinach
& Pea Soup; Slow-cooked Fennel Soup*

Roast Tomato Soup
with Salsa Picante

The pleasure in your bowl is two-fold here. First, it's just a damn fine, honest tomato soup, with a proper tomatoey flavour that's intensified by pre-roasting the toms. But against that smooth and calm background comes a cunning contrast from the bright, biting salsa that tops it off. Only make this from July to October, when tomatoes are at their best. And yes, I know a tomato's not a vegetable.

A summer starter for 4 (see photo, previous page)

12 vine-ripened or gorgeous
    plum tomatoes, halved
1 red onion, cut into 6 wedges
2 shallots, halved
3 garlic cloves, unpeeled
good glug of olive oil
1 tbsp chopped rosemary
1 tbsp chopped thyme leaves
500ml light veg stock (diluted if
    using bouillon or a cube), hot
S & P

For the salsa:
½ pepper (red or green), cut
    into small dice
1 spring onion, halved
    lengthways then thinly sliced
1 garlic clove, minced
a thumb of cucumber, deseeded
    and cut into tiny dice
½ chilli, deseeded and finely
    chopped
½ tbsp sherry vinegar or red
    wine vinegar
splosh of extra virgin olive oil
S & P

Preheat the oven to 190°C/fan 170°C/Gas 5.

Put the tomatoes in a roasting tray with the red onion, shallots and garlic cloves. Do a bit of fairly liberal free-pouring with the olive oil (but not so it's all swimming – about 3 tablespoons) and then scatter on the rosemary and thyme, giving it all a good season with salt and pepper. After a brief toss, turn them all cut-side up, cover with foil and bake in the oven for 20 minutes. Then whip the foil off, give them a shuffle and roast for another 15–25 minutes until the veg has softened and is just beginning to pick up a little bit of colour.

Meanwhile, knock-up the salsa by mixing all the ingredients together in a little bowl. Make sure it's properly seasoned.

To finish the soup, pick out the garlic, squeeze it out of its skin, and just tip everything else into a blender or food processor (or use a stick blender) and blend with the hot stock – you'll probably need to do it in two batches. Tip it back into a bowl or pan to mix it all together, season to taste then serve up with a spoonful of the kicking salsa on top.

Very Green Spinach & Pea Soup
(and other expressions of chlorophyll)

A blended green soup should be a vibrant green, and there are a couple of tricks that will ensure your end product is pulsating with chlorophyll. You may cook all hell out of the vegetable base, but when it comes to the blending, put a big handful of baby spinach in at the last moment, either at the bottom of the blender before you ladle in each batch of the hot soup, or if using a stick blender, just directly into the soup. Whizz until it's completely disappeared into the soup, i.e. there are no little green flecks.

If you're making your soup ahead of time, you need to cool it immediately after blending to keep the bright green. Putting it directly into the fridge ain't on from a food safety perspective (it raises the temperature of the whole fridge), so instead half-fill your sink with very cold water – iced is even better – then float or sit a mixing bowl in it. Pour the soup from the blender directly into the bowl, and stir from time to time until the soup is cool. Removing the heat quickly like this keeps your soup good and verdant.

Serves 4 as a handsome starter or hearty lunch (see photo, page 173)

splash of olive oil
2 celery sticks, halved lengthways then thinly sliced
1 leek, halved lengthways then thinly sliced and washed
3 garlic cloves, chopped
small handful of parsley, stalks and leaves chopped small
1 litre half-strength veg stock
150g frozen peas, defrosted
500g spinach, washed (ideally 400g big spinach and 100g baby)
good grating of nutmeg
S & P
Greek yoghurt or crème fraîche, to serve

Heat the olive oil in a wide pan then tip in the celery, leek and garlic. Sweat them over a medium heat, stirring from time to time so that they soften but don't colour. Add the parsley stalks and stir briefly before pouring on the veg stock and bringing to a simmer. Let it bubble gently for about 10 minutes, then stir in the peas, spinach leaves (keeping back a massive handful of big, or all the baby spinach, if using), nutmeg and some seasoning.

Bring back to a simmer and cook for just enough time to wilt the spinach and warm the peas through – 5ish minutes – then either chuck the reserved spinach into the blender and ladle the hot soup on top, or if using a stick blender directly into the soup, and blitz until totally smooth. Taste and adjust the seasoning. If you want to reheat, do so very gently as a fast boil will give it a grainy look. A blob of dairy rounds it off nicely.

Leek & Potato Soup (hot)
+ Bonus Vichyssoise (cold)

Leek and potato soup is owed a big apology from couldn't-care-less chefs who have done their damndest for years to sully its good name. When made well, and with love, it's simple, warming and utterly delicious. Then of course there's the cool, Continental version (Vichyssoise), which has long been one of my summer standards.

For 4–6 as a starter or light lunch

25g butter
splash of olive oil
2 large greengrocer leeks or
    4 smaller supermarket ones,
    thinly sliced and well washed
1 big onion, chopped small
2 celery sticks, halved
    lengthways then sliced
2–3 garlic cloves, chopped
3 medium–large spuds (600g in
    total), peeled and cut into
    1–2 cm chunks
2 bay leaves
1 litre veg or light chicken stock
    (your call)
S & P

Melt the butter and oil in a wide pan, then chuck in the leeks, onion, celery and garlic. Cook over a medium heat until it's all beginning to soften nicely (about 5–7 minutes) but without browning at all.

Now add the spud chunks and bay leaves, stir well then turn down the heat to medium–low and stick a lid on. Give it a stir every couple of minutes and after about 10 minutes the spuds should have begun to soften around the edges. Pour on enough stock to cover and bring to a simmer. Cook at a steady but not manic bubble for 10–15 minutes until all the veg are tender.

Blitz a third to a quarter of the soup in a blender or food processor (or use a stick blender), then stir back in to what's left in the pan and have a good taste – this soup needs a good amount of both salt and pepper (but less if you used a stock cube).

To turn this soup into Vichyssoise, just blend it all until completely smooth then chill. Stir in 125ml double cream and 20g of finely chopped chives, and revisit the seasoning before serving – most dishes take a bit more when they're cold.

Jerusalem Artichoke Soup

Few ingredients look so unappealing yet have such an unexpectedly magnificent and, frankly, posh flavour as Jerusalem artichokes. They belong to the horticultural family that includes sunflowers and dandelions, as well as being a distant cousin to regular artichokes. They also have nothing at all do to with Jerusalem. It's thought the name came from a mispronunciation of 'girasol', which is Spanish for 'sunflower'. (In American English they're known as sunchokes). Anyway, whatever they're called they are god-given to souping, and here they have the simplest of support bands as they perform their magical transformation.

For 4 as a starter or simple sophisicated lunch

25g butter
1 leek, white part only, halved lengthways, washed well and thinly sliced
1 shallot, halved and thinly sliced
2 garlic cloves, chopped
1 kg Jerusalem artichokes, peeled and cut into chunks
1.2 litres chicken stock (go half strength if using cube or concentrate)
S & P

In a wide pan, melt the butter and gently fry the leek, shallot and garlic for a happy 10 minutes until all is softened but not browning at all. Add the Jerusalems and carry on cooking, stirring regularly, for another 8–10 minutes – you want the artichokes to just begin to soften at the edges – then pour in the stock. Bring to a simmer with a lid on and keep it ticking over nicely for 10–15 minutes, until the artichokes are tender when you stick a knife into them.

Blitz completely to a purée in a blender or food processor (or use a stick blender), adding a cup more stock or water as necessary if it's too thick. Tip back into the pan, if necessary, to reheat. Season and serve, resisting the urge to ruin it all with some cheap truffle oil, as is the unfortunate trend these days.

Beefed-up French Onion Soup

Sweet slow-cooked onions, beefy bits for backbone, and a great big cheesy crouton on top – what's not to love?

For 4 FOS lovers

3 tbsp olive oil, plus an extra drizzle for the croutons
400g beef (braising steak or chuck), cut into 1–2cm cubes
1.5kg onions (red, white or shallot – a mix works well), sliced
4 large garlic cloves, roughly chopped
2 bay leaves
handful of thyme, tied together with string
200ml white wine
1 litre chicken or beef stock (home-made or buy fresh)
4 slices of baguette or ciabatta
big handful (about 60g) Gruyère cheese, grated
1 tbsp brandy
S & P
handful of flat-leaf parsley, finely chopped, to serve

Heat the olive oil in a heavy-bottomed saucepan until it's smoking. Season the beef well then gently lower it into the hot oil and brown evenly over about 10 minutes, stirring it after about 4 minutes and again a few minutes later. When you have decent colour on most fronts, lift it out with a slotted spoon and set aside on a plate, leaving the pan on the heat.

Now tip in the onions, keeping the heat up high, and stir regularly for about 10 minutes until they start to collapse. Add the garlic, bay leaves and thyme, and keep turning the onions over until they are just beginning to brown, then reduce the heat to low–medium. After another 25–30 minutes, the onions will have begun to caramelise, becoming sticky and soft. At this point, tip the beef back in, turn the heat back up to high and mix well. Season with gusto, then pour in the wine, give it a good stir and let it reduce until there's no more liquid in the pan.

Now go in with the stock and when it starts to simmer turn the heat down to the lowest setting, put a lid on and leave for 1¼–1½ hours, until the beef is very tender.

When the soup is ready, turn the heat off to give it a bit of a rest and preheat the oven to 180°C/fan 160°C/Gas 4.

Put the bread slices on a tray, season and drizzle with olive oil. Bake for 8ish minutes, until golden, then share the cheese between them and stick back in the oven until it's melted and just beginning to brown.

Stir the brandy into the soup, and if you think it's looking a bit thick and more like a stew than a soup, loosen with a few shots of hot water. Have a last taste for seasoning before serving up with one of those naughty croutons floating aloft and pretty parsley.

Minestrone

This is the best winter warmer ever. It keeps for days and the flavours keep improving (though it rarely lasts that long in our house). These ingredients are just a guide; really the only key things are the home-made stock, some pasta and some veggies, though I argue a strong case for the extra virgin and Parmesan too.

For 4 as a generous starter

1.5 litres home-made chicken
    stock (see page 373)
1 red onion, cut into small dice
1 carrot, peeled and finely diced
2 celery sticks, halved
    lengthways then sliced
1 courgette (or other green veg
    like French beans, asparagus,
    Savoy cabbage or fennel),
    roughly diced
1–2 garlic cloves, chopped
a small rosemary branch, leaves
    picked and finely chopped
2 bay leaves
2 tomatoes, roughly chopped
a large piece of Parmesan rind
40g small pasta (orzo, little stars
    or broken-up spaghetti)
couple of handfuls of frozen peas
big handful of flat-leaf parsley
    leaves, chopped
big handful of basil, chopped
80–100g fontina cheese (optional)
good extra virgin olive oil
compulsory Parmesan
S & P

Heat the stock in a large pan and throw in everything except the peas, parsley and basil, then bring to a simmer.

Pick the leaves from the parsley and basil and chop the leaves and stalks separately. Throw the stalks straight into the soup and keep the leaves for later.

Simmer the soup for 45 minutes, until everything is totally tender. Turn off the heat, stir in the peas and chopped basil and parsley, then taste for seasoning.

Let the soup sit for about 15 minutes before serving. If you fancy the fontina, cut it into small dice, and put it in the bottom of the bowls, then ladle on the soup and finish with a healthy slosh of extra virgin and some finely grated Parmesan.

Clockwise from top right: Minestrone; Bootsie's Chicken Noodle Soup; Ribollita

Ribollita

'Ribollita' literally means 're-boiled'. The origins of this peasant Tuscan soup were drummed into me when I worked at The River Café; it's all about having a big old pot of water on the hob, into which you chuck whatever's knocking around the kitchen: some pulses and aromatic herbs, a few root veggies, a carcass or two, some greens, a bit of bacon, bread, etc., until the soup is thick and rich. The remains are topped up each day and added to again, and so on and so forth, hence the name. But in the real world, you probably won't want this hanging around on your stove endlessly, so just let any leftovers cool and keep in the fridge for a couple of days (or in the freezer): it gets even nicer after a bit of hanging around.

For 4 hungry peasants (see photo, page 181)

a few slices of decent white bread, preferably ciabatta, crusts cut off

good extra virgin olive oil

1.5 litres home-made chicken stock (see page 373)

70g cured pig: pancetta, bacon, ham or even salami

2 garlic cloves, chopped

1 large carrot, peeled and cut into small dice

400g dark green cabbage (Savoy, cavolo nero or kale), sliced about 2cm thick

1 x 400g tin borlotti or cannellini beans, drained

1–2 tbsp chopped rosemary, thyme, sage or parsley or ½ tsp dried oregano

a good pinch of chilli flakes, if you like a bit of bite

1 x 400g tin of peeled plum tomatoes

finely grated Parmesan, plus a bit of rind if possible

S & P

Preheat the oven to 180°C/fan 160°C/Gas 4.

Tear the bread into chunks, place on a baking sheet and drizzle well with olive oil. Bake in the hot oven for 15–20 minutes, until golden on the outside and dried out but not totally desiccated.

Meanwhile, put the stock on to heat and throw in the pig bits, all the veg, beans, herbs, chilli (if you fancy it), and tomatoes, breaking the tomatoes up roughly in your hands as they fall in.

If using, chuck a big piece of Parmesan rind in to infuse.

Bring to a simmer, pop on a lid and leave to bubble away gently for about 45 minutes, then stir in the toasted bread and leave for another 5 minutes before turning off the heat. Let it sit for 15 minutes with a lid on, then taste for seasoning and slosh on a couple of tablespoons of extra virgin (ideally it's best left for an hour or even overnight at this stage).

Ribollita is supposed to be a very thick soup – I've even been given a knife and fork to eat it with in Tuscany, but if you want to keep it spoonable, then you may want to ease it with a mug of stock or even hot water. Finish with flutterings of Parmesan, a crack of black pepper and, inevitably, more extra virgin olive oil.

Panacea for the Poorly

Whether you've got a sore throat, dodgy tum or an all-over body ache, the sustenance that soothes almost universally is of a liquidy nature. Simple vegetable soups, fresh juices (particularly veg-based to boost immunity) and anything involving chicken stock came up again and again when I surveyed my family and friends for their fail-safe healing potions. The entrance to the road to recovery is your mouth, so if you're feeling under the weather, the simple answer is to eat yourself better. This particular soup is also known by the shamans of Irkutsk as 'Thai Dragon Juice'. Fact.

Makes 2 fierce cold remedies

1 chilli, halved, plus extra slices to serve if you want it feisty
a thumb (about 20g) of fresh ginger, peeled
1 lemongrass stalk, fat end only, outer leaves peeled off
2 Kaffir lime leaves (worth hunting down in Asian shops and some supermarkets)
couple of handfuls of quick-cook veg (such as mangetout, French beans, courgettes, spring onions, corn, bok choy, cabbage), chopped into bite-sized pieces or shredded
zest and juice of 1 lime
1 tbsp light soy sauce

Put the chilli in a small pan with the ginger, lemongrass, lime leaves and 500ml of water. Bring to the boil then turn down to a relaxed simmer for 10 minutes.

Use a slotted spoon to lift out the solids, which you can chuck out as their work is done. Put the infused stock back on the heat. Toss in all the veg and lime zest, bring to a speedy boil, then immediately turn off the heat and season with soy and lime juice to taste (you can add some more sliced chilli now if, like me, you think the burn helps). Eat straight away – it's never going to be as good for you as it is right now.

Doctor's Orders Stracciatella

Stracciatella is Italian for 'little strands'. This soup is so called because as you quickly whisk the egg into the stock it forms shapes like comet tails. These attract all the fatty bits and other solids, drawing them out of the liquid, thus 'clarifying' it, and making even the cloudiest stock clear to the bottom of the bowl, which is very satisfying. It's the simplest of pauper's soups – just what you want when feeling poorly – and it always reminds me of my dad, who was a doctor, which is a fine endorsement for its healing properties.

It's made in the *alla Romana* style, which means plenty of cheese and pepper please.

Makes 2 soothing bowlfuls for a flu sufferer

500ml home-made chicken
    stock (see page 373)
2 eggs
big handful of finely grated
    Parmesan
scraping of nutmeg (optional
    but good)
handful of flat-leaf parsley,
    finely chopped (optional
    but helpful)
S & P

Pour the stock into a saucepan and while it is coming up to a simmer, beat the eggs in a little bowl or mug with most of the Parmesan, the nutmeg and some seasoning.

Using a whisk, stir the hot stock fast in one direction for a second, so it's swirling round like a vortex, and then continue doing so as you slowly dribble in the beaten egg. Once it's all in, turn the heat off, and stir in the parsley, salt to taste, quite a good amount of pepper and the last of the Parmesan. Very good healing.

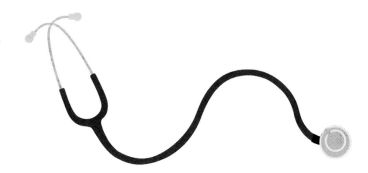

Bootsie's Chicken Noodle Soup

Bootsie, my dear friend Danny's mum and a feisty lady of East End extraction, learnt her soup-making craft half a century ago from the Jewish community associated with that neck of the woods. She suggests making this soup from either a chicken carcass (ask your butcher), leftover bones from a roast chicken, or a dozen or so chicken wings.

It's a two-part operation; you need the stock to cool completely before turning it into soup so that you can scrape all the fat off once it has solidifed. Don't be afraid to make a lot – a happy household always has home-made chicken stock in the freezer.

Serves 4 handsomely (see photo, page 181)

For the stock:
chicken bones (see intro, above)
1 onion
2 carrots, washed and cut into
    large chunks
2 celery sticks, cut into large
    chunks
1 leek, washed well, trimmed
    and cut into chunks
6 peppercorns

For the soup:
2 carrots, peeled and cut into thin
    matchsticks
2 leeks (or 1 big one), quartered
    lengthways then washed well
    and chopped finely
1 chicken stock cube (adding
    this to home-made stock feels
    so wrong but tastes so good!)
2 handfuls (about 60g) of
    vermicelli (durum wheat, not
    rice), capellini or angel
    hair pasta
S & P

First get the stock going. In a large pan, cover the chicken bones with 2.5 litres of cold water, bring to the boil and skim off any scum. Add all the veg and the peppercorns and simmer for 2–3 hours, then strain the stock into a bowl. Once cool enough to handle, pick any chicken meat from the bones, set it aside and then chuck out the bones and veg.

When the stock has cooled to room temperature, put it in the fridge so that all the fat comes to the top and solidifies so it can be scraped off with a spoon.

Tip the fat-free stock back into a saucepan and add the carrots and leeks for the soup, topping up with water if the veg aren't covered. Crumble in the stock cube and simmer for 30–40 minutes, until the veg is well cooked.

Meanwhile, put a second pan on to heat with enough salted water in it to cook the pasta and bring to a boil. Tip the pasta in, give it a stir and cook for about 7 minutes until soft. Drain and stir into the soup along with the picked chicken meat, then season and serve. 'Enjoy,' says the formidable Bootsie (and I'd do what she says!).

A Flash in the Pan: finishing flourishes to up your soupy game

I'm such a die-hard soup fan you'd think I'd set up a soup cult. I always chuck a little something extra on top to round it off, either for flavour, looks or both – because, let's face it, a bowl of soup is somewhat uniform in appearance. Here are some of my favourites:

- **Olive oil**: a good zig zag of your best extra virgin suits most soups. It goes hand in hand with a twist of black pepper. (For the record, I don't believe in white pepper, or truffle oil. EVER.)

- **Herbs**: a small handful of anything sympathetic to the soup brings welcome brightness in both colour and flavour. If you're not sure which to reach for, it's hard to go wrong with chives (or their big sibling, spring onions, finely chopped). Pesto also falls under the banner of 'herbs' and a lobbed-in blob works for many soups.

- **Cheese**: so many soupy situations are improved by finely grated Parmesan on top. Crumbled feta gives sheepy, salty acidity, and grated Gruyère adds nutty French meltiness. Or reverse the whole thing and put the cheese in the bottom of the bowl and pour the soup on top – mozzarella or something stringy like Comté or fontina work well.

- **Pig**: make your own little porky crunchies; they add so much to just about any soup. They're best made from lardons, pancetta or streaky bacon, fried till golden, then drained of excess grease. A spoonful scattered on top is only a good thing.

- **Egg**: poach an egg directly in your soup while it's simmering on low; just crack it in and pop a lid on. After about 3 minutes, when the clear bits have turned white, use a slotted spoon to lift the egg into your serving bowl. Breaking the yolk brings a new level of richness.

- **Bread**: croutons are making a deserved comeback after a post-seventies lull in popularity. I prefer them small in my soup and chunky in my salads. Make them in the oven, rather than frying, and in my opinion, white works best. Oh, and back to cheese; bread and cheese is never wrong, best illustrated by classic French Onion Soup (see page 178 for my twist on it).

- **Dairy**: few soups aren't improved with a little cow-made richness. These days it's not so much the old-school Coffeemate-style swirl of double cream, but more a blob of crème fraîche or Greek yoghurt.

- **Nuts** and seeds: flaked almonds, a scattering of pine nuts, chopped walnuts, pumpkin, sunflower and hemp seeds are all good, and can be used raw or toasted. Raw is healthier, but toasting gives more crunch and, well, nuttiness.

- **Last, a slightly posher one** that I save for entertaining – chanterelle mushrooms, sautéed in butter, scattered sparingly on top. They really lift a soup when out to impress, as they look pretty, taste wonderful and are a textural joy. Mushrooms go with many flavours, including meaty soups and almost every veg soup from artichoke to zucchini. Tread carefully with fish soups; though chanterelles are light in flavour, you don't want to walk all over those delicate sea flavours.

Bun in the oven

I got pregnant more than two decades after my mum died, and though my heart had healed quite a bit by then, the whole business of carrying a child, giving birth and being the sole lifeline for this little helpless babe was so amazing and mind-blowing and miraculous that it made me miss my mum deeply all over again. Questions that I wanted to ask her about pregnancy, birth and caring for a newborn came into my head all the time. And of course more than any of that, once my daughter arrived I just wanted to show her the perfect little girl I'd made, who looks more than a little bit like her.

Most of the thinking around pregnancy and eating doesn't exactly fill any mum-to-be with gastronomic excitement: there's sickness, not being able to eat many of your favourite things (sushi, quality cheese, pâté), more sickness; and the indignity of coal butties to look forward to, which you can't even wash down with a glass of Pinot.

Some people say pregnancy made them eat differently, some say there was no change, some say the smell of food made them sick, others couldn't stop eating. Some craved junk food, some needed minerals and others had no discernible cravings at all – they just took the opportunity to do some intense indulging (and there's nothing wrong with a bit of that).

What follows is a fairly random bunch of recipes that were relevant either while I was up the duff or during the crazy few months following the main event, because on some level they were useful either to me or to Delilah-to-be.

Bun-in-the-oven Buns

Until I was pregnant I was a thoroughly wholemeal kind of a girl, but the minute I got knocked up, all I craved was crappy refined white flour. My preggers friends were wolfing down tangerines or kale juice like it was going out of fashion, but no, I had a trailer-trash baby who demanded I eat the lowest common denominator, farinaceously speaking. But Delilah was born a healthy weight and seems to have inherited my ox-like constitution ... and she still craves the white stuff.

These can be made by hand but the very wet dough takes quite of a lot of kneading (10ish minutes). It's a lot easier in an upright mixer, but doesn't give the same sense of having worked for the treasure.

Makes a circle of life in 6 buns (or enough for one massive craving)

250g plain flour, plus extra
    for dusting
35g caster sugar
25g butter, softened
1 egg
1 x 7g sachet fast-action
    dried yeast
1 tsp salt
150ml whole milk, warmed

For the glaze and icing:
1 egg yolk
1 tbsp milk
100g icing sugar

Put the flour, caster sugar, butter, egg, yeast and salt into a free-standing mixer and mix on a slow speed with the dough hook until it's all roughly come together. Slowly pour in the warm milk. Once incorporated, turn the speed to high for 4–5 minutes until your dough is smooth and coming away from the side of the bowl.

Scrape the dough on to a well-floured surface (it's a super-wet dough so don't be alarmed) and bring together into a fat, floppy sausage shape, then cut into six equal pieces.

Flour your hands and roll each piece between your palms in circular motions until worked into a tight ball; the surface of the dough should be smooth and not cracked. Arrange the buns in a circle on a lightly greased baking tray, about 1cm apart so there's room for them to expand.

Cover with a tea towel and leave in a warm place for 45 minutes to 1 hour, until each bun is cuddled up to the next and the dough bounces back slightly from a gentle prod.

Preheat the oven to 190°C/fan 170°C/Gas 5.

For the glaze, beat the egg yolk with the tablespoon of milk and give the buns a quick brush. Bake for 12–15 minutes until their bases are dry and golden. Leave to cool completely, then mix the icing sugar with 1–1½ tablespoons water for a thick but runny icing and spoon it liberally over the room-temperature buns. Pregnant or not, these are just so devourable.

An Early Introduction to Curry/Spice/Chilli

After a bit of random straw-polling, it turns out that I wasn't alone in loving spicy food during pregnancy. I've always been a fan of chilli, but my craving went further with a need to add cumin, garam masala, turmeric, ground coriander (and cinnamon, which I'm usually not keen on at all) to dishes for which they just weren't appropriate. Like porridge and poached eggs.

Introducing your baby to the wonderful world of spices at the antenatal stage can only be a good thing, I think. The earlier the better, say I. What follows are a couple of contrasting curries – the first is mild and mellow and absolutely scrummy; the second is fiery, deep and very interesting. (As an endnote, 'spicy one!' is one of my two-year-old daughter's favourite exclamations.)

Butter Chicken

There are a lot of spices here but plenty may already be lurking in your cupboard. If not, it's worth a trip to the shops because this recipe is a) fricking delicious and b) fricking easy. Quick, too.

For 6 (see photo, overleaf)

a thumb (about 20g) of fresh
    ginger, peeled and chopped
    into smallish pieces
5 garlic cloves
1 red chilli, deseeded and chopped,
    or 1½ tsp chilli powder
3 cloves
4 cardamom pods
150ml natural or Greek yoghurt
    (if using Greek, water it
    down a bit)
50g ground almonds
3 bay leaves
1 tsp garam masala
½ tsp ground turmeric
¼ tsp ground cinnamon
250ml chicken stock
1kg chicken thighs, each one
    skinned, boned and cut into
    6–8 pieces (ask your butcher)
40g flaked almonds
splash of plain oil, like rapeseed
    or groundnut (sunflower or
    vegetable at a push)
75g butter
2 onions, diced
50ml double cream
small bunch of coriander, roughly
    chopped
S & P

Put the ginger, garlic, chilli, cloves and cardamom in a spice grinder or pestle and mortar and grind to a paste.

In a mixing bowl, stir together this paste with the yoghurt, ground almonds, bay leaves, garam masala, turmeric, cinnamon and chicken stock. Before the raw chicken gets involved it's a good time to taste for seasoning, making sure it's got enough of what you like: add more garlic, ginger or chilli as you wish.

Now chuck in the chicken pieces and give it all a great big stir so it's well coated. This is super-yummy cooked straight away, but if you have up to an hour to set it aside to marinate, it only improves the flavours.

In a saucepan big enough to hold your finished curry, gently dry-toast the flaked almonds to a lovely golden brown, then tip them out into a bowl.

Pour in the oil, melt the butter in it and fry the onions until soft – about 5 minutes. Tip in the chicken plus its marinade, making sure you don't leave any of the marinade behind. When it starts to bubble, turn the heat down and simmer for 15–20 minutes, until the chicken is just cooked, then stir though the double cream, as well as most of the coriander and toasted almonds, saving a sprinkling for the top.

Taste for seasoning, scatter on the rest of the coriander and almonds and serve with rice.

Flash Fried Sesame Spring Greens, p359

Beef Rendang

Butter Chicken

Beef Rendang

It was a happy day when I first came across the rendang style of currying: deep and earthy, and very different to most South-east Asian curries we know. To be honest I felt a little smug about having 'discovered' it. Then a friend went to Anna Hansen's excellent Modern Pantry in Clerkenwell and told me about her fantastic brunch of beef mince rendang with a crispy fried egg. On toast. I smiled, but inside I was crying, as Anna's eggy idea is genius, and makes this spectacular curry Utopian in its yumminess.

For 4

2 tbsp oil (groundnut is traditional here)
750g braising steak, cut into 2cm dice
6 Kaffir lime leaves
1 x 400ml tin coconut milk
1 tbsp brown sugar
S & P
4 fried eggs, to serve (optional but reluctantly encouraged)

For the curry paste:
1 tsp coriander seeds
½ tsp ground turmeric
a large thumb (about 25g) of unpeeled fresh ginger, washed and roughly chopped
4 whole garlic cloves, peeled
1 large onion, roughly diced
2 bird's eye chillies, seeds in (or regular chillies are a little milder)
2 lemongrass stalks, tough end discarded then roughly chopped
1½ tsp salt

Put all the paste ingredients in a food processor with just enough water to bring it together (about a tablespoon or two) so that it's thoroughly blended.

Pour the oil into a heavy-bottomed lidded pan and turn the heat up high. Season the meat, and when the oil is really hot fry it in two or three batches so that it browns nicely all over – about 5 minutes per batch. When all the meat is done, set it aside.

Turn the heat down and tip the paste into the pan. Fry it pretty gently for 10 minutes, chucking the lime leaves in along the way and stirring from time to time, until wonderfully aromatic and starting to dry out. Tip in the coconut milk and seared beef and stir in the brown sugar. Bring to the boil, then put the lid tightly on the pan and turn the heat down to the lowest setting.

Cook for about 3 hours, stirring regularly: this kind of curry requires a bit of patience as the coconut milk simmers away and the liquid level lowers. The end game is the darkest, stickiest, most fragrant meat; soft as you like, enriched by the paste and coconut milk, which have given all of themselves to tenderise and flavour the beef. Only add a splash of water towards the end if it's going a little fast and the liquid is leaving the building before Elvis is out of his dressing room.

Because when The King is ready, I just can't help believin' that this is one of the best curries ever. Thank you very much.

Seared Mackerel
with Raw Beetroot & Walnut Mezze

Omega 3s meet superfoods in a fabulously tasty way.

For 1 massively hungry mum

1 batch of Raw Beetroot
    & Walnut Mezze (see
    page 363)
1–2 mackerel fillets,
    depending on size,
    skin on and pin-boned
olive oil
½ lemon
S & P

First knock up the raw beetroot and walnut mezze, which improves with a little time sitting at room temperature.

Season the mackerel and put a heavy-bottomed frying pan on the hob to get good and hot. Pour in a couple of tablespoons of oil, and once it's smoking, lay the fillets in, skin-side down. ress with a fish slice for a few seconds so they sit flat but don't move them at all; let the fish tell you when it's ready to be turned (3ish minutes) as it will lift away from the pan without coaxing – don't force it or you will ruin a potentially perfect crispy skin.

Flip them over and cook for just another minute, then take out of the pan and serve with the yummy-meets-healthy beetroot mezze and half a lemon.

More than Miso Soup

Growing a baby is a tiring thing; there are times when you feel it's literally sucking the life out of you to feed itself. Having a tub of miso in the fridge made this my go-to answer for instant emergency nourishment.

For 1 (see photo, overleaf)

1 tbsp white miso paste (fresh is
    MUCH nicer than dried and
    lasts forever in the fridge)
a big handful of greens (such as:
    mangetout, French beans,
    broccoli, edamame), chopped
    into bite-sized pieces

Put the miso paste into a suitably comforting vessel to hold. Pour over boiling water to about two-thirds of the way up and stir until the miso has dissolved.

Stir in the chopped veggies and cover the bowl with cling film for 2 minutes so they can soften up a bit. Uncover, give it one last stir and relax.

A Salad with Integrity & Value
(not to mention a truly different kind of dressing)

This is wall-to-wall goodness. It's great noshing and not chore-like in the slightest, plus you get bonus virtue points for giving your work-in-progress what it needs, too. I ripped off the crazy avocado mint dressing from a place in California where they know a thing or two about healthy eating. This salad is almost too good to be true.

Makes 2 grown-up helpings

½ head of broccoli, cut into big
   florets
2 big handfuls of watercress
1 x 400g tin chickpeas, drained
2 handfuls of seeds (pumpkin,
   sunflower and hemp are good)
100g whole almonds, skin on,
   very roughly chopped
1–2 red chillies (depends on
   how hot you like it), deseeded
   and thinly sliced
100g feta cheese (pasteurised),
   crumbled
4 spring onions, sliced quite
   finely
S & P

For the dressing:
1 really, really ripe avocado,
   mashed
75g Greek yoghurt
small bunch of mint, chopped
juice of 1 lime
2 tbsp extra virgin olive oil
S & P

Put a pan of lightly salted water on the stove and once it's at a rolling boil drop in the broccoli florets. Cook for just 3 minutes, then drain and run under cold water until cool. Pat the florets dry then put into a big mixing bowl with all the other salad ingredients and some seasoning.

Knock up the dressing either by hand in a bowl or in a food processor: simply combine everything, then stir in 3–5 tablespoons of water to loosen it up and give it a good season. It's not the prettiest dressing, but it's damn tasty and very good for you.

Put half the dressing into the salad bowl and toss lightly, then either in the bowl or once you've plated, spoon over the rest of it.

Shown with: More than Miso Soup

PPP
(Penne with Potatoes & Pesto)

This is the perfect one-pot supper: yummy, filling, quick and easy. Leftovers are excellent cold the next day with an extra squeeze of lemon and some more seasoning. In Italy, this is called *penne alla Genovese* as it hails from the region around Genoa.

For 2 and a bump

4 tbsp pesto, or to taste (bought is okay, but home-made is much better, see page 368)
1 tbsp olive oil
200g penne (not quick-cook)
200g new potatoes, washed and sliced no more than 1cm thick
extra virgin olive oil
good squeeze of lemon juice
finely grated Parmesan
S & P

If you're using home-made pesto, take 10 minutes to get this out the way first.

Bring a medium saucepan of salted water to a rolling boil with a lid on. Once it's up to speed, slosh in the olive oil, drop in the pasta and spud slices and give it a brief stir so that nothing sticks to the bottom or its comrades. Check the packet instructions: the pasta should take about 12 minutes, by which time the spud slices will be cooked. Drain, and leave to steam dry for a few minutes, then tip back into the pan, but not on the heat.

Stir in the pesto briskly so that some of the spuds break up, then season and pour in a good glug of extra virgin olive oil and a healthy squeeze of lemon juice. Taste, adding more seasoning or lemon if you like, then spoon into warmed bowls and serve with some finely grated Parmesan on top.

Lambs Gamboling in Fields of Barley
(Lamb, Prune & Pearl Barley Casserole)

One-pot stews and braises like this and the next recipe are perfect for this time in your life, both before and after the new arrival. They're easy to knock up before D-day then freeze in smaller containers so you don't have to cook for a while after baby arrives; they are pretty hardy – once cooked, the oven can be turned right down or off and the pot will just wait for whenever your Small has nodded off; they have a fridge life of about 5 days (the flavour even improves), and they freeze well too. But most importantly, they are complete meals of loving, nourishing goodness. And for all these reasons they also make very welcome drop-off dinners for new parents. Sweet and sharp, rich and multi-layered, spicy and fruity – this great casserole is home-cooking at its best.

For 6 hearty meals

2 tbsp olive oil
400g lamb, cut into 2–3cm dice
1 large red onion, cut into large
    dice
3 garlic cloves, chopped
½ tsp chilli flakes
handful of sage, chopped
100ml white wine
1 x 400g tin plum tomatoes
1 litre light chicken stock (diluted
    if using a cube)
2 bay leaves
½ butternut squash (about 500g),
    peeled, deseeded and cut into
    4cm chunks
½ small Savoy cabbage (about
    300g), cut into large irregular
    pieces
150g prunes, stoned
100g pearl barley
S & P

Preheat the oven to 160°C/fan 140°C/Gas 3 and put your best casserole dish on a high heat on the hob.

Pour in the olive oil and, as it heats up, season the lamb well with salt and pepper. Fry the lamb until browned – about 7 minutes – then lift out with a slotted spoon and put aside while you fry the onion and garlic for a couple of minutes, adding a splash more olive oil if it's looking dry in there.

Stir in the chilli flakes and sage, and once the onion has begun to soften pour in the wine. As soon as that comes to the boil add the tin of toms, breaking them up a bit with your hands as they plop in, then pour on the chicken stock, followed by the bay leaves and lamb. Stick a lid on and bring back to a simmer.

Season well and pop in the oven for an hour, then take out and stir in the squash, cabbage, prunes and pearl barley. Cook for another hour until the lamb, squash and pearl barley are all soft and welcoming. Check the seasoning and leave to sit for at least 15 minutes before getting stuck in or setting up your takeaway station.

Top: Chicken, Chorizo & Butterbean Stew
Bottom: Lamb, Prune & Pearl Barley Casserole

Chicken, Chorizo & Butterbean Stew

This trio of classic Spanish ingredients are familiar bedfellows: a perfect example of give and take with an end result that is far more than a sum of its parts.

Makes 4 really satisfying meals (see photo, page 204)

4 chicken legs, split into thighs
   and drumsticks, skin on
2 tbsp olive oil
150g cooking chorizo sausage
   (you need the raw kind),
   sliced 1–2cm thick
1 large onion, sliced
2 carrots, peeled and cut into
   bite-sized pieces
3 garlic cloves, chopped
2 sprigs of rosemary, leaves
   picked and finely chopped
2 tbsp tomato purée
120ml white wine
2 x 400g tins plum tomatoes,
   broken up a bit
2 x 400g tins butter beans,
   drained and rinsed
250ml chicken stock
big handful of flat-leaf parsley,
   roughly chopped
S & P
extra virgin olive oil, to finish

Preheat the oven to 170°C/fan 150°C/Gas 3½ and season all the chicken pieces. Heat the olive oil in a large pan, and once hot, fry the seasoned chicken thighs, starting with the skin side. Don't turn or fiddle with them until they're a deep golden brown (which takes 5ish minutes), then flip and fry on the other side for a similar amount of time.

Now set them aside and do the same with the drumsticks, which take a bit less time to reach a similar shade of loveliness. Put the drummers with the thighs, and tip most of the oil out of the pan, leaving just about a tablespoon or so.

Chuck in the chorizo slices and fry for a few minutes until they are golden brown. Fish them out with a slotted spoon, set aside, then go in with the onion, carrots, garlic and rosemary. Give them a shove from time to time for the 10ish minutes it takes them to begin to soften, then add the tomato purée and coat the veg in it. Stir pretty constantly for a couple of minutes so that the purée doesn't catch, then pour in the wine, mixing it in well with the other ingredients.

Once the wine has pretty much reduced away, pour in the tins of toms, butter beans and stock and bring to a simmer. Chuck in the chorizo, stir and then slide in the chicken pieces. Give it all a bit of a season and, once it's come back to a simmer, pop in the oven for 1¼–1½ hours until the chicken is tender and comes away from the bone with little coaxing.

Taste for seasoning, stir in the chopped parsley and, once in the bowl/plate/container, add a little splash of best extra virgin olive oil too (as the Spaniards do).

And After the Main Event ...
Breast-feeding Porridge

Rolled oats are easiest to get hold of and quickest to cook, but using ground oats of a medium or fine texture doesn't take much longer and gives a pleasing, comforting texture. Oat aficionados would say this is the right time in your life to indulge in pinhead oats – the only true, proper porridge in their eyes. All oats are a good source of iron, calcium and fibre. As for what else goes into the porridge, dairy is all about vitamin D, which helps grow strong bones, and many old-school midwives will tell you that fennel and caraway seeds help your milk production.

Makes a big bowl for 1 hungry, feeding mum

1 small ramekin (or anything roughly that size) of oats
2 ramekins of whole, organic milk
pinch of salt
handful of blueberries
spoonful of golden syrup or honey
handful of roughly chopped nuts (walnuts are great, so are pecans but any will do)
sprinkling of caraway and fennel seeds

Pour the oats and milk into a small saucepan over a medium heat and add a pinch of salt as it comes to a simmer. Turn down to the lowest heat and pop a lid on. Cook for about 10 minutes, stirring occasionally, until all the milk has been absorbed and the oats are soft.

Stir though half the blueberries and cook for just a couple of minutes more until they have popped. Tip into your bowl and use your spoon to make a hole in the middle, so you can see the bottom. Quickly pour in the golden syrup to make a 'treacle well', as we used to call it. Now you can see the importance of swift spoon action: the faster you move, the bigger the hole stays and the more treacle you can get into it!

Scatter on the nuts, seeds and the rest of the berries and get stuck in. This is quite a big helping. When porridge is this fun, room temperature is no bad thing: I often keep my brekkie bowl on the go till past elevenses.

FAMILY
9
FAVOURITES

THE definition of 'family' has definitely loosened up over the last few decades, which is a strength of our changing society. A mum, a dad and 2.4 kids is no longer the key template. There are child-free families, single-parent families, steps in all generational directions, and of course, extended family with super-special people with whom one shares no DNA whatsoever. I've folk in my life who have neither married into nor are part of my blood family, yet they are totally and indisputably 'family' to me. Whatever and whomever you have in your family, sharing a home-cooked meal made with love while talking, listening, catching up and having a laugh are the things that make those bonds the lasting ones.

This chapter is like the ultimate Greatest Hits album ever: wall-to-wall belters that make you want to shake your culinary booty. The dishes I've given here are the informal crowd-pleasers upon which our nation was built. Some are just my versions of the classics, others I've given a small McEvedy make-over and I've also laid down some future cult dishes for a new generation of family cooks.

My big sister and I always ate with our parents in the evenings. Our dad was a psychiatrist and a history writer, and came home from work at about six o'clock to be greeted by my sister and me thundering down the hall. He'd pick us up, carry us through to the sitting room and drop us with an exciting bump on to one of the soft chairs in the sitting room. After pouring himself a glass of wine he'd disappear into his study and at half-past seven our mum would shout 'suppertime!'. Then, we would all convene as a family for the first time that day. Sometimes Pa would read us the words he was working on, about the building of the lighthouse at Alexandria or how the Visigoths charged on Europe, or the great courage of the Spartans. All of this magnificent history, recounted with genuine emotion, went down against a backdrop of shared spoonfuls that were as laden with love as Pa's stories.

Except for the terribly exciting times when my dad and I would walk down to the local Indian or the kebab shop for a take-away,

Mama always cooked. Many of her trademark suppers are included in this chapter, such as shepherd's pie, lasagne, toad-in-the-hole and fishcakes. The names (if not the execution) have been the same in households up and down the country for decades, and having passed the test of time with flying colours for generations of British families.

After supper we'd clear the table and then sit down again to play cards (which I loved and my sister hated), with a jolliness and togetherness lingering in the kitchen that just could not have existed were it not for the meal that preceded it. Everything starts with suppertime: the act of sitting down and eating together is key. Preferably with peas. And ketchup.

Bloody Big Bol

In terms of family cooking, bolognese sauce is pretty much the template for feeding a crowd: it's not expensive, everybody loves it and if you make a huge batch then you're quids-in for an easy life. The point is to have a good old cook-up then freeze some. Interestingly – or mildly so – according to my sister the frozen batch tastes even better.

Makes a massive batch (3kg): enough spag bol for 4–6, plus plenty left to freeze for a lasagne, see next page, and/or more spag bol another day (see photo, overleaf)

about 3 tbsp olive oil

2 onions, finely chopped

4 celery sticks, finely chopped

2 massive carrots or 3 regular, peeled and chopped small

2 garlic cloves, chopped

4 bay leaves

1kg beef mince

3 tbsp tomato purée

large glass (250ml) red wine

3 x 400g tins plum tomatoes

750ml beef stock (concentrate is better than cube)

S & P

Heat the oil in a wide pan and fry the onions, celery, carrots, garlic and bay leaves for about 8–10 minutes until softened.

Tip the meat in, breaking it up with a wooden spoon and fry over a medium–high heat until well browned all over, which takes a fair amount of time – up to about another 10 minutes depending on the water/fat content of the mince.

Once there's no more redness to be seen, splodge in the tomato purée and stir well to coat all the meat and veggies, then pour in the wine and let it bubble. When the wine has almost totally reduced, go in with the tins of toms, breaking them up a bit in your hands on the way in, and let it come up to a simmer before pouring in the stock.

Give it a season and a stir as it comes back to the boil, then turn down to the lowest heat so that it bubbles away very gently for an hour. Whip the lid off and let it slowly reduce for another 30–50 minutes until it looks like your perfect bolognese. Leave to sit for 10 minutes before giving it a final taste for seasoning.

Lasagne As You Like It

Few meals in life are loved as universally as a really good lasagne, and this is a *really* good lasagne.

6–8 happy helpings

½ batch of Bloody Big Bol
    (see previous page)
1 batch of Basic White Sauce
    (see page 369)
150g Parmesan, finely grated
250–300g dried lasagne sheets
    (buy the kind you don't have
    to pre-cook)
drizzle of extra virgin olive oil

Preheat the oven to 190°C/fan 170°C/Gas 5.

Start by knocking up the bolognese and the white sauce. Now choose your dish – it needs to be about 30 x 22 x 6cm – and ladle in about a third of the bolognese so that it covers the bottom.

Next, spread on roughly a quarter of the white sauce, sprinkled with a quarter of the grated Parmesan. Cover it with pasta sheets – you'll probably need to break some to get a full layer.

From now on it's just more layering: bolognese, white sauce, Parmesan, pasta, and so on until you run out of everything. Just make sure that you have enough white sauce for that to be your top layer, and a good amount of Parmesan to cover it – there should be no raw pasta sticking out uncovered.

Drizzle lightly with olive oil, then sit the dish on a baking tray and bake for 35–45 minutes until the top is golden, the sides are bubbling and a sharp knife meets with little or no resistance when you push it into the middle.

Serve with a crisp, lightly dressed green salad, not chips!

Shown with: Bloody Big Bol

The Lighter Side of Chicken Pie

This is a particularly fine example of the species, considerably less nap-inducing than you'd expect.

Makes 6–8 biggish helpings

1 free-range chicken, about
   1.5kg, or 2 legs and 2 breasts
2 carrots, peeled
2 celery sticks, halved crossways
1 large greengrocer or 2 smaller
   supermarket leeks, halved
   crossways and washed well
1 onion, peeled and halved
2 garlic cloves, smashed
2 bay leaves
50g butter
300g mushrooms (chestnut are
   lovely for this, but button or
   any will do really), halved
   or quartered
1 tbsp plain flour
1–2 tbsp tarragon, chopped (it's
   a pretty intense herb so it
   depends how much you like
   it, and if you don't like it at
   all, use parsley)
a blob of wholegrain mustard
   (if you fancy it)
3 tbsp sour cream or crème
   fraîche
500g puff pastry
1 egg, beaten
S & P

Put the chicken into a large saucepan with the carrots, celery, leek, onion, garlic and bay leaves, then pour in water to cover by about 2cm, so about 2–3 litres in total. Bring to a simmer and let the chicken poach gently until cooked – a whole chicken will take about 50 minutes. If using portions, the breasts should be lifted out after 30 minutes and the legs after 45.

Take the veg out with the chicken and set both aside, then turn the heat up and allow the stock to reduce to about half a litre. Tip it into a jug, give the pan a quick clean and then fry the mushrooms in the butter until soft and golden.

Preheat the oven to 200°C/fan 180°C/Gas 6. When cool enough to handle, pick the chicken into nice chunks, chucking out any skin, bones and gristly bits.

Stir the flour into the cooked mushrooms until sticky and well coated, then slowly add the stock, a ladleful at a time. Start this with a wooden spoon, then as more liquid goes in, move over to a whisk to keep the sauce smooth. When all the stock has been incorporated, bring to a gentle simmer for a couple of minutes, then turn off the heat. Roughly chop the stock veg, then stir into the sauce along with the chicken, tarragon, mustard, sour cream/crème fraîche and seasoning.

Taste, then tip into a pie dish measuring about 35 x 25 x 7cm. On a lightly floured work surface, roll out the pastry to just under 1cm thick. Brush the edges of the dish with beaten egg then lay the pastry on top and trim off the excess. Make a little hole in the middle to let steam out, and now brush the top with the egg wash. Score it lightly with partners of parallel lines (if you like geometry and/or Blondie) and bake for 30–40 minutes until golden and irresistible.

Coronation Kedgeree

We, as a family, are particularly fond of a good kedgeree, and we, as a nation, have a small obsession with coronation chicken: both are dishes that have their roots in the Raj, when Britain began its love affair with curry. For all intents and purposes this is just a damn fine kedgeree, though the addition of sultanas and almonds nicked from coronation chicken gives it a fruit and nut angle that appeals to little 'uns.

Abundant for 6

600g undyed smoked haddock, skin on
1 onion, sliced
couple of bay leaves
about 500ml whole milk
knob of butter
a slug of oil (it doesn't matter what type, just nothing too strong)
2 tbsp curry powder
½ tsp ground turmeric
400g basmati rice
100g sultanas
6 eggs
handful of coriander, leaves picked, stalks chopped
handful of flaked almonds, toasted (see page 74)
S & P
mango chutney, to serve (sounds odd but highly recommended)

Cut the fish into three pieces and put skin-side down in a wide pan, with the onion and bay leaves. Pour on enough milk to just cover (don't worry if a bit sticks out), pop a lid on and put over a medium heat. Once steaming, poach for 5–6 minutes until only just cooked, i.e. flaking, but still slightly translucent. Carefully lift out the fish and set aside to cool, then strain the milk, keeping both the onions and milk but chucking out the bay leaves.

Stick the kettle on to boil. Clean the pan and put it back on a medium heat to dry out. Once dry, melt the butter with a splash of oil and gently fry the spices for a minute. Tip in the rice and mix it all well together. Chuck in the sultanas, then pour on hot water from the kettle to cover the rice, plus about 2cm. Give it a stir and a season, and pop a lid on as it comes to the boil, then turn down to a simmer and cook for around 8 minutes.

Pour all the poaching milk into the rice, stir well to be sure it's not sticking to the bottom, and cook for another 3–5 minutes, until tender. Meanwhile, bring a pan of water to the boil, lower in the eggs and cook on a busy simmer for 6 minutes, then drain and run under cold water before peeling and cutting in half.

Chop the onions from the poaching milk and add to the rice. The fish will now be cool enough to handle, so flake it into the rice, throwing away any skin and bones. Stir in some seasoning and the chopped coriander stalks, then taste again, splashing in more milk as necessary to make your kedgeree good and creamy. Serve up with the eggs, a scattering of coriander leaves and flaked almonds. And it really is very good with mango chutters.

Ali's Authentic Aubergine Curry

Children's meals are often centred around meat, but in truth we should all be eating a bit less moo (or oink, baa or bwak) and more veg (which generally don't make any noise at all). My friend Alison first made this for me: she hails from Bolton but channels her Goan granny in the kitchen. It's a great way to give youngsters a gentle introduction to the wonderful world of spice, and the aubergines make it taste kind of meaty, too.

For 6

4 aubergines, 2 whole and 2 cut into big chunks
2 tbsp vegetable or groundnut oil, plus extra for coating
1 heaped tsp mustard seeds (yellow or black)
1 heaped tsp cumin seeds
1 tsp ground turmeric
1 tsp chilli powder (or not)
1 small onion, roughly chopped
½ a thumb of ginger, finely chopped
3–4 curry leaves (available dried in most supermarkets)
200g split peas or green/brown lentils
1 x 400g tin chopped tomatoes
1 litre hot veg stock (or boiling water will do)
2 large carrots, peeled and roughly diced
2 courgettes, sliced lengthways then cut into half-moons
2–3 tbsp tamarind paste or lemon juice, to taste
3 tbsp soft dark brown sugar
salt
chopped coriander, to serve
some natural yoghurt, to serve

Preheat the oven to 190°C/fan 170°C/Gas 5. Pierce the whole aubergines all over and put on a baking tray. Toss the two cut aubergines in a little oil and salt, lay out on a second baking tray and stick both trays in the oven for 45 minutes to 1 hour.

Heat the vegetable oil in a saucepan over a low–medium heat and gently fry the mustard and cumin seeds for a few minutes until fragrant and popping. Stir in the ground spices and cook for another couple of minutes before adding the onion, ginger and curry leaves. Fry for a further 5 minutes until the onion begins to soften, then add the split peas or lentils and give them a hearty roll around in the oil.

Plop in the tomatoes and hot stock/water, and simmer for 30 minutes until the pulses are soft (split peas take longer than lentils). Meanwhile, the cut aubergines should now be soft, so take them out of the oven and leave to cool. Check the whole ones too, and when they're squidgy they should also come out.

Once the pulses are beginning to soften, add the carrots and courgettes and more hot water as necessary to just cover. Simmer for a further 25–30 minutes: the sauce should thicken up nicely, so stir it to make sure it doesn't stick on the bottom.

Halve the whole roasted aubergines, scoop out the soft flesh with a spoon and stir it into the curry along with the chunks of aubergine, tamarind or lemon juice and brown sugar. Season well with salt. Bring briefly back to a simmer, then turn off and rest for 15 minutes to a day. Serve with chopped coriander on top and a blob of natural yoghurt if you fancy it (I usually do).

Toad-in-the-hole with Cidery Onions

Although I have distant memories of my mum making this, I'd basically forgotten about toad-in-the-hole until I started thinking about recipes for this book. Then it all came flooding back: Mama's kind, satisfied smile and our oohs and ahhs as her toad came out of the oven, all gloriously puffed up around the edges. And I remembered my joy at what has to be one of the best kiddie suppers ever: a family-sized Yorkshire pudding, with sausages to boot. Cooking this for my daughter produces a slightly confusing cross-generational moment, as really, it makes *me* want to be the child again.

Handsome supper for 4

For the onions:
splash of olive oil
large knob of butter (about 25g)
3 onions, sliced
1 sprig of rosemary, leaves picked
    and chopped
250ml cider (any kind except
    Diamond White)
250ml chicken stock
S & P

For the toad:
110g plain flour
2 eggs
300ml whole milk
½ tsp salt
black pepper
4 tbsp plain oil (like veg or
    sunflower) or animal fat,
    as in duck, pig, beef, etc.
8 decent-quality pork sausages
    (thick, not chipolatas)

Preheat the oven to 220°C/fan 200°C/Gas 7.

Get the onions going first: put a wide pan on a medium–high heat and pour in a good splash of olive oil. Melt the butter in it and once it starts to froth, throw in the onions. Stir them from time to time until they have started to collapse and soften (about 10 minutes), then turn the heat down to medium and keep cooking them for another 15–20 minutes, at which point they should be golden brown, caramelised and smelling sweet.

While the onions are doing their thing, knock up the toad batter: sift the flour into a bowl then whisk in the eggs and slowly start pouring in the milk, whisking all the while. Once it's all smooth, season with ½ tsp salt and quite a bit of pepper, then cover the bowl with cling film and put it in the fridge – you want it to have about 30 minutes chillin' in the fridge.

Find yourself a roasting tray measuring about 30 x 20 x 5cm. Pour the plain oil into it and stick it in the oven to get hot.

Once the onions are looking lovely, stir in the rosemary, followed a minute or two later by the cider. When it starts to bubble, pour in the chicken stock, bring back to the boil, then turn down to a steady, slowish simmer: it'll take about another 22–25 minutes to be the sauce we want it to be.

Meanwhile, pop the sausages into the hot oil and stick them in the oven for 10–12 minutes to brown on the outside, giving them a shuffle halfway through.

CONTINUED

CONTINUED FROM
PREVIOUS PAGE

When the bangers have decent colour all over, move them all away from the edges of the tray and, giving it a quick whisk first, pour the cold batter into the hot oil. Cook in the oven for 20–25 minutes, but don't open the oven door until 20 minutes to give the batter a fair chance to do its thing: you're looking for it to be risen and crisp on the outside with no soggy bits in the middle, so once you've had a peek, stick it back in if not there yet.

Have a butcher's at the onions. Taste for seasoning and turn off the heat when you're happy with the consistency – oniony sauce, rather than sauce with a few floating onions, if you know what I mean. Serve as soon as the batter is cooked in the middle – couple of toads, a square of hole and a ladleful of loveliness to bring it together. Pride on a plate.

Macaroni Cheese

Look, I know you don't really need a recipe for macaroni cheese, but I'm never going to write another book like this, a Book for Life, so forgive me. Macaroni cheese is important, and I just need it to be in here for my own peace of mind.

For 8ish (depending on age and tummy size)

splash of olive oil
1 batch of Cheese Sauce
   (see page 369)
500g macaroni
knob of butter, for greasing
50g Parmesan, grated
50g fresh breadcrumbs
S & P

Preheat the oven to 190°C/fan 170°C/Gas 5. Put a big pan of water with a lid on to boil with a good pinch of salt and a splash of olive oil.

Now make your cheese sauce, but I wouldn't bother infusing the milk, just use the basic white sauce recipe then stir in the cheese.

Once the water is boiling, tip in the macaroni, give it a quick stir and cook it for 2 minutes less than it says on the packet – it's going to have some oven time, so it can finish cooking in there.

Drain the pasta, keeping 250ml of the cooking water, then in the saucepan mix together the pasta, cheese sauce and reserved pasta water. Seasoning levels vary depending who you're cooking for so bear that in mind. Choose your baking dish, erring more towards the flatter rather than higher variety, and grease it lightly with butter. Pour the cheesy pasta in and give it a firm bang on the table to make sure it's relatively evenly spread.

In a little bowl, mix the Parmesan with the breadcrumbs and scatter all over the top. Put it on a baking tray (it's so boring if it dribbles over into your oven) and bake for 25–30 minutes until golden on top and bubbling round the edge.

CAUTION: Filling is HOT.

Spaghetti & Meatballs

When I lived in New York, I found an amusing difference between Italian dishes I'd had in Italy and the food I experienced in 'Little Italy' (or 'Liddleidaly' as New Yorkers say). Two or three generations of American living has produced a marked influence on their cooking. This is one of those dishes now owned by Italian-Americans, not the motherland. Goodfellas and Goodfamilies, fill ya boots.

For 6 family-loving folks

300g pork mince
300g beef mince
50g crustless white bread, ripped
  into chunks
50ml whole milk
extra virgin olive oil
500g spaghetti
double batch of 15-minute
  Tomato Sauce (see page 369)
big handful of flat-leaf parsley,
  chopped
60–80g Parmesan, finely grated
S & P

In a biggish bowl, mix both minces with quite a lot of seasoning. Put the bread in a separate little bowl with the milk and squish with the back of a spoon. Once the bread has soaked up all the milk, stir it into the meat. Split the mix into four, divide each quarter into 8–10 walnut-sized balls so you have 32–40 of them in total and roll them very briefly between the palms of your hands with a fair amount of pressure.

Meanwhile, fill a big pan with hot water, hurl in some salt and put over a high heat with a lid on. Once it comes up to a rolling boil, slosh in a bit of olive oil and slip in the spag. Give it a quick stir so it's not stuck together, then cover and simmer for 12–15 minutes, until al dente. Drain, saving a cup of the cooking water.

While the spag is cooking, knock up the tomato sauce. When it's simmering and no longer needs your full attention, pop a wide, preferably thick-bottomed, frying pan on a high heat for the meatballs. Slug in some olive oil and when just smoking, fry the balls in batches – enough to cover the bottom of the pan but not all piled up. You want them roughly browned on all sides, but keep the tempo up so they don't cook through.

As each batch of balls is looking lovely, plop them into the gently simmering tomato sauce. Let them braise for 7–10 minutes, then tip the drained pasta into the balls 'n' sauce, splashing in a bit of the pasta water if it seems a bit too thick – this will restore the gloss and make it a more pleasing consistency if it's over-reduced.

Chuck in the parsley and taste for seasoning. Finally, get into your best Italian Mama outfit and serve up in an appropriately family-sized bowl with generous flufflies of Parmesan.

Pork, Cashew & Sugar Snap Stir-fry

We never had stuff like this when I was growing up, but times have changed, as has the ethnic make-up of our country: these day stir-fries are commonplace, and much loved by children. This one goes down particularly well with kids: the hoisin sauce and honey make it a touch sweet and the cashew nuttiness is generally a hit too, though it's also loaded with a parent-pleasing amount of veg.

For 4 adults, or 2 bigs and 4 smalls

350g pork tenderloin, trimmed of any sinew
1 tbsp dark soy sauce, plus more to taste
2 tbsp hoisin sauce
1 tbsp clear honey
1 tbsp sesame oil
2 tbsp groundnut, sunflower or vegetable oil
2 garlic cloves, sliced
2 carrots, peeled and cut into matchsticks
2 peppers, deseeded and cut into strips
150g sugar snap peas
2 spring onions, chopped
big handful of cashew nuts, chopped a couple of times

To serve:
long-grain rice (see page 358)
chilli sauce (but maybe not for the kids)

Slice the pork lengthways then into bite-sized chunks and toss it in the soy sauce, hoisin, honey and sesame oil. Give it all a good coating and leave to marinate.

Bring the rice into action before the main event as the stir-fry doesn't take very long.

Now conquer your veg prep. When everything is ready (which it needs to be because this is a quick-cook), heat a tablespoon of the groundnut oil (or whichever variety you are using) in a wok or very wide frying pan. As the oil approaches bloody hot (extraction on, open the window now), chuck in the cashews and fry for a scant minute, moving them all the time until they are lightly browned.

Lift them out using a slotted spoon, set them aside and tip in the saucy pork. Fry it quickly, stirring pretty much all the time for 2–3 minutes: you want it to pick up a bit of colour and be cooked about three-quarters of the way but still a bit pink in the middle.

When you're happy with the pork, take it out with your trusty slotted spoon, then go in with the garlic, carrots, peppers, sugar snaps and spring onions. Toss and fry until they have all just crossed the divide from raw to cooked (as in still very crunchy), then tip the pork back in. Give it a last stir-fry to bring it all together, then check the seasoning: a touch more soy will probably go down well. Scatter over the cashews, serve at speed and I'd leave the question of chilli sauce up to the recipients.

A Barbecue Feast:
Burgers, Coleslaw, Corn & Smoky Beans

Everybody loves a barbie, and this fine spread is all you need for the best kind of family day in the garden. Just add sunshine. And beer.

All my barbecue recipes feed 5 adults and 5 kids, so re-work if necessary to suit your party

The Burgers

about 1.2kg beef mince
1 onion, finely diced (optional –
   I tend not to)
squirt of ketchup (up to you, but
   never goes amiss)
S & P
10 burger buns (or as required)

Put the beef in a big mixing bowl, season with salt and pepper, and add either or both of the optional extras as you choose, then give it a good mix.

Grab a medium handful of mince for an adult burger (about 150g) and a smaller one for the kids (about 75–100g, though as burger-eating kids range from ages 2 to 15, this is not an exact sport) and shape them into the appropriate form.

Cooking times on a barbecue are always hard, but they're roughly 3 minutes a side for the big burgers (for medium-rare) and 4 minutes for the kids' ones, cooked through.

Danny's Coleslaw

Coleslaw can be one of those things where home-made never tastes as good as the dirty bought stuff, but my great friend Danny has absolutely cracked it, so yah boo sucks to the supermarkets!!

1 carrot, peeled and finely grated
½ small white cabbage (about
   400g), finely shredded
½ small red onion, finely sliced
4 tbsp mayo
2 tbsp salad cream
S & P

In a big bowl, mix the carrot, cabbage and onion with the mayo, salad cream and a bit of seasoning. Stir it all together really well, then taste for seasoning.

Leave to sit for at least half an hour for the veg to soften up a bit (overnight is even better, though in that case add the onion and seasoning the next day), but check seasoning before serving.

PTO FOR MORE
BBQ FEASTING

Smoky Beans

This quantity is enough as part of my barbecue feast (for 5 adults and 5 kids), but if you're doing these as a standalone side for something like a piece of grilled chicken, which you might well do once you've tried them, it's probably only enough for 4–6. It's also a fab one for vegetarians; just ditch the bacon.

(See photo, previous page)

3 tbsp plain oil (like vegetable or sunflower)
1 large or 2 small red onions, diced
2 garlic cloves, chopped
80g smoked streaky bacon/ lardons/pancetta, diced (but not for veggies)
½ tsp smoked paprika*
1 tbsp maple syrup
4 tbsp barbecue sauce
2 x 400g tins beans (borlotti, kidney, pinto or black – or a combo), drained and rinsed
1 x 400g tin plum tomatoes
S & P

*And I'd add ½ tsp chilli flakes if it's a grown-ups' do

In a wide pan, fry the onion, garlic and bacon vigorously in the oil for 5ish minutes until the bacon is browning, the onion has softened and it's all getting a bit sticky in there.

Stir in the paprika, maple syrup and barbecue sauce and bring to a simmer, then add the beans. Tip in the toms, breaking them up a bit on the way in, then fill the tin with water and pour that in too. Stir and season as it comes back to a simmer, then keep it bubbling away gently for 35–45 minutes, stirring occasionally to make sure it doesn't stick on the bottom.

Taste for seasoning. It's ready when the beans are good and soft, and the sauce has come together and is down to a binding consistency.

Cheesy Barbecue Corn on the Cob

Of course you can just grill it plain, but you really would be missing out ...

(See photo, page 229)

8 corn cobs, preferably still in
    their husks
4 tbsp mayo
50g Cheddar, grated
1 garlic clove, finely chopped
small handful of mint, finely
    chopped*
small handful of parsley, finely
    chopped*
juice of ½ lime
S & P

* It's quite possible that small
    kids might like these better
    without the green stuff, but to
    me it's the making of them.

If they're husked or partially so, just whack the cobs straight on the grill or barbecue; if they're naked, they cook better with a metal bowl over them so they steam a bit as they grill. Cook on all sides, turning them regularly, for about 10–15 minutes.

In a bowl, mix together the mayo, cheese, garlic, herbs (if using), lime juice and seasoning.

When the corn comes off the grill, peel off any husks and halve three of the cobs for the kids. Use a teaspoon to splodge and spread the cheesy mix all over them and have a bunch of napkins on hand as they're a good and messy eat.

Shepherd's Pie

As well as being slap-bang yummy, this recipe has the added bonus of a little hidden veg that veg-phobic kids will hardly notice. The anchovies might also slip under the radar: I promise your pie won't taste fishy – they just do a very good job as a flavour enhancer where lamb is concerned.

For 6–8

about 2 tbsp olive oil

2 onions, diced

2 carrots, peeled and cut into chunks

2 celery sticks, halved lengthways and diced

2–3 garlic cloves, chopped

1 tbsp rosemary leaves, finely chopped

4 anchovies, chopped (optional)

750g lean lamb mince

1 tbsp tomato purée

small glass (125ml) white wine

1 litre hot chicken stock

1½ tbsp Bovril (to make it meaty)

good splash of Worcestershire sauce (which has anchovies in it anyway)

2 handfuls of frozen peas, defrosted

handful of flat-leaf parsley, chopped

S & P

For the mash topping:

1kg spuds, peeled and quartered

125ml milk

50g butter, melted

Heat the olive oil over a medium–high heat in a large, wide pan and fry the onions for 5–7 minutes, stirring regularly. Once it has started to soften, go in with the carrots and celery and fry for a few minutes until bright and shiny. Add the garlic, rosemary and anchovies and stir for a couple more minutes until the anchovies have melted and the garlic and rosemary are fragrant.

Now tip all this into a bowl and get the pan good and hot again before plopping in the mince. Season the meat as it fries, and once it has all browned, take a look at the amount of fat in the pan: a little bit is fine, but if there's lots then spoon it off or dab it up with kitchen paper.

Next, stir the tomato purée in well, followed by the wine. Let this reduce away, then pour in the hot stock, add the Bovril (not key but recommended) and splash in some Worcestershire sauce. Give it all a good mix, bring to the boil with a lid, then turn down to a fairly busy simmer, lid still on. Give it a helpful prod every now and then, and after about 45 minutes whip the lid off. Stir in the veggies from earlier and let it reduce for 25–30 minutes or until it looks like the bottom of a Shepherd's Pie should, but slightly runnier. Take off the heat, taste and season.

Now get your mash on: put the spuds in a pan of plenty of cold water with a bit of salt. Stick a lid on, bring to the boil then take the lid off and turn down to a busy simmer until cooked, about 10–12 minutes (a knife should go in without much resistance). Drain and leave in the colander to steam-dry for a few minutes.

CONTINUED ☞

Shown with: Spiced Winter Braised Red Cabbage, p359

CONTINUED FROM
PREVIOUS PAGE

Pour the milk and half the melted butter into the pan then tip the spuds back in and mash until smooth, seasoning to taste.

Preheat the oven to 190°C/fan 170°C/Gas 5. Stir the peas and parsley into the meaty base and tip into a suitable dish (I use a big oval dish measuring about 36 x 24cm), remembering you have to fit the mash on top too.

Spread the mash on top, fluff up with a fork, then brush with the rest of the melted butter. Put the dish on a baking tray and bake for 30–40 minutes, until golden brown on top and bubbling enticingly round the edge.

And your option to cottage:

Shepherds obviously look after lambs and sheep, but do cottagers look after beef? And why do I keep humming 'Careless Whisper'?

As Shepherd's Pie except:

∗ Use beef mince instead of lamb.

∗ Finely dice the onions, celery and carrots instead of leaving them chunky.

∗ Ditch the anchovies, Worcestershire sauce and tomato purée.

∗ Swap the rosemary for thyme.

∗ Use red wine instead of white, and double the amount.

∗ Use beef stock, not chicken (so there's no need to add Bovril either).

∗ Peas are out, parsley stays.

Mrs Johnson's Cheese Pudding

Arabella Boxer's *First Slice Your Cookbook* was unlike any other cookbook on my mum's shelf. It had a crazy design that I can't begin to describe, with *Alice in Wonderland*-type illustrations, an intriguing Appendix that I spent a long time studying (which was the inspiration behind the appendices in this book) and this fine recipe, which was a firm family favourite.

Boxer doesn't give us any information at all about Mrs Johnson, but for the record she makes a very mean, very rich cheese pudding. (Inevitably I have tinkered with it slightly – I do hope Mrs Johnson and Mrs Boxer won't mind.)

Serves 6

knob of butter, for greasing
5–6 slices of slightly stale white bread, crusts off
1 tbsp mustard (English preferred, but Dijon is good too), plus a little more for brushing on the bread
6 eggs
125ml double cream
75g Gruyère, grated
100g Cheddar (mild or medium – mature is just a bit much here), grated
3 spring onions, thinly sliced
1 tsp picked thyme leaves (optional – good for grown-ups; kids are less bothered)
pepper

Preheat the oven to 190°C/fan 170°C/Gas 5.

Butter a 1.5 litre pudding basin and line with the bread. It's fine to cut pieces to make a patchwork, but you do want the basin to be completely covered, i.e. no holes. And there to be corners of bread sticking up around the edge (these go fantastically crunchy during the baking).

Brush the bread lightly all over with mustard – or not, if your audience mostly still have their milk teeth.

In a separate bowl, beat the eggs with the cream, grated cheese, a splodge of mustard (this one is more compulsory, but for real youngies use Dijon), spring onions, thyme, if using, and quite a lot of pepper. Pour into the bread-lined basin, making sure some corners of bread are sticking up above the liquid. Cover with buttered foil, making a fair dome at the top for the pud to rise.

Bake for 1 hour, then whip the foil off and have a look for both colour and cookedness: visually it should be puffed up and golden brown, so give it another few minutes if necessary. It's cooked when you give it a little shake and the outer parts are set firm but there's a small but discernable amount of wibble in the middle. Get in there immediately before the puff falls (though it's also yummy cold).

Salmon & Leek Fishcakes

My first job in a professional kitchen was at Green's Champagne and Oyster Bar, a London institution. The menu was mostly comprised of old-school British classics and their signature dish was fishcakes, made to a particularly brilliant recipe by executive chef Beth Coventry. Beth was culinary royalty at the time, having co-founded the legendary Langan's Brasserie with her friend Peter, before going on to take the helm at Green's, owned by another well-connected mate, Simon Parker-Bowles. Beth's fishcakes had a massively loyal following, and as junior commis it was my job to breadcrumb 60–80 of them every morning. Though this is pretty much that recipe, it's from a 20-year-old memory, so it's technically not a direct crib (and my friend Beth wouldn't mind anyway!).

Makes 12 – roughly speaking allow 2 for a grown-up and 1 for a child (and they freeze really well)

3–4 spuds, about 450-500g, peeled and quartered
1 x 450–500g piece salmon fillet, skin on, pin-boned
1 onion, chopped
small glass (125ml) white wine
150–200ml milk
80g butter
1 large greengrocer or 2 smaller supermarket leeks, halved lengthways, washed well and thinly sliced
80g plain flour, plus an extra handful
few scrapes of nutmeg or ¼ tsp ground
2 eggs, 1 of them beaten
100g fresh breadcrumbs
about 2 tbsp sunflower oil
S & P

Shown with: Beetroot, Parsley & Sherry Vinegar Salad, p362

Preheat the oven to 210°C/fan 190°C/Gas 6½. Put the spuds on to boil in a slightly bigger pan than is necessary, with cold salted water to cover. Put the lid on, and once boiling, turn down and simmer for 10–12 minutes until cooked, then drain and leave in the colander to steam-dry.

Meanwhile, lay the salmon snugly in a roasting tin. Season, then scatter the onion around and pour over the wine. Cover tightly with foil and bake for 10–15 minutes, depending on thickness, until just cooked on the outside, but still a bit raw in the middle (it gets cooked more later). Lift out and tip all the liquid in the tray through a sieve into a measuring jug, keeping the onions. Top up the jug with milk to 250ml.

When you've drained the spuds, give the pan a quick rinse or wipe, then put back on a medium heat. Once dried off, melt the butter and fry the leeks for about 5 minutes, stirring regularly, until softened and a gorgeous bright green – don't let them brown. Scatter in the flour, mix well for a minute or two, then slowly pour on the winey milk, stirring constantly until it has a smooth glue-like consistency.

Tip the spuds into the leek glue, then mash. Season with salt, pepper and nutmeg, then stir in one beaten egg, plus the onions. Break up the now-cool salmon into largish flakes, fold gently

CONTINUED

CONTINUED FROM
PREVIOUS PAGE

into the mix and taste for seasoning. Scrape on to something flat and put in the fridge for half an hour to firm up – overnight is even better – as the next stage is a nightmare if it's too sloppy.

Now prepare your breadcrumbing station. For this you need three wide, shallow bowls or similar. Into the first goes a handsome handful of plain flour, plus quite a bit of salt and pepper. Break the remaining egg into the second bowl and beat with 2 tablespoons of water. The breadcrumbs go into the third bowl. You'll also need a flat tray of some description for a landing pad. Sprinkle a thin layer of the breadcrumbs on this too.

Split the rested mix into 12 balls and, four at a time, move them through your production line: first coat all over with flour, and dust off any excess. Then put them in the egg bowl, making sure they are fully egged before moving them into the breadcrumbs. Once thoroughly tarred and feathered, pop them on the flat tray, not worrying if they've lost a bit of shape, and give your hands a quick rinse before doing the next lot. When all are done, stick the tray in the fridge for 20–30 minutes to firm up again.

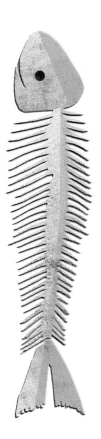

Preheat the oven to 180°C/fan 160°C/Gas 4. Put a big ovenproof frying pan on the hob. Take the fishcakes out of the fridge and give them a quick re-shape. Freeze any you don't need straight away. (Small tip – stacking them between sheets of greaseproof paper lets you defrost them individually.)

Pour a couple of tablespoons of sunflower oil into the pan, and once it's hot lay in the fishcakes (if they don't all fit, you can cook in batches). Fry for a few minutes until their underside is golden and crispy, then flip over and put the frying pan in the oven. Cook for 5–7 minutes, again until the underside is golden and crispy.

To do another batch, transfer this lot to a baking tray on the lowest shelf in the oven. Give the frying pan a quick wipe with kitchen roll, splash in a bit more oil and go again. Or, if you're plating up inmediately, give them all a quick drain on kitchen roll to soak up excess oil. Serve with peas and ketchup or a sharply dressed rocket salad, depending on the tastes of your diners ... which incidentally have nothing to do with age.

Cheesy Lucky Dip

This is a recipe my mum made up. Presumably it was born from her children's love of cheese sauce, because that's basically what it is – a baked dish of extreme cheesiness with the added fun of not quite knowing what the serving spoon is going to emerge with. Happy and fond youthful memories.

For 4

1 batch of Cheese Sauce
    (see page 369)
3 medium spuds, peeled
4 vine-ripened tomatoes, halved
4 eggs, soft–hard-boiled
    (see page 353)
100g thick-cut ham, roughly
    diced
S & P

For the topping:
1 medium spud, peeled and
    grated
50g Cheddar, grated
handful of flat-leaf parsley,
    finely chopped

First make the cheese sauce, but don't bother infusing the milk, just make it up then stir in the cheese.

Preheat the grill to medium. Quarter the spuds (except the one for the topping) and put in a pan with cold salted water to cover. Bring to the boil with a lid, then turn down to a simmer and cook for 10–12 minutes until a knife goes in with little resistance.

Meanwhile, sit the toms under the grill, cut-side up and season. Grill for about 5 minutes, until they begin to soften and some of the water has come out of them, then take them out and leave to sit. Preheat the oven to 190°C/fan 170°C/Gas 5.

When soft, drain the spuds and leave to steam-dry for a few minutes in the colander while you get on with peeling your eggs.

Choose an ovenproof dish that's good for serving at the table and put the cooked spud chunks in the bottom. Scatter over the ham then lay the grilled tomato halves and the whole eggs on top. Pour over the cheese sauce and give the dish a gentle shuffle so that the sauce falls into all the nooks and crannies.

For the topping, squeeze all the water out of the grated spud and put in a little bowl with the grated cheese, chopped parsley and some seasoning. Scatter this all over the top, then put the dish on a baking tray and bake for 20–30 minutes until golden, crispy and bubbling around the edges. Nursery food at its finest.

10

Nursery Puddings

THESE are the cult classics: traditional British puddings that are big on comfort and low on frills. More than any other in this book, this chapter has made me a very special kind of happy. The natural assumption, therefore, is that I am a pudding person, and a rather old-school one at that, but actually the exact opposite is true.

When I started my chef training back in 1990, it was pretty unusual for women chefs to be in the mosh-pit of the main kitchen. Instead, women were gently encouraged to head more towards the pastry section. With hindsight I can see the attraction: generally speaking you're left to do your own thing; pastry kitchens tend to be places of calm, monastic silence and pastry chefs often get to knock off earlier, as opposed to the after-midnight finish in the main kitchen. All in all, it is a gentler life than the fire and brimstone of the hot kitchen.

But as an upstart commis with a fair whack of attitude and a nose for trouble, I didn't see any of that. I saw the subjection of women through crème patissière and spun sugar, and vowed I would not be a part of the evil plan to keep women from grilling meat and throwing pans (and, of course, in truth my rebellious side found the shenanigans and shouting of the main kitchen most appealing). So, even though as a youngster I loved a pudding, by the age of 20 I pretty much turned my back on them, and it's taken the same amount of time again for me to take another look. After all, I couldn't write a Cookbook for Life and not have the Great British Pudding fairly represented. And so, a love was reborn.

Over my career I have clearly had to write lots of pudding recipes, and I don't want you to think I did them begrudgingly; in fact, I'm rather proud of some of them. But I wrote them then with an internal attitude that they were the fries, rather than the burger; a necessary bit on the side but not the part I really wanted to get my teeth into, so to speak. However, I have here, for the first time, got totally and utterly stuck in, and have loved every sticky, lip-licking mouthful. Letting myself become wrapped up in the sweet smells emanating from my oven induced flashbacks to being a small girl sitting at the kitchen table, watching my mum – who was a pudding queen – whisk and fold and roll and bake. And I'm so grateful to have reconnected with a very special something that has the ability to make people happy and joyful and playful in a way that no amount of savouries ever could.

Auntie Jam's Lemony Lattice Treacle Tart

My beloved Auntie Jam wasn't my auntie. Genealogically she was a remote cousin on my mum's side, but most importantly she was my godmother. Cornish through and through, she died knocking on 90, and till the end still played the best boogie-woogie I've ever heard. Man, she was cool.

I asked the family if I could have her recipe books and what turned up some months later was too good to be true: a foot long 1960s' filing box, with all her recipes on Rolodex cards in her own characterful handwriting, fastidiously organised into sections from batters, birds and cocktails to savouries, vegetables and yeast. In it I found this excellent recipe, and looking through them all gave me the kind of feeling that I aspire to with this book for future generations of my family.

Makes a happy 12–16 squares

For the pastry
350g plain flour, plus a little extra
    for rolling out the pastry
85g butter, cold and cubed
85g lard, cold and cubed
pinch of salt
zest of 1 lemon
2 eggs
3 tbsp milk

For the filling
650g golden syrup
75g dried breadcrumbs or panko
    (now available in most
    supermarkets)
3 lemons; zest of 1 and juice
    of 2½
a touch of sugar (demerara
    ideally, but anything that's
    not dark will do)

First sort the pastry. Put the flour, butter, lard, salt and lemon zest in a food processor and whizz for just a minute until combined and looking sandy. Crack in the eggs, one by one, then the milk and pulse gently to combine. Scrape into cling film, wrap tightly and rest in the fridge for at least an hour.

Preheat the oven to 180°C/fan 160°C/Gas 4 and lightly grease a shallow 34 x 25 x 2cm baking tin. Scatter a little flour on to a flat surface and roll out the pastry to around 3mm thick. Line the tin, pressing the pastry into the corners and trimming off the excess around the edges; keep the off-cuts to use for the latticing. Poke the bottom all over with a fork then pop it (and the off-cuts) back in the fridge for 15–20 minutes to firm up again.

Once rested, cover the pastry with scrunched-up greaseproof paper, fill with baking beans and blind bake (see page 370) for 10 minutes, then lift out the paper and beans and bake for another 5 minutes. Don't worry if the base has puffed up, just press it back down with a palette knife. While the pastry is cooking, mix all the filling ingredients (minus the sugar) in a bowl.

Let the case cool completely before adding the filling, as a hot filling won't support the lattice. Roll the off-cuts into strips and lay on the treacle in your best Tudor-style lattice. Brush with water and sprinkle with the sugar, then bake for 35 minutes until the filling is firm and the lattice is golden and delicious. Leave to cool almost completely, then cut into squares.

BBB & BP

[Best Brioche Bread & Butter Pudding]

Apologies for the overexcited alliteration but this is a total tum-thumping triumph. Sadly it's not one I can take credit for, as talented patissière Queen Deniz came up with it for me after Delilah made it pretty clear this was her idea of pudding heaven. I'm a big believer in delegation when you know someone who will do a better job than you!

Makes 6–8 people very, very happy

50g sultanas
20ml rum, brandy or Madeira
400ml double cream
250ml milk
½ vanilla pod, seeds scraped out
zest of ½ orange
few scrapes of nutmeg
5 egg yolks, plus 1 whole egg
150g caster sugar, plus extra for
    sprinkling
400g brioche loaf (or any kind
    of brioche to make up the
    same weight, preferably
    slightly stale)
butter, for greasing and dotting
    on top
icing sugar, for a pretty
    snowstorm

Put the sultanas in a little pan with the booze, bring to the boil then turn off the heat and cover with cling film.

In a separate pan, mix the cream, milk, scraped-out vanilla pod and seeds, orange zest and nutmeg, and heat up to the point where they're steaming but not boiling.

Put the yolks and egg into a big mixing bowl and whisk with the sugar until pale. Slowly at first, pour the warm dairy concoction through a sieve on to the eggs, whisking after each addition, until all incorporated, then give it a bit of muscle at the end to aerate.

Tear the brioche into big chunks, stir into the custard and leave for 20ish minutes to soak up. Preheat the oven to 150°C/fan 130°C/Gas 2.

Choose an ovenproof dish that's big enough to hold the brioche compactly. Grease generously with butter and sprinkle with a little caster sugar. Once the brioche is good and squidgy, lay half of it in the dish, scatter on most of the sultanas, then top with the rest of the brioche and last of the sultanas, pouring any extra custard over the top. Dot the top with little knobs of butter, cover with foil and bake for 30–35 minutes, then take the foil off and cook for another 10–12 minutes, until golden. The custard shouldn't be completely set, nor too loose.

The final flourish is a snowstorm of icing sugar. Eat straight away, keeping any leftovers in the fridge for a few days as they reheat rather well (cover with foil and heat at 170°C/fan 150°C/Gas 3½ for about 15 minutes depending on how much is left).

How To Crumble ... And the Best Example
(Blackberry & Apple)

There are different schools of thought on crumbling: old-timers tend to load up the dish with raw fruit on the bottom and lay the crumble mix on top, leaving it to sort itself out in the oven.

Contemporary crumblers generally see it more as a two-stage construction, giving the fruit a blast in the oven first. How you make it also depends on the fruit, as cooking times vary not only between fruits, but also varieties thereof. I'm generally a mix of old-school and modern, but with this recipe I have found I get a better result from giving the fruit a bit of oven-love first. As for why this is my favourite crumble: the Lord paired blackberries and apples together seasonally for a reason, and quite simply, this is it.

Serves 4–6

800–900g apples (about 4), Bramley is the classic, but just choose anything with some proper flavour – no Golden Delicious, please!

up to 50g soft light brown sugar, to taste (if using Bramleys you might need all 50g, most other apples need just a couple of tablespoons)

1½ tsp vanilla extract

squeeze of lemon juice

120g blackberries

½ batch of Better-than-Bird's Custard (see page 249), to serve

For the crumble:
80g butter, at room temperature
80g soft light brown sugar
40g rolled oats
120g plain flour

Preheat the oven to 180°C/fan 160°C/Gas 4.

Peel, core and cut the apples into chunks – size doesn't really matter here. Put them into a suitable crumbling dish, which will preferably be ceramic or anything thick-sided that conducts heat slowly and evenly, oval and about 25 x 20cm. Sit the dish on a baking tray (this stops any juices dripping on to your oven shelf), then sprinkle the sugar, vanilla extract and lemon juice over the apples. Bake in the oven for 25–30 minutes, until some apple chunks are breaking down and others are still firm.

Meanwhile, knock up the crumble by mixing together the butter and sugar with a wooden spoon in a biggish bowl. Chuck in the oats and flour and ditch the spoon to use your fingers, rubbing the mix gently through your fingertips until it naturally forms small clumps. Feels nice.

When the apples have had part 1 of their cooking experience, scatter over the blackberries, then cover the whole lot with a blanket of crumble. Bake for another 25–30 minutes, until the top is golden and crispy. Thus providing you with the perfect window to make your custard, which is over the page.

Baked Apples with
Oats & Stem Ginger

Blackberry &
Apple Crumble

Baked Apples with Oats & Stem Ginger

It doesn't really get much more nursery than this and I remember adoring these baked apples as a youngster. Back in the seventies, ginger, especially stem ginger, was considered pretty sophisticated – imagine!

Makes 4 (see photo, previous page)

3 good-sized nuggets (about 45g) stem ginger, finely chopped,
2 tbsp syrup from the ginger jar
2 tbsp dark soft brown sugar, plus a bit more
large handful of rolled oats
4 Bramley apples, cored (as easily done with a thin sharp knife as with a corer)
about 20g butter, at room temp
Better-than-Bird's Custard, to serve (see opposite; optional)

Preheat the oven to 160°C/fan 140°C/Gas 3.

Mix the ginger and syrup with the sugar, oats and 2 tablespoons of water to make a paste.

Grease the outside of the apples with butter and lightly dust them in a little more of the dark sugar. Stuff them with the oaty mix then put on to a baking tray, reasonably closely packed but not touching. Cover tightly with foil and bake for 1 hour, then whip the foil off and give them a further 10 minutes to get a bit of colour. For maximum pleasure and good times, serve with Better than Bird's Custard.

Top Tip

Leftover baked apples can be blitzed in a food processor and the purée frozen for another time, like when you next have roast pork: apple and ginger flavours just rock that piggy.

Better-than-Bird's Custard

As a youngster, Bird's was the yardstick by which all custard-like things were measured. But with all due respect, it's a bit too cornflour-claggy for me now, not to mention an almost scary kind of nuclear yellow, so here's my calmed-down version that's a little more attuned to our times.

Makes about 1 litre, enough for a small kitten to bathe in (see photo, page 247)

800ml whole milk
200ml double cream
1 vanilla pod, seeds scraped out
6 tbsp caster sugar
10 egg yolks
(2 tbsp cornflour*)

* Cornflour makes a thick, set custard, for things like trifle. For pouring custard (i.e. for crumble-like situations), leave it out.

In a saucepan, heat the milk, cream, vanilla seeds and pod with half of the sugar to the point where it's steaming but not boiling.

In a large bowl, whisk the yolks and the rest of the sugar by hand until pale, then whisk in the cornflour too, if using.

Pick out the vanilla pod from the pan and, slowly at first, pour the infused milk and cream on to the beaten egg yolks, whisking all the while, then pour it all back into the pan.

Your tool of choice now should be a rubber spatula (though for centuries people coped fine with a wooden spoon). Keep stirring over a low heat, making sure it doesn't catch on the bottom. It should never approach a boil and will just thicken as you stir. Don't walk away; just keep it moving and in about 5–7 minutes your custard will be ready: the best way to check is to coat the back of the spatula and run your finger across it – if it holds its shape and doesn't drip down through the track left by your finger, then it's ready.

Your custard is now fully operational, so you can either serve it up straight away, or keep it warm until you need it, or leave it to cool (if you're making trifle, as overleaf). For these last two options just cling film it, with the cling film sitting directly on the custard's surface so it doesn't form a skin (unless you're one of those weirdos who likes custard skin).

'Brass-up-your-manners-for-Granny' Trifle

My maternal grandparents were Cornish. Whenever we visited them, we crossed the Tamar next to the railway bridge and passed the statue of its engineer, who had the coolest name ever (Isambard Kingdom Brunel). As we crossed from Devon into Cornwall, Mum would look over her shoulder at her misbehaving daughters, listless from hours in the car, and say, 'Now girls, brass up your manners for Granny.' Trifle is the only food I can ever remember eating there.

For a party – 10ish

1 x 135g packet jelly (arguably it has to be red), to make about 500ml
1 batch of Better-than-Bird's Custard (see previous page), cooled
2 x 400g tins peach halves in juice (rather than syrup)
75ml cream sherry
200g sponge fingers
200–300ml double cream (depending on the width/depth of your dish)
2 tbsp caster sugar
handful of flaked almonds, lightly toasted (see page 74)
handful of glacé cherries (compulsory)

In a jug, make up the jelly according to the packet instructions, then leave to cool in the fridge for 1–1½ hours – you need it still on the runny side, not set firm. Meanwhile, make the custard and leave it to cool as well.

Pour the juice from one of the peach tins into a bowl with the sherry. Dip the sponge fingers in it so they become a bit soft, then use them to line the base of your trifle bowl (which should be a bit fancy and made of glass), packing them quite tightly.

Put the peach halves on top of the sponge fingers, and once your jelly is sufficiently wibbly, pour it on to the peaches. Pop in the fridge until the jelly is totally set – about another hour or so.

When it's good and firm, next up is a layer of the cooled custard (you may not need it all, depending on the size of your dish, but spare custard never hangs around for long). Finally, whip the cream with the sugar until soft peaks form. Carefully spoon on and spread with a hot palette knife. Finish with a flourish of almonds and cherries.

Silly, but splendid!

Cornish Saffron Cake

Having some Cornish blood in my veins, I have no doubt the locals of yesteryear got their mitts on this rarest of spices, weight-for-weight more expensive than gold, by good old-fashioned piratical looting. Well, it would be mad not to take advantage of that craggy coastline full of clandestine caves in which to stash your booty. This recipe makes a brilliant yellow loaf with a nice crust. It's fabulous eaten warm, but like most things Cornish, it's pretty resilient and carries on toasting well for days. The general consensus is that jam is superfluous – even my two-year-old says, 'No jam, Mama!'

Makes a handsome loaf of 10–12 slices

300ml full-fat milk, plus extra for brushing the top
½ tsp saffron threads
500g white bread flour (though you can do it with plain flour)
150g cold butter, cut into 3cm cubes
a big pinch of salt
80g soft light brown sugar
¼ tsp ground or grated nutmeg
1 x 7g sachet fast-action yeast
100g currants
50g candied peel
a good sprinkling of demerara sugar

In a saucepan, infuse the milk with the saffron over a low heat for a few minutes, then turn the heat off and cover with cling film. Tip the flour into a big mixing bowl, add the butter cubes and salt and work with your fingertips until it looks like breadcrumbs, then stir in the brown sugar and nutmeg.

Gently warm the milk again then stir in the yeast. Make a well in the middle of the flour and fill it with the milk. Mix slowly until it's come together in a ball, then tip on to a floured surface and knead for about 10 minutes until it's a smooth dough.

Mix the currants and candied peel together and throw a third in. Knead a couple of times, then do the same with the next third and repeat with the last lot for good random distribution.

Grease a 900g loaf tin (23 x 13 x 7cm) and knock the dough into a rough loaf shape. Plop it into the tin with the smoothest part on top, then put the whole thing in a plastic bag and tie loosely. Leave to prove somewhere warmish for 1½–3hrs until the dough has risen and springs back up when gently pressed.

Preheat the oven to 180°C/fan 160°C/Gas 4. Brush the top of the loaf with milk and sprinkle with the demerara sugar, then bake for 45 minutes to 1 hour until well risen and slightly brown. To check it's ready, gently tip the loaf out of the tin and make sure the base is cooked, coloured and sounds hollow when tapped. If it's not there yet, stick it back in the oven and try again in a bit. Cool on a wire rack for 15 minutes but don't miss the opportunity to slather butter on a slice warm from the oven.

Sussex Pond Pudding

This classic English steamed pudding is definitely of a superior nature to most of its steamy brethren: the sweetness and richness of the pastry is balanced out by a whole lemon inside, which goes a special kind of soft and sweet after spending hours enveloped in sugar and suet. I'm not sure how successfully I'm selling this to you, but if I say it's the only steamed pudding I ever make, and I need to make it at least once a winter, maybe that'll tempt you.

For 4–6

100g cold butter, diced, plus
    a knob for greasing
170g self-raising flour
100g fresh breadcrumbs
pinch of salt
2 large juicy lemons, preferably
    unwaxed
120g suet
135ml whole milk, plus a little
    extra for brushing
100g demerara sugar

Grease a 1-litre pudding basin with a knob of butter. In a large bowl, mix the flour, breadcrumbs, salt, zest of 1 lemon and suet, then slowly pour in the milk and stir to make a flaky ball of dough. Cut off a third and put aside for the lid.

On a lightly floured surface, roll out the rest of the dough to 5mm–1cm thick, and big enough to line the basin, allowing for an overhang of about 2cm all round. Plop it in and use the flats of your fingers to press down any bits that are folded up double, so it's roughly the same thickness all over – it doesn't matter if the overhang gets a bit scraggy as it will eventually be the base.

Put half the sugar and half the diced butter into the basin, then roll the unzested lemon on the table to release its juices and poke holes all over it with a toothpick. Pop it into its hiding place in the basin and cover with the rest of the sugar and butter (see photo 1, overleaf). Your basin probably won't be full to the brim but that's fine.

Choose a large saucepan that's big enough to hold the basin. Half-fill with water, then bring to a boil with a lid on. Meanwhile, roll out the bit of dough you put aside for the lid, sit it on top of the filling, then brush all round the edges of the lid with milk. Flip the overhanging dough on to the lid and press all around the join with your fingertips to seal and make it airtight (shown in photo 2, overleaf).

CONTINUED

CONTINUED FROM
PREVIOUS PAGE

Cut a piece of greaseproof a lot larger than the lid, grease with butter then fold a crease into it (photo 3) to give the pudding room to rise. Cover the basin with it, buttered-side down, and tie tightly around the rim with string, leaving the paper a bit baggy on top (photo 4).

Turn the heat down under the pan of water – it needs to be steaming, not boiling, when the pudding goes in. Gently lower an upturned saucer into the bottom of the pan and sit the basin on it. The water should come half to two-thirds of the way up the sides of the basin, so adjust with hot water from the kettle, if necessary. Pop a lid on the pan, or cover tightly with a dome of foil if your lid will squish down the greaseproof paper too much – the pudding definitely needs room to expand a bit as it cooks.

Cook for 3 hours, topping up the water level every now and then from the kettle. Turn off the heat and leave the pudding in the steaming water until you're ready to serve.

When the moment comes, lift the pudding out of the pan. Take off the paper, sit a flat serving plate on top of the basin, hold them together and flip over. The pudding should fall right out (easiest done when it's hot). Slice into it straight away, making sure everyone gets some lemon, and for proper old school have a jug of custard present (see page 249), or it's also excellent with vanilla ice cream because although this is a steamed, nursery-ish pudding, it has delusions of the dining room too.

Mango Jelly

When I was a young 'un, jelly was all about Rowntree and E-numbers. Though jelly will never, ever go out of fashion with the under-fives, our tastes and food knowledge have developed. My daughter's favourite fruit is mango so whenever jelly is centre stage in our house (as opposed to lost in the middle of a trifle), I make this one for its cross-generational appeal.

Made in a 1-litre jelly mould, easily enough for 6–8

8 gelatine leaves
750ml unsweetened mango and
    passion fruit juice
juice of 2–3 limes (about 70ml)
150g caster sugar
1 ripe mango, peeled and cut
    into rough chunks

Fill a small bowl or jug with cold water and individually drop the gelatine leaves into it to soften.

Heat the mango and passionfruit juice with the lime juice and sugar over a low heat, until it is warm and the sugar has dissolved – don't let it get anywhere near bubbling.

Lift out the gelatine leaves, giving them a brief, firm squeeze to get rid of any excess water, and whisk them one by one into the warmed juice.

Put the mango flesh into the bottom of a 1-litre jelly mould, then pour about a quarter of the jelly liquid on top, leaving the rest in the jug at room temperature, and put the mould in the fridge to set (this way the mango chunks should stay at the top when you turn it out). When that bit is totally solid (after about an hour or two max), gently pour in the rest, cover with cling film and pop in the fridge overnight to set good and solid.

Burnt Camp Rice Pudding

Camp Coffee is one of those really crazy ingredients – it tastes like coffee but is actually made from chicory root: even Heston would be proud of that one. I used to love it just stirred into a glass of milk after school, and my mum did a memorable child-friendly coffee junket with it, which is the reason I'm opting for it here over espresso, so the kids can join in too.

I've burned the top of my rice puddings (intentionally!) since I got a lesson from the Turks on how they do theirs. The bitterness really works with the super-sweet rice, and even more so with the coffee flavour.

For 6–8

230g pudding rice
700ml whole milk
100ml double cream
125g demerara sugar, plus 2 tbsp
3 tbsp Camp Coffee

Put the rice into a saucepan with plenty of cold water and leave to stand and swell for 20 minutes.

Once swelled, give it another good rinse, tip back into the pan and cover again with fresh water to come about 2cm above the rice. Bring to the boil, lid on, then turn the heat down and simmer for about 10 minutes until almost all the water has been absorbed, before stirring in the milk and cream.

Keep cooking the rice on a slow, steady simmer over a low heat for 12–15 minutes until it is approaching ready, then add the sugar and Camp Coffee and cook at the same tempo for a few more minutes, stirring until the sugar has dissolved.

Preheat the grill to hot. By now the rice should be thickening up nicely, with a pleasing 'nursery' consistency. Taste – it should be good and soft, and if it's not sweet enough for you then stir in more sugar if you fancy. Scrape the whole lot into a deep ovenproof dish (mine's round and 20cm across but use whatever suits) and sprinkle the last 2 tablespoons of sugar all over the surface. Put under the grill for 10ish minutes, until the top is bubbling up with exciting burnt bits.

The serving temperature for rice pud is a matter of worldwide contention, but it doesn't matter really as it's always good, whether hot, warm or chilled.

"CAMP"
COFFEE
AND
CHICORY
ESSENCE

Mama's Meringues

Our mum was famous for her puddings, most of all her meringues. When I was trying to remember her signature dishes to include in this book, I asked her friends what their strongest memories were of her cooking and with a wistful sigh many of them said, 'Oh, those amazing meringues.'

Mama's meringues were truly legendary: crunchy on the outside with a decent bit of chew in the middle. I never thought to ask for the recipe when she was alive, and all these years later, it's no exaggeration to say that it took about 30 attempts to get anywhere near. But I've made my peace and am happy that this is as close as I'll ever get. It's damn close too, just not quite as awesome as I remember hers being, but 30 odd years can do things to your memory ... And in a funny way I don't really want mine to be better than hers. Some things should always remain sacred.

Makes 4 massive meringues, or 6–8 kiddy-sized meringues or 1 x 25cm pavlova (see pages 328–9)

3 egg whites
200g caster sugar
1 tsp white wine vinegar
1 tsp cornflour

To fill:
500ml double cream
2 tbsp caster sugar

Preheat the oven to 120°C/100°C/Gas ½ and line a baking sheet with greaseproof paper. Clean your chosen whisking bowl with a drop of lemon juice, to degrease it.

Whisk the whites in an upright mixer or with an electric hand whisk on top speed. When they start to go frothy, add the sugar a tablespoon at a time, whisking constantly. Once the mix has thickened and all the sugar is in, stir the vinegar and cornflour together in an egg cup and tip this in too. Carry on whisking at full pelt for about another 3 minutes until firm and glossy.

As soon as the mix is ready, dollop on to the prepared tray. For individual meringues, use a large serving spoon or spatula to make 4 Willy Wonka-esque constructions or 6–8 kiddy-sized ones. For a pavlova, dollop the whole lot into the middle and spread out to a circle roughly 25cm across, with a higher rim around the edge and a lower, flatter plateau in the middle.

Bake for 1¼ hours, *without opening the oven at any stage*, then turn the oven off and *keep the door shut*. Leave the meringue/s in there until the oven has cooled completely. If you've made a pavlova, now turn to page 328. Otherwise, when meringue munching time is near, whip the cream with the caster sugar until thick but still a touch floppy. Use it as extravagant glue to stick two meringues together and watch with joy as small jaws try their hardest to wrap themselves around the prize.

A Week of
SUNDAYS

Seven timeless Sunday lunches,
including the mythical art of gravy-making

OUR mum always put on what can only be described as a 'proper Sunday lunch', complete with a cracking pudding (her culinary speciality and favourite to make). Straight after eating and on the stroke of 3 o'clock, my father's friend and his daughter would arrive and the fathers and daughters would go off to Chiswick Park. As the men walked and talked intently with their hands clasped behind their backs, we three girls would run round in circles, make camps in the undergrowth, climb trees and, best of all, spy on the dads. Meanwhile, back home, Mama would magically replace the lunch detritus with a full-on tea of crumpets, cakes, biscuits, sandwiches, scones and jams, ready for us when we piled home in our muddy wellies.

Given these origins, it's not surprising to me that Sunday lunch is sacred. Quintessentially British, it's relaxed, family-oriented and, by a clear mile, my favourite time of the week to cook, provide and share. Done right, this mighty meal is, quite simply, epic. More than any other, it's one not to miss, whether lunching at a friend's, in the pub or best of all in your own home with those you love. Sunday lunch punctuates the week in a positive way – a bit like that Friday feeling – but with a slow Sunday tempo. And being lunch, there's time for a full recovery before bedtime and the beginning of another week.

The secret to putting on a good Sunday lunch is down to a small amount of planning – no excuses of running from the office or being too tired after work to cook. You've had all of Saturday to plan and get to the shops. This is also a definite occasion where it's worth going to a proper butcher: never is the quality of meat better shown off than in the cold cuts that you'll be snacking on as leftovers for the days to follow.

This is a meal that works for everybody – even our vegetarian brethren: it's the one time where I don't have to worry about them going hungry as, in my opinion, a good Sunday lunch involves three accompanying veg: a carb, usually potatoes of some sort (though it's nice to swap this for rice or even supplement it with some flavour-laden pulses, particularly if there are vegetarians coming round). Then, a slow-cooked classic like braised red cabbage, cauliflower cheese or roasted roots, and finally a green, seasonal offering, just blanched and buttered with a bit of salt and pepper. I usually do a seasonal mix of whatever's caught my eye in the shops, or just anything that needs using up in the veg box, such as greens and mangetout in spring; broad beans and runners in summer; broccoli and spinach in autumn; and Savoy and purple sprouting broccoli (PSB) in winter. The ensemble is usually bumped up with some peas from the freezer: everybody loves peas. So really, the vegetarians are well looked after, though of course, cook them my Contemporary Nut Roast (see page 281) and you'll have friends for life.

But to most, Sunday Lunch means meat, and you'll be selling yourself short if you don't do right by your roast by knocking-up its traditional and well-tested accompanying sauce (horseradish/bread/apple/mint). And the final furlong to this family feast is the all-important gravy.

I also regularly need to go off-piste and break with tradition: it's not that far a leap from a roast to a glossy, rich, be-dumplinged beef stew, which is one of my all-time fave winter Sunday lunches. By contrast in summer, when a roast just doesn't hold quite the same allure, I serve up something inspired by faraway flavours, which is always met with an enthralled and grateful look from my guests.

It doesn't matter what big dish you've opted for, the deal with Sunday lunch is that it has to be one made for sharing. No other meal has this so innately at its heart: breakfast and weekday lunches are largely individual affairs; supper can go both ways; but for Sunday lunch eaten in the home, the shared spread is a prerequisite, and, like a weekly mini-Christmas, helps to give it that sense of special occasion. Which is exactly what it is.

Roast Pork & Crackling

As you may or may not have gathered by now, in our house, pig is king. Not just in terms of cooking; for us it's a term of endearment, perhaps inspired by the A. A. Milne stories we had read to us as children. For whatever reason, when I was a nipper, both my sister and I were called 'piglet', and for my 18th birthday my father and sister gave me a signet ring with a pig on it, like a family crest. Now, my daughter holds the title, and just like mine was, her bedroom is a shrine to all things porcine.

Here are a couple of my fave joint options. Whichever cut you go for, make sure the skin is well scored by your butcher, as it requires a very sharp-pointed knife as well as a firm wrist.

Makes lunch for 6 plus a few sarnies the next day

This is a proper roast pork joint, with darker meat than loin and more fat running through, which makes it tastier. Get it boned and rolled by your butcher for more even cooking as well as ease of carving.

Makes lunch for 8 plus another supper of leftovers

This is a very tender, lean meat, which contrasts well with the crackling. Loin is considered the premium cut, so is a tad more expensive than other joints, as roasting pork goes. It's a bit of a whopper, though, so not one for small appetites. Get your butcher to take it off the bone and then tie it back on – meat always cooks better this way, as the bone imparts flavour during cooking and also acts as a barrier between the very hot tray and the flesh, thus preventing it from drying out. (Note that the bone adds about half a kilo to the weight, so check your cooking time.)

FOR COOKING TIMES, SEE NEXT PAGE

Shown with: Pommes Boulangère, p355;
Cauliflower & Broccoli Cheese, p360;
Rosemary Apple Sauce, overleaf

Cooking the Shoulder

**For the pork support and
   gravy-making:**

2–3 carrots, peeled and cut
   into 2–3 pieces
1–2 onions, unpeeled and halved
olive oil
coarse sea salt (such as Maldon)

For the accompanying veg:

6–8 banana shallots, unpeeled
3 carrots, peeled and left whole
3 small red onions, peeled and
   halved
1 garlic bulb, unpeeled

Preheat the oven to 220°C/fan 200°C/Gas 7. If you don't know
the weight of your joint, weigh it now.

Make a closely packed little carpet of carrots and onions for the
meat to sit on in the roasting tray. Roll them in a little oil then
push together into the middle of the tray. The bonus is that as
well as protecting the meat, you've also got a starter pack going
for the gravy. You're missing a trick if you don't put some veg
around the joint as well: these are for serving and look great
nuzzled up to the joint on the serving dish. (They'll cook in about
an hour, so remember to take them out or you'll be looking at
shapes of blackness, discernible only using carbon dating, by the
time the pig is ready.)

With your pig in place on top of the veg, very lightly oil the skin
then use your fingertips to aggressively rub in a tablespoon or so
of sea salt all over, but especially into the scored slashes. Cook
for half an hour without opening the oven door, then turn down
to 180°C/fan 160°C/Gas 4 and give the joint a good basting all
over. Turn the exposed veggies and rotate the roasting tray 180°.
The meat will take another 30 minutes or so per kilo (depends
on how you like it) with regular basting. When the veg has had
its hour, take it out, cover with foil and keep in a warm place.

To check your pork's done, poke a skewer right into the middle
of it and look for the oft-cited 'juices running clear' or use my
tried-and-tested 'McEvedy's Lip Service' method on page 125.

Once you're happy the pork is cooked to perfection, move it to a
pre-warmed serving dish and cover with foil, then leave it to rest
for 15–20 minutes while you get on with the gravy (see page 273).

Cooking the Loin

The cooking is exactly the same as the shoulder, but ...

There's no need to make a veg pile for the loin to sit on as it's been tied back on to the bone to provide a barrier between pan and flesh (though you'd still be wise to whack some hardy veggies around the joint as it roasts, such as whole onions, parsnips and butternut, for serving).

Cook for an initial 30 minutes at 220°C/fan 200°C/Gas 7, then baste well and turn the oven down to 200°C/fan 180°C/Gas 6. After another 30 minutes baste thoroughly again, then turn the oven down to 180°C/fan 160°C/Gas 4 and cook for a final 45 minutes.

Rosemary Apple Sauce

If a pig were going out for a night on the town it would slather itself in apple sauce to show off its best attributes. Fat is also a vital part of a good pig; and a discernable sharpness is the hallmark of a great apple sauce, which is why the two are made for each other.

(If there's more left than you'll need for your cold pork sarnies, try it on ice cream or whizzed up in a blender with yoghurt, milk, ice and a banana for a fab smoothie.)

For 6 (see photo, page 267)

4 Bramley apples (about 800g), peeled, quartered and core cut out
1 sprig of rosemary, leaves picked and chopped
1–2 tbsp honey or sugar, to taste
S & P

Put the apple pieces in a wide-ish pan so they're not stacked up too much, then tip in two eggcups of water and the rosemary. Cover with a lid and put on a medium heat for 5–10 minutes, stirring occasionally until the apples start to soften.

Once they start to break down, take the lid off and turn the heat right down. As the apples make their journey to apple sauce, stir in some sweetness and if they're being obstinate (as opposed to mushing nicely), give them a brisk stir, breaking up the bigger pieces. Resist the urge to play with the sauce too much as it will inevitably lead to apple purée. Chunkier is better for home-made apple sauce: you'll know when the time is right. Taste again for sweetness, season a little, and serve just above room temperature.

Roast Forerib of Beef, Yorkies & Proper Horseradish

If I don't have beef, Yorkies and proper horseradish either at home or in a decent pub for Sunday lunch once a month, I start to get this nervous, rising feeling that I'm just not doing my life right.

Good for 4 adults, 2 kids, seconds all round and a sarnie or two tomorrow if you're lucky
(the Yorkie recipe makes 7 handsome ones)

1 x 2-bone forerib of beef, between 3–4kg
veg for a 'gravy starter pack': 1–2 carrots, 1 onion, a bit of celery, all unpeeled and halved or quartered
couple of sprigs of rosemary
splash of extra virgin olive oil
sea salt and pepper

For the Yorkies:
110g plain flour
2 eggs
300ml whole milk
½ tsp salt
about 60ml goose, duck or other animal fat, though sunflower/ vegetable oil will do

For the horseradish:
120g fresh horseradish root, peeled, or 75g grated horseradish from a jar (not 'creamed'; we don't go there)
good squeeze of lemon juice
80ml double cream

Preheat the oven to 200°C/fan 180°C/Gas 6 and weigh your joint.

If you're using fresh horseradish then start by grating it (very good for the nasal passages) so that it has time to macerate. Squeeze on the lemon juice (though not if you're using jarred horseradish, which is already acidulated) and stir well, then cover with cling film and stick in the fridge.

In the roasting tray, make a little base of veg for the beef to sit on – the celery does best not directly on the tray but sitting between the beef and the onions and carrots. Splash a little olive oil on the veg, rub a little more all over the beef and season the meat heartily with sea salt and pepper.

Once the oven is up to temperature, roast the beef for 30 minutes then turn the oven down to 160°C/fan 140°C/Gas 3 and cook for 10 minutes per 500g for rare, and 12 minutes per 500g for medium-rare. At the time when you turn the oven down, put in the Yorkie muffin tray to heat.

Knock up the Yorkie batter by sifting the flour into a big bowl, then whisk in the eggs. Carry on whisking as you slowly incorporate the milk, then add the salt and a few cracks of pepper. Once you're happy it's all smooth as silk, pop it in the fridge for no less than half an hour.

Whip the cream for the horseradish to the stage where it's soft and has just crossed the line from liquid to solid. Use a spatula to gently fold in the horseradish and season well with S & P.

Shown with: Orange & Caraway Roast Parsnips, p365

CONTINUED FROM
PREVIOUS PAGE

As soon as the meat is done, whip it out and turn the oven up
to 200°C/fan 180°C/Gas 6. Fill seven holes of the Yorkie tray
with ½ teaspoon of whatever fat or oil you're using and put back
in the oven to get hot. Move the beef to a warmed serving dish,
press on a double layer of foil and let it have a nice, warm rest.
Put the tray of veg on the hob for gravy-making (see opposite).

When the oven is up to speed, carefully pour the cold Yorkie
batter in to just below the rim of each hole – it's this cold hitting
hot that gives them a great crust. They'll take 20–22 minutes in
the oven but NO opening to look until 20 minutes, during which
time you can busy yourself with everything else: getting the
gravy made, heating plates, cooking your greens, etc.

So, roast forerib of beef, prize-winning Yorkies and proper
horseradish: a triple swoon factor.

The Mythical Art of Gravy Making

Goodness me there's a lot of huff 'n' puff when it comes to gravy. Given how easy it is to make, I can only point an accusatory finger at the manufacturers of instant gravy for intimating that it's harder than it is. Either that or we're all just a lot lazier than I like to think. A good gravy should be pretty much free: veg from accumulated offcuts (carrot tops and tails, parsley stalks, celery stubs, roots of onions, etc.) and stock made from the previous roast dinner's carcass. The post Sunday-lunch ritual in our house is that the stock goes on as the washing up goes down, and leftover gravy is frozen to be added to next week's roasting tray at the simmering stage.

Makes a good amount for 8 people (about half a litre)

the roasting tray from your joint (save the carcass for next week's gravy stock)

veggie offcuts, like carrot tops, celery ends, onion, garlic (unpeeled)

the cooked 'gravy starter pack' (see recipes, pages 268, 271, 274 and 305)

giblets, if possible

winter herbs, like rosemary and thyme sprigs, on the branch

couple of bay leaves

2–4 tbsp plain flour (depends on how thick you like your gravy)

1 glass of wine (150–250ml; white for chicken/pork/lamb; red for beef)

1 litre stock (chicken for chicken/pork/lamb; beef for beef!)

½–1 tsp clear honey, to taste

splash of sherry vinegar

S & P

Once your joint has come off its roasting tray to rest, pour any fat left in the tray into a small bowl. Put the roasting tray across two burners on the hob on a medium heat. Chuck in any veggie offcuts to join the cooked 'gravy starter pack', plus the giblets if you have them, tipping back in just enough fat to coat. Fry everything for a good 5 minutes, stirring continuously and chucking in the herbs along the way, until it's all properly hot.

Now sprinkle in the flour and give it a good roll and coat – the flour will absorb the fat, so you may need to add a splash more of what you set aside to prevent it catching and burning. Don't leave the tray at all, just stay there stirring for a minute or two, adding another teaspoon of fat or oil if it begins to look a bit dry. Now pour in the wine. Sizzle, sizzle.

Let the wine reduce by two-thirds, which takes a few minutes max, then follow it with the stock. Bring to a fast simmer and let it bubble away for about 15 minutes until it gets to a consistency you like. Stir in the honey and a splash of vinegar, then simmer for just a minute or two more to burn off the acidity.

Strain the gravy through a sieve into a bowl and taste for seasoning. My tip is to serve it in a teapot; this pours better than most gravy jugs and keeps it nice and warm – especially if you pop a tea cosy on.

Roast Chicken Dinner (the Simple Way) …

Rookie cooks cite timing as the hardest aspect of pulling off a good roast, so here I've simplified it right down so that the major accompanying veg (a foolproof yummy medley of spuds, squash, onions and garlic) get roasted around the bird. With the bird and primary veggies already working in the oven, you get a clear hour and a bit to concentrate on your bread sauce, and when the end of the cooking gets closer, to deal with whatever green veg takes your fancy.

Once the chicken and veg are out and resting, all that remains is to quietly get on with conquering the mythical art of gravy-making (see previous page).

Good for 2 grown-ups and 2 kids + a sarnie or two

½ lemon
3 garlic bulbs, halved across the middle
small handful of thyme sprigs
big knob of butter
1 medium free-range chicken, about 1.5kg
½ butternut squash (ideally the bulbous end), quartered and seeds scraped out
2 red onions, halved
2 medium spuds, about 400g, scrubbed and quartered
splash of extra virgin olive oil
a bit of veg for a 'gravy starter pack': 1–2 carrots, 1 onion and a bit of celery, unpeeled and halved or quartered
3ish sprigs of rosemary
S & P
1 batch of We Love Bread Sauce (see overleaf)

Preheat the oven to 210°C/fan 190°C/Gas 6½ and choose a suitable roasting tray for all the ingredients.

Shove the lemon half, one garlic half, the thyme and the butter inside the chicken. Put the squash in the roasting tray along with the rest of the garlic, the onions and spud chunks. Splash on a bit of olive oil and season well, before getting your hands involved to make sure everything is well coated. Push all these veggies to the edges of the tray, then pile the unpeeled veg for the gravy starter pack in the middle (the celery does best not directly on the tray but sat between the chicken and the onions and carrots). Lay the rosemary sprigs on the celery and sit the bird on top.

Once the oven is up to temperature, pop the tray in and roast the chicken for 45 minutes, then turn the oven temperature down to 180°C/fan 160°C/Gas 4 and briefly take the tray out to turn the serving veg (taking out any that look good to go) and give it a baste. Put it back in for a last half hour to finish it off, then take out, baste again and rest it under foil for at least 10 minutes.

While your bird is resting, all you need to do for the simplest, completest of roast dinners is cook some green veg and knock up a gravy (and after lunch don't forget to make a stock with the carcass for next week's gravy, thus making yourself a member of 'The Cyclical Sunday Stock Club').

Shown with: Autumnal Savoy & Bacon, p359; We Love Bread Sauce, overleaf

We Love Bread Sauce

Although my mum really was an ace cook, I've never understood why she always made her bread sauce from a Knorr packet (which, incidentally, we loved, especially as she used to let us 'make' it!). My sister still uses packets, but with a young child I'm always swimming in milk, so I find this a good way to use up the dregs of the week's supply before the milkman comes again on Monday morning. Small daughter not only *loves* bread sauce (it's bread and milk – what's not for a todddler to like?) but gets double joy, as her favourite Sunday afternoon activity is throwing the crusts at the ducks in our local park.

Plenty for 6 (see photo, previous page)

500ml whole milk
2 cloves (resist the urge to go for a third – they're potent little buggers)
couple of bay leaves
1 small onion or 2 shallots, roughly sliced
1 garlic clove, unpeeled and smashed with the side of the knife
a small handful of whatever hardy herbs you have around – rosemary, thyme or sage
5 slices, about 125g, white bread, crusts cut off
S & P

Put everything except the bread into a saucepan and heat it to the point of steaming. Now turn the heat down as low as it goes and leave for a good 20 minutes.

Strain the infused milk into a bowl, and use the back of a serving spoon or ladle to really press down and extract the flavour from the onion. Pour the milk back into the pan, and with the heat still low, toss the bread in, tearing it into bite-sized chunks as you go.

Stir with a wooden spoon until the bread has broken down into the milk, then turn off the heat and taste for seasoning – salt and pepper will both be needed. It can sit like this for ages and although it will firm up a little, can easily be brought back to the right creamy texture with a splash more milk.

I serve bread sauce warm rather than piping hot, and usually in the pan I cooked it in so it keeps the heat.

Sunday Lunch Soup (from a Roast Dinner)

Leftovers are great, but sometimes there are some spuds, parsnips, cabbage or carcass that you're just a little bored of picking at, and that's where this great invention (not mine) comes in handy. The theory? Anything goes in, including bread sauce! It's also very nice with dumplings floating in there, like the ones on page 285.

For 6–8

leftover veg (greens, roasted
    roots, spuds, onions, etc.)
a mug of gravy or stock
leftover meat
½ quantity of Caraway
    Dumplings (see page 285),
    if you fancy
S & P

Chop the veggies irregularly but small (random chopping, not precise slicing) and put in a pan with the gravy or stock. Top up with water to cover, bring to a boil, then turn down to a simmer, dropping in the dumplings now if you've gone down that route.

Meanwhile, chop the meat into similar small pieces. When the soup has been bubbling gently for 15-20 minutes, turn it off, stir the meat through and taste for seasoning (which it probably won't need) before tucking in.

Aga Khan Lamb (with or without the Aga)

This is the story of a slow-cooked shoulder of lamb with a slight Persian/Middle Eastern inflection – and they know a bit about cooking lamb over there. I thoroughly approve of their pairing it with spice and sticky dried fruit, and in this super-slow braise it all comes together in the tenderest way.

This only needs simple seasonal greens to round it off. In the Middle East, they would serve salad with it and probably a rice dish too, like the Chickpea Pilaf on page 74, but seeing as there are already spuds in here, that may feel like a carb too far unless you're really out to impress.

For 6

1 shoulder of lamb, about
    1.5–1.8kg
glug of olive oil
5 banana shallots, or 10 regular
    ones, peeled and left whole
about a dozen or so garlic cloves,
    peeled and left whole
750g new potatoes
½ butternut squash, left
    unpeeled and cut into
    3–4cm chunks
1 tsp ground cumin
1 cinnamon stick, or ½ tsp
    ground cinnamon
4 sprigs of rosemary, leaves
    picked and chopped
500ml chicken stock
100g dried apricots
S & P

Preheat the oven to 160°C/fan 140°C/Gas 3. Rub a little olive oil all over the lamb and season liberally with salt and pepper.

Choose a wide casserole dish or thick-bottomed roasting tray big enough for the meat and all the veg, and put it over a high heat with about a tablespoon of olive oil – no more as lamb can be pretty fatty. As it starts smoking, lay the meat in and seal all over until well browned – allow a good 10 minutes and be sure to have the extraction fan on or window open.

Lift the lamb out and chuck in the shallots, garlic cloves, spuds and butternut, adding a splash more oil if needed to give them all a light sheen. Once it's all hot, go in with the cumin, cinnamon and rosemary, making sure everything gets well coated.

When the spices are smelling really good (a minute or two max), pour in the chicken stock and stir well, scraping the bottom with a wooden spoon to incorporate all the flavour lurking there. Chuck in the apricots and give it a bit more seasoning before nestling the lamb back in there too. The veg should be largely under the joint, with a little coming up around the edges, and the shoulder mostly above the level of the liquid.

Pop a lid on or double-foil the tray tightly, then stick it in the oven for 4–4½ hours. You want the meat so tender it's forkable so I wouldn't bother checking it at all for 3 hours. When you're happy the lamb is there, lift it out and set aside. Use a slotted spoon to move all the veg on to a suitably dramatic serving dish, sit the lamb on top and ladle over the juice. Simply magnificent.

Contemporary Nut Roast

I'm holding my hands up – for 30 years I've been wrong about nut roast, making it the butt of cruel cheffy jokes (along with lentil bake and vegetarian sausages). But when I canvassed my veggie friends about what they really like for Sunday lunch, I nearly laughed my head off when this is what they came back with. So I had a go, resulting in a full-on Damascene moment. I've seen the light, and now have no doubt that this classic will still be in fashion when Small Daughter is going through her obligatory teenage vegetarian phase.

The roast lasts for ages wrapped tightly in the fridge: if you cook it for Sunday lunch, it'll still be fine for breakfast the following weekend. Fry up a slice or two along with an egg and tomato, then hit it with a splodge of HP. Sooo good on the tum, and a bit of a hangover buster too.

Makes 8 good slices

100g almonds, skins on
100g hazelnuts, skins off
50g pecans
1 large leek, trimmed
150g vacuum-packed cooked
  chestnuts
splash of regular olive oil
1 shallot, chopped
1 heaped tbsp thyme leaves,
  chopped
100g Jarlsberg or Comté cheese,
  grated
1 eating apple, halved, cored and
  grated
handful of flat-leaf parsley,
  chopped
2 eggs, beaten
20g Parmesan, finely grated
drizzle of extra virgin olive oil
S & P

Preheat the oven to 190°C/fan 170°C/Gas 5. As it's heating, lightly toast the almonds, hazelnuts and pecans on a baking tray for 12–15 minutes, until they've browned a bit and a nutty smell greets you when you open the oven, then tip them on to a plate.

Slice the leek in half lengthways, then chop as thinly as possible. Wash thoroughly in a colander and drain well.

Blitz the nuts in the food processor until you have a good mix of fine and chunky pieces. Chop the chestnuts by hand to a similar size (they go a bit sticky in the machine), then mix all the nuts together in a biggish bowl.

Put a splash of olive oil into a wide pan over a medium heat and sweat the leek, shallot and thyme for 10–12 minutes until wonderfully softened, adding a splash of water if they start to stick. Stir into the nuts along with the cheese, apple, parsley, eggs and a good amount of seasoning.

Line a 450g loaf tin (20 x 10 x 6cm) with greaseproof paper, then butter the paper. Spoon the mix in, gently packing it down, then top with grated Parmesan and a drizzle of extra virgin olive oil. Bake for 25–30 minutes, until the top looks irresistibly golden. Leave to sit for 10 minutes before lifting out and slicing.

Shown with: Alternative
Roast Med Veg, p364

Vietnamese Pot-bellied Pig with Pickled Veg

Times are a-changing, and even though Sunday lunch is usually one to play close to home, every now and then it's nice to surprise your family or guests by going totally off-piste. There is nothing traditional about this, unless you're Vietnamese, of course. The flavours are a complete breath of fresh air ... but fresh air never tasted this good – especially on a Sunday. (And by the way, before folks start rattling their hoes at me, it doesn't really involve a pot-bellied pig.) Ideally, pickle the veg the day before as it really is much better when left to sit overnight.

Happy for 8

2.5kg piece of pork belly on the
    bone, skin closely scored
olive oil
4 garlic cloves
1–2 red chillies (your call)
a thumb (about 20g) fresh ginger,
    tough bits trimmed off
1 lemongrass stalk
3 tbsp fish sauce
3 tbsp light soy sauce
8 banana shallots, peeled and
    sliced thickly, or 16 regular
    ones, halved
500ml chicken stock
1 tbsp rice wine vinegar
long-grain rice for 5–6 people,
    (see page 358)
good handful of coriander leaves
good handful of mint leaves

For the pickled veg:
150ml rice wine vinegar
1 tbsp caster sugar
1 red chilli, thinly sliced
salt
2 large carrots, peeled
1 cucumber

To make the pickled veg, heat the vinegar, sugar, chilli and a couple of good pinches of salt in a saucepan with 2 tablespoons of water until the sugar and salt have dissolved. Leave to cool a little as you attend to the veg.

Over a big bowl, use a peeler to shave the carrots and cucumber into wide ribbons. Pour the liquid on top and leave to sit, stirring occasionally as the veg soaks up the pickling liquor. If you're using them today, keep at room temperature, otherwise tip into a big jar and keep in the fridge – they will last for up to a week.

Preheat the oven to 220°C/fan 200°C/Gas 7. Lightly oil the skin of the pork then rub a couple of big pinches of salt all over. Finely chop the garlic, chilli, ginger and lemongrass together, put in a bowl and stir in half the fish and soy sauces. Rub this all over the bones and belly flesh, as opposed to the skin side.

Pile the shallots in the middle of a roasting tray that will hold the pork snugly. Sit the piggy, skin-side up, on top of the shallots, making sure they are all are tucked in under the meat. Roast for 40–45 minutes until the skin is starting to get a good crackling, then turn the oven down to 150°C/fan 130°C/Gas 2 and give the pork a baste to make its skin shiny. Pour the stock around but not over it, along with the remaining fish and soy sauces and stick it back in for about another 3 hours. You need to baste the skin with the liquid every half an hour or so.

CONTINUED

CONTINUED FROM
PREVIOUS PAGE

Towards the end of the cooking time, check the liquid as you don't want it to dry up completely, in which case just splash in a little more stock or boiling water as necessary. About half an hour before the pork time is up, get your rice going.

To see if the pig is ready, gingerly poke a fork into its side and the meat should come away easily in shreds. Ideally, your crackling will now be picture perfect too, but if it's not, just turn the oven up to full whack for as long as it takes to get it super-crispy, anything between 5 and 15 minutes depending on the beast.

Now lift the meat out and pop it on a baking tray. Strain the cooking liquor through a sieve into a jug, so that the shallots stay in the sieve and put both aside. Cut away the sheet of crackling and leave that to one side for now too.

Using a couple of forks, break up the meat, picking out and discarding any white sinewy pieces or flabby fatty bits, of which there will be quite a bit because this is exactly what makes pork belly so delicious. Once you've got a pile of boneless, tender meat, put it in a mixing bowl and stir in the cooked rice, shallots and two-thirds of the drained pickled veg. Turn your attention to the cooking juices: the fat will have risen to the top, so use a spoon or ladle to chuck out as much of it as possible before pouring the good stuff below into the bowl with everything else.

Pile high on a pretty serving dish and scatter on the rest of the pickled veg, the crackling (chopped into whatever shape and size you fancy) and the herbs to complete this dish of contrasts: slow-cooked and fresh, soft and crunchy, sweet and sharp. Rather special, really.

Beef Stew with Caraway Dumplings

Is it a stew? Is it a casserole? Would you like it more if I called it 'Bourguignon'? I think, on reflection, this dish has elements of all three: the dumplings are borrowed from stew, the cooking style from a casserole, and the booze, bacon and baby onions are all pinched from a classic boeuf Bourguignon. Whatever. From November to March, this never fails to hit the spot.

Mash is the compulsory side with this (see page 357) – and I think it's really yummy with a blob of Salsa Verde (on page 368) if you're the type who likes a tangy, fresh contrast to rich, lethargic meat.

Feeds 8, happily (see photo, overleaf)

700g braising beef, cut into
    3–4cm dice
half a bottle (375ml) red wine
2 bay leaves
1 bunch of thyme sprigs, tied
    tightly with string
a few tbsp of olive oil
100g sliced streaky bacon or
    lardons
3 large carrots, scrubbed and
    thickly sliced
10–12 shallots, peeled and
    left whole
3 tbsp plain flour
2 garlic cloves, sliced
100g mushrooms (button or
    chestnut), de-stalked and left
    whole unless they're monster
1 litre beef stock
S & P

For the dumplings:
100g self-raising flour
½ tsp baking powder
50g suet
small handful of flat-leaf parsley,
    finely chopped
1 tsp caraway seeds

Marinate the beef overnight in the wine, bay leaves and thyme.

The next day, heat a tablespoon of olive oil in a casserole pan and fry the lardons over a medium heat for a few minutes until they start to give out their fat and firm up. Chuck in the carrots and shallots and cook in the bacony fat for a good 5 minutes – you want them glossy and just beginning to pick up a bit of colour.

Meanwhile, tip the beef into a colander, letting the marinade drain into a bowl below. Put the thyme and bay leaves into the wine marinade, then scatter the flour over the beef and give it a brief stir/toss to get it all lightly coated.

When the veggies are beginning to soften, stir in the garlic for just a minute, then lift them all out with a slotted spoon and put them aside, leaving the pan on the heat.

Season the beef enthusiastically with salt and pepper. You need the bottom of the pan to be coated with fat, so if necessary pour in a little more olive oil. Once the fat in the pan is properly hot, gently lower in about a third of the beef to brown on all sides.

When batch one is done, put it with the carrots and shallots and go on to batch two, adding a splash more olive oil to the pan if necessary. Repeat for batch three, and once it's good and browned throw the rest of the beef and veggies back into the pot along with the mushrooms. Stir till hot then pour in the wine

CONTINUED

CONTINUED FROM
PREVIOUS PAGE

marinade along with the bay leaves and bunch of thyme. As it
bubbles up and reduces away use a wooden spoon to scrape up
any bits that have stuck to the bottom – they're all good flavour.
Hit the stew with a tad more seasoning, then once the wine
has reduced by half, pour in the stock, pop a lid on and bring to
the boil. Turn down to a steady tick-tick (steaming with some
bubbles but all quite lethargic), keeping the lid on.

Have a look at your stew after 2 hours – the beef needs to be
pretty much fully cooked and super-tender when you put the
dumplings in, so give it longer if necessary – you can't hurry
beef, and it's all dependent on the age, breed and quality of the
beast in question.

Meanwhile, knock up the dumpling dough by mixing all the
ingredients in a bowl with quite a bit of seasoning, and add just
enough cold water (4–5 tablespoons) to bring it together. Lightly
flour your hands, then divide and roll the dough into 8 balls.

When it's time to dumpling, the key thing is that they need to
be mostly submerged, so sink them into the stock and press
gently with the back of a spoon. If there's not enough liquid, you
can just top up with a little more stock or water, though don't
add any more than necessary. Stick the lid back on and give the
dumplings 20 minutes of uninterrupted low-level simmering
before turning the heat off.

Check the seasoning, and ideally let the stew sit for 15 minutes
to half an hour before getting stuck in. Overnight works too, in
which case you should make the dumplings the next day when
re-heating the beef.

12

The Art of Entertaining

High Days & Holidays

Part 2

WHEN we were growing up, my sister and I decided that our parents each had to have 20 presents in their Christmas stockings. Let me tell you that on £4-a-week's pocket money, this was a struggle, but as a family we came up with a rule that home-made counted double.

Whatever the occasion, some 30 years later, I still wholeheartedly believe that sentiment holds true, and while saying it with flowers is okay, saying it with flour is so much more touching. That's why no amount of posh Selfridges baubles can compare with the stained glass window biscuit tree decorations on page 312 that Delilah, Susi (her other mother) and I make every year.

The experience of and attitudes to big annual holidays and events change so much throughout our lives: when I was a child, Mother's Day was always a flurry of arts and crafts, yet after she died it became a day that I dreaded. It took becoming a mother myself for the dread to turn once again to joy, albeit always with some loving but sad thoughts for my mum too.

Inevitably perhaps, my Christmasses have followed a similar pattern: youthful, unblinkered pleasure, then 20 years of stepping into my mother's shoes as the family cook, providing for my father, sister, her kids and some faithful family friends too. But the role of lunch-maker on that Biggest of Days was mine a little too early in life, and for years I went through the motions of putting out an

impressively cheffy Christmas dinner at home without much inner joy. And I'm sure I'm not alone there. Now though, I'm in Act III, and Small Daughter has re-ignited my festive felicity. Although she's a bit wee to appreciate the finer nuances of my stuffings, the whole event – picking the tree, decorating the house, filling the stockings and even present-shopping – all give me pleasure now because I can't wait to see that little face I love so much light up in wondrous joy.

In this chapter I've put together my favourite foods for specific celebrations that are designed to spread a little happiness to those who mean so much to us. Undeniably, some of these recipes take a bit more making, but what better reason do you need to spend a little dedicated time in the kitchen than cooking something truly special for those you love?

Profiteroles for the People, or a Mini Croquembouche for St Valentine

This recipe gives you choux pastry two ways – first for profiteroles, and then stacked up into a croquembouche – a tower of choux buns bound together with caramel ... surely the ultimate declaration of love.

Choux pastry is the easiest of all pastries to make and the hardest to fuck up, but here's a quick heads-up: there's no way to fill a choux bun without a piping bag (you'll also need one to pipe the pastry on to the tray). Traditionally, the balls are filled with whipped cream for profiteroles and crème patissière (a slightly floury custard) for a croq, but I've opted for whipped cream for both, because it's sexier, easier and more fun – some of my mainstays in life. If you're going the distance to the croqembouche, you'll need a sugar thermometer too – it's a moody caramel thing. Since it's unlikely the finished structure will fit in your fridge, ball-filling and building should only happen a few hours before the love-in starts. Whether you're making a croq or simply fun-filled profiteroles, my advice is to serve with chocolate sauce – you really can never go wrong with rich, molten chockie.

Profiteroles

Makes 30–40 balls, which is good for 8 folks

For the choux pastry:
75g butter, cubed
pinch of salt
120g plain flour
pinch of caster sugar
3 eggs

For the chocolate sauce:
100ml double cream
150g dark chocolate (70% cocoa solids), roughly chopped
2 tbsp golden syrup
40g butter

For the filling:
350ml double cream
2 tbsp caster sugar

Preheat the oven to 180°C/fan 160°C/Gas 4.

Whether making profiteroles or the croquembouche, start with your choux pastry. Put the butter into a medium-sized, thick-based pan with 200ml cold water and a pinch of salt. Gently bring to the boil, making sure that all the butter has melted before it gets to bubbling.

Tip in the flour and sugar and use a wooden spoon to bring it all together – keep stirring as it begins to dry out. When it's all a golden colour and uniformly mixed, check the clock and keep beating for about another 3–4 minutes, until it has formed a ball and comes away cleanly from the side of the pan. Take off the heat and leave to cool for about 10 minutes.

CONTINUED

CONTINUED FROM
PREVIOUS PAGE

Now beat in the eggs, one by one, either mechanically using the paddle attachment in an upright mixer, or by hand. (If by hand, crack the eggs straight into the pan one by one and go at it with a balloon whisk). At first the pastry will reject the eggs, but keep beating (or watching the mixer) until the first egg is entirely incorporated, then go in with the next. When all the eggs are in you should have a silky, glossy, smooth mix, and use a spatula to scrape it all into a piping bag with a small nozzle/hole.

Grease two baking trays lightly with butter and pipe the mix into walnut-sized piles, spacing them about 2cm apart. Dampen your finger and run it over the tops so they are smooth and rounded. Arrange your oven shelves so that both trays are in the top half of the oven and bake for 22–25 minutes until golden, puffy and dry: it's really important you don't open the oven before 20 minutes – the steam that's captured inside the balls is what makes this pastry rise and puff up.

When you're happy with the way they look, keep the oven on with the buns in there but open the oven door and leave for 5 minutes. Then take out and cool on the tray and go through the same drill with your next batch.

While the buns are cooling, knock up the chocolate sauce. Gently heat the cream over a low heat, throw in the chopped chocolate and stir until it's all melted and smooth. Pour in the golden syrup and drop in the butter, then mix gently. Once smoothness has been restored, turn off the heat, cover with cling film and leave somewhere warm.

Now, ball-filling time. Whip the cream with the sugar until you have soft fluffy peaks. Load it into a piping bag with the same small nozzle/hole and get filling: you need to poke a hole into the base of each ball, either with your piping nozzle or something sharp and pokey, then stick the nozzle in and squeeze till the ball is full (it's remarkably quick and satisfying once you've got the system). If your aim is profiteroles, your work is done; just warm up the chockie sauce and you're off. But to make your lover fall in love with you that little bit more, we've a bit more work to do...

Mini Croquembouche

Makes 1 tower-ette of love (see photo, page 292)

Profiteroles and chocolate sauce
　　(see previous page)
300g granulated sugar
2 tbsp clear honey
seasonal flowers, buds and
　　leaves, to make it pretty

First make the profiteroles as per the previous recipe. Then, for your caramel, put the sugar in a very clean pan with the honey and 150ml water and bring up to 160–165°C over a high heat (yup, this is where you need the sugar thermometer). It'll take 8–10 minutes to get to 120°C, then will fly up to 160°C in another 2–3 minutes, so don't walk away. Have a bowl/sink of cold water on hand to dunk the base of the pan into when it hits the right temperature. If you don't shock it like this, it'll carry on cooking and will burn. CAUTION: caramel is a crazy hot beast: be careful.

Choose a presentation plate to build your love palace on, find a comfortable place and have all your raw materials ready around you (filled buns, an empty tray and a little bowl of cold water to dip your fingers in when you burn them, which you will).

When the caramel pot has been in water for a couple of minutes, lift out and rest it on a tea towel in front of your construction site, tilting slightly so that the caramel pools to one side. Dip each ball lightly in the caramel on the presentation side and leave to set on the landing tray. If the caramel becomes too thick to coat, then gently warm it up to loosen it again.

Once all the buns are dipped, start building from the bottom up in concentric rings, now using the caramel as glue: dip two balls into it on one side each (not the pre-dipped bits) and stick together. Position on the plate with the now-solid pretty dipped bit on the outside. Dip and stick one ball at a time, using 9–10 balls for the bottom ring. Then do the next layer, building up and inwards for 7ish layers until you reach a single ball at the top.

The finishing touches are what make this a show-stopper: weave some seasonal flowers, buds and leaves into the holes of the tower. By the time you've dressed your croquembouche to the nines it should look like some Wicker Man-esque fertility symbol. Just don't get so carried away that you forget the chocolate sauce, which is probably best served in a jug on the side, but if you're really going for it just use your imagination.

Sea Bass Baked in Herbs & Salt

For Mother's Day

If you've never tried it before, cooking fish in salt is a revelation. It's fantastically quick and easy, un-mess-upable and very, very impressive, but the real joy is what it does for the fish: it keeps it so pure, clean and healthy. I'm sure this is why I put it as my number one all-time women-pleasing, lady-loving dish. They just go nuts for it.

Big whole bass are beautiful but they're not the cheapest option due to their being wild not farmed (all the portion-sized bass you see are farmed), which is also why this recipe is perfect for Mother's Day ... Because she's worth it.

For 6–8 (any leftovers are gorgeous tossed in a simple salad)

handful of thyme sprigs
handful of parsley (curly or flat-leaf)
few sprigs of rosemary
½ garlic bulb, unpeeled, cut in half through the equator
2kg rock salt
2–2.5kg sea bass, gutted and cleaned
Salsa Verde (see page 368), to serve

Preheat the oven to 200°C/fan 180°C/Gas 6.

Chop all of the herbs together, leaving a few sprigs of each whole to put inside the fish.

Put the cut garlic bulb into the fish cavity and stuff any unpeeled loose cloves in too, along with the whole herb sprigs.

Mix the salt with the chopped herbs, and stir in a couple of tablespoons of water, until it is all just wet. Scatter a thin layer of it across the bottom of a roasting tray that's large enough for the fish to lie in flat. Sit the fish on top and methodically pack all of the remaining salt around the fish so that all of the flesh is covered in a salt crust (there's no need to cover the head or fin part of the tail). Cook for 25–30 minutes, or until a skewer stuck into the thickest part (a few centimetres from the back of the head) comes out warm.

Leave to sit for 10 minutes before breaking into the sarcophagus: as you crack it all over, the salt should come away in biggish pieces. Clear all of it off, making sure you also brush off any rogue bits of salt, before pulling back the skin. Now just lift off the beautiful white flesh in tranches. For my ideal meal, serve it up with some salsa verde, simply boiled new potatoes and a few sharply dressed salad leaves.

Shown with: Gratin Provençal, p364

Wellington for Waterloo

Psychiatrist by day, historian by night, my dad was a truly impressive man. At just 24, he had his first historical atlas published, and went on to write over a dozen books, with about a million sales in his lifetime. His older brothers also both went into the medical profession, and their love of history was another common thread between them. Dad would tell us a story about Mark, the eldest, waking the entire house as he sleepwalked one night, shouting, 'Blücher proved a traitor at the field of Waterloo.'

Wellington was, of course, the hero of Waterloo, and whether for historical reasons or those of appetite, I could tell from the look in my dad's expressive watery blue eyes (which are, by the way, the only physical mark my daughter bears of him, my eyes being brown) that he regarded my Beef Wellington as something similarly heroic. In fact, I've yet to meet a man who hasn't looked at me slightly doe-eyed when chowing down on my Wellie – it's just one of those dishes whose route to the stomach is definitely via the heart.

Cuts into 8 bloody handsome slices (see photo, overleaf)

1kg beef fillet, ideally from the
    middle so it's even in width
    (can be two pieces), at
    room temperature
plain flour, for rolling
700g puff pastry
1 egg beaten with 1 tbsp milk
    (known as egg wash)
S & P

For the mushroom layer:
600g button mushrooms, cleaned
60g butter
400g shallots, cut into small dice
3 garlic cloves, finely chopped
small bunch of thyme, tied
    tightly with string
300ml Madeira (cream sherry or
    Marsala work too)
50ml double cream
S & P

First crack on with the mushroom layer. In a food processor, whizz the mushrooms to little pieces, not mush. Heat the butter in a wide pan over a medium heat and fry the shallots, garlic and bunch of thyme for 5–10 minutes until the shallots are golden but not browning. Tip in the mushrooms and turn the heat up high. Give it a good stir. At first the mushrooms will release quite a bit of water; you want all of this to evaporate, so keep stirring every now and then for 10–12 minutes.

When it begins to stick to the pan and is on the drier side of mushy, pour in the Madeira and give the bottom a good scrape with a wooden spoon to lift all the dark, sticky bits, which have great flavour. Turn the heat down to medium and let it soak up all the booze. Then slosh in the cream and stir from time to time until you have a delicious, clumpy-looking dry mushroom pâté.

Season well with salt and pepper and taste, but try not to nosh too much! Tip the mix out on to a large plate to cool to room temperature then stick it in the fridge. Don't wash the pan.

Preheat the oven to 200°C/fan 180°C/Gas 6 and move on the beef, which hopefully you remembered to get out of the fridge to come to room temperature.

For the jus:

500ml beef stock, half strength (if cube or concentrate)

250ml red wine

3 garlic cloves, smashed with the side of a knife

another small bunch of thyme, tied tightly with string

1 tbsp sherry vinegar

2 tsp clear honey

Put a heavy-bottomed frying pan on a very high heat and season the meat heartily on all sides. Keep the pan dry (i.e. no oil) and once smoking-hot lay the fillet in it and don't fiddle with it (this is a good time for the extraction fan/open windows and doors). Imagine your fillet has three sides, and sear it on each side for 3 minutes, but don't do the ends. Turn it off and lift the meat out (again, don't wash the pan). Set aside to rest in a cool place until it's at room temperature (it's easier to work with everything at room temperature, rather than too hot to handle).

Lightly dust your work surface with flour and roll out the pastry to about 30 x 35cm and 5mm thick. Brush it all over with the egg wash, then take about a third of the duxelles (proper name for the mushroom mix) and put it in the middle of the pastry. Pat it into a shape the same size as the fillet, then sit the meat on it. (If any juices came out of the meat as it was resting, tip them into your beef stock). Briefly lift the sides of the pastry up and over the beef to check they meet. If not, now is your last chance saloon to do a bit of emergency rolling to extend both flaps.

Scrape every last bit of mushroomy goodness off the thyme before throwing it away, then press the rest of the mushroom mix all over the beef, including the ends if you have enough. Lift the sides of the pastry up and around the beef, and where the two sides meet, press together tightly, like a giant Cornish pasty. Crimp the pastry between your fingertips to make it pretty, making sure the ends are tightly sealed, then cut off any excess.

Transfer the Wellie-to-be to a baking tray, and, if you fancy it, cut some leaves from the leftover pastry, sticking them on with some of the egg wash, then brush more egg wash all over. Bake for 30 minutes then stick a skewer into the middle of the meat, leave it there for 5 seconds and put it to your top lip. For rare beef it should be warm but not hot or cold. Given these timings, it won't be hot, but if it's cold, put the meat back in the oven for 5 minutes then repeat the test. This will give you a perfect rare, which is how this dish should be.

CONTINUED

CONTINUED FROM
PREVIOUS PAGE

Meanwhile, get on with the jus. Put both the mushroom pan and the beef pan back on the hob. Once both are hot, pour the stock into the mushroom pan and the red wine into the beefy one. Drop the garlic cloves and second bunch of thyme into the wine, then bring both liquids to a fierce simmer. The aim here is that while the liquids are bubbling, you are scraping away at the bases of the pans to release all the flavour that is stuck there.

When the wine has pretty much completely reduced, tip the hot stock into the pan, along with any bits, and keep simmering at a reasonable tick. As you're approaching a saucy consistency (this is not intended to be a thick gravy, just an intensely flavoured sauce, which is why I call it the more delicate name of 'jus'), turn the heat down low, stir in the sherry vinegar and honey and taste for seasoning. All in all you should get about 50–100ml, just enough for a tablespoon or two per plate. Once you feel you're there flavourwise, turn the heat off.

When you're happy with your skewer test, take the mighty Wellington out, rest for 10 minutes (covered with a tea towel not foil), warm the jus and call up the bugler to bring the troops to table.

Bonfire Chilli con Carne

I still live in the London borough in which I grew up, and for as long as I can remember I've been watching the same fireworks display in the park down the road. Where we now live has a clear view of the sky above the park from our flat roof, which is much more civilised than rubbernecking in the crowded, cold, muddy park. Over the years, increasing numbers of friends have cottoned on to this, and a few days before Guy Fawkes Night I start getting calls about our now-expected Bonfire Night party, for which I always make a load of this chilli. It's undoubtedly the right dish for the occasion – and much the better for making early and hanging around for a day or two in the cold garden.

For 8–10

2 tbsp olive oil
2 carrots, peeled and cut into thick half-moons
2 red onions, chopped
2 garlic cloves, chopped
1 tbsp chilli powder
2 tsp smoked paprika
1½ tbsp ground cumin
1 tbsp dried oregano
750g beef mince
2 x 400g tins kidney beans, drained and rinsed
2 peppers, roughly chopped
3 tbsp tomato purée
2 x 400g tins of plum toms
1 litre beef stock
30g dark chocolate (70% cocoa solids), grated
S & P

To serve:
one of the two carb suggestions in last paragraph of method

Heat the oil in a large, wide, heavy-bottomed pan and fry the carrots, onions and garlic in it for 5ish minutes, until softened. Lob in the spices and oregano and cook for another few minutes before adding the beef. Break up with a wooden spoon as it fries and browns on all sides – it will need a good 8–10 minutes. Add the beans and peppers, give it all a good roll around so that it's nice and hot before stirring in the tomato purée thoroughly. Tip in the tins of toms, roughly breaking them up, then pour in the beef stock and give it a hefty season.

As it starts to bubble, turn the heat down low-ish to a very slow simmer – some bubbles and lots of steam – and leave for 1½ –2¼ hours (depending on the beef and how wide your pan is) until rich and thickened. Turn the heat off and finish by stirring in the chocolate and having a last taste to check the seasoning.

Serve up generously either with my Best Jackets (on page 355), which are decidedly bonfire-ish, plus chopped chives, or go the more Mexican route – long-grain rice, fresh coriander and pieces of lime. Either way, sour cream is a must for its cool creaminess, and hot sauce is compulsory for the over-12s.

Top: Bonfire Chilli con Carne
Bottom: Pumpkin & Coconut Curry

Pumpkin & Coconut Curry

By Halloween and Guy Fawkes Night we're pretty much into the first throes of winter, but this veggie alternative to the meatilicious Chilli con Carne (previous page) is a suitably appreciative last hurrah for autumn's greatest mascot.

Makes 6–8 bowls or about 12 mugs (see photo, previous page)

splosh of plain oil, such as
   sunflower or vegetable
2 red onions, diced
big handful of coriander
2 tsp curry powder
1½ tsp coriander seeds
1kg pumpkin, peeled and cut into
   3cm cubes
1 x 400ml tin coconut milk
2 peppers (preferably 1 red and
   1 green but it doesn't really
   matter), cut into bite-sized
   pieces
40g sultanas
50g ground almonds
50g frozen peas, defrosted
1 red chilli, halved, deseeded and
   thinly sliced
1 lime
handful of pumpkin seeds, husk
   on or off, toasted (see page 55)
S & P

Heat some oil in a wide pan and fry the onions over a medium–high heat for about 5 minutes, stirring regularly until softening.

Meanwhile, chop the coriander stalks and put the leaves aside for later.

Chuck the coriander stalks, curry powder and coriander seeds into the pan and stir well. Keep the heat up as you fry the spices for a couple of minutes, then tip in the pumpkin. Coat it in the flavoured oil and spices and once it's all warm on the outside, pour in the coconut milk. Bring to a simmer then turn the heat down to medium and cook for 25–30 minutes with the lid on.

Add the peppers, sultanas and ground almonds and cook for another 10–12 minutes, until the pepper is softening but still has a bit of bite to it. Turn the heat off and stir through the peas, chilli, a squeeze of lime juice and half the coriander leaves.

Season, taste and re-season as necessary (it may need more lime juice as well as salt) then serve up in mugs or bowls with the last coriander leaves and toasted pumpkin seeds scattered on top.

Stateside our Side
Thanksgiving Dinner, incl. a Decent Roast Turkey

My daughter's grandmother on her other maternal side is an expat American, so Thanksgiving is now firmly in our calendar. Whereas at Christmas there are other meats in the potential mix for our dinner, Thanksgiving really does need a turkey. However, that doesn't change the fact that, anatomically, this bird is not suited for roasting. The combination of lean meat, a massive breast and slow-cooking legs makes it a toughie to get your head or your chops around the cooking: the timings of various parts simply do not work together. It's our fault really, not the turkey's; it never said it was built for roasting – we did. But I got my best people on it and essentially the method below counteracts the turkey's basic form as best possible to produce something pretty darn tasty.

(Variables: oven, bird, how often you open the door, what else is sucking up oven heat, temperature of bird when you start, whether it's stuffed, how much you've had to drink … disclaimer over.)

Feeds about 6 adults and 4 kids, so adjust as necessary assuming 1 adult portion = 2 kids (see photo, overleaf)

1 batch of Golden Breadcrumb & Herb Stuffing (optional, see page 318)
1 x 6kg turkey (weight without giblets, which you also need)
half a pat of butter, at room temp
a little olive oil
bit of veg for 'gravy starter pack':
    1–2 carrots, 1 onion and a bit of celery, all unpeeled and halved or quartered
300g unsmoked streaky bacon
S & P

First make the stuffing, if you fancy it. Now to the bird: know how much she weighs, remove the giblets if inside and have her at room temp – you might as well give yourself every fighting chance to make the end result moist. Starting with a fridge-cold bird means you'll have to cook it for even longer, which doesn't help in the fight against dryness.

Preheat the oven to top whack 220°C/fan 200°C/Gas 7, or whatever full throttle is for you.

This is the slightly gruesome bit: going in at the neck end (the one without the big gaping cavity) and starting on one side of the breastbone at a time, work your hand in between the skin and the flesh – it's much easier if you take any rings off and wet your hand … and I'm not even going to go there. It will need a fair amount of finger wiggling – near the beginning you'll encounter some membrane barriers but all will give in to you with gentle perseverance, allowing your hand to fully separate the flesh and skin, right up to the top, thin end of the breast. Now do the same

CONTINUED

CONTINUED FROM
PREVIOUS PAGE

on the other side. When both are done, give your hands a good wash and have a well-deserved gin and tonic.

Season your soft butter with salt and pepper and get back under that skin (you know you want to), smearing three-quarters of it directly on to the breast meat. Retract your hand and spread the rest of the butter all over the legs. Now lightly drizzle the whole bird with olive oil and season well with salt and pepper.

If you're planning on stuffing your bird, then do it from the neck end thereby not stuffing the main cavity at all. This is because contemporary thinking is that the bird cooks better if it's not stuffed full of gubbins – it's to do with the air flow and all that.

Pile your starter pack of gravy veg into the middle of the roasting tray and sit the bird on them. Drape overlapping slices of streaky bacon all over the breast and legs and loosely rest some foil on top.

Stick it in the oven on full pelt for about 20 minutes, then turn down to 180°C/fan 160°C/Gas 4 and cook for 23–25 minutes per kilo – there's no need to baste during this time as that's what the butter and bacon are for. Whip the foil off for the last 20ish minutes so she can get a good tan (keep the foil), and check she's cooked by inserting a thin knife into the point at which thigh meets breast and following 'McEvedy's Lip Service' on page 125.

When you take her out, give her a thorough basting, then move her straight on to your serving dish. Sit the foil on top again, covered by a tea towel or two, and rest for 15–20 minutes, while you get on with the all-important gravy (see page 273).

Once your bird and all the appropriate accoutrements are served up, there is one final tradition to be observed. Take a moment to think about your life: they call it Giving Thanks, we call it Counting Your Blessings.

Clockwise from top left: Spot-on Mash, p357;
Roast Turkey; Cranberry Sauce, overleaf;
Sweet Potato & Marshmallow Pie, overleaf

Sweet Potato & Marshmallow Pie

The first time I saw this Thanksgiving must-have was at my friend Jodi's Jewish grandmother's apartment on the Upper West Side of New York, circa 1997, and I thought they were winding the Brit up (a regular pastime of theirs). How a vegetable dish topped with melted marshmallows was ever allowed into the lexicon of great American cooking just astounds me. But having said that, it's an absolute hit every year.

Enough for everyone at Thanksgiving dinner to double their blood sugar levels (see photo, previous page)

2 large sweet potatoes (about 1kg)
1 tbsp maple syrup
25g butter, plus extra for greasing
¼ tsp ground cinnamon
¼ tsp ground nutmeg
100g pecans
100g marshmallows (the regular size work better than mini)
S & P

Preheat the oven to 180°C/fan 160°C/Gas 4.

Roughly prick the sweet potatoes all over and bake in a roasting tray until sugary goo is oozing out of them and they are squidgy when you squeeze them – anything from 1 hour to 1½, depending on the size of your spuds. Take them out but leave the oven on.

When they are cool enough to handle, peel and then tip the flesh into a food processor. Pour in the maple syrup, butter, spices and seasoning and whizz to a purée.

Scrape into a buttered dish (I use a 28cm square dish), making sure that it doesn't come more than two-thirds of the way up. Spread the pecans out on a baking tray. Put both in the oven with the sweet potato above and the pecans below, and after 15 minutes take them both out, give the nuts a quick chop, then scatter on top of the sweet potato.

Cover the top with marshmallows, loosely foil the dish and bake for 7–10 minutes until the marshmallows have melted. Take the foil off and cook for a further 5 minutes or so, until the top is golden, or as golden as pink and white marshmallows can be.

Cranberry Sauce

When it comes to meat and fruit, in the States cranberries are to turkey what apples are to pork over here; that is to say pretty much compulsory. They're more interesting than apples though, as their flavour covers a baseball field of bases: fruity, bitter, bright and tart. All of which makes them a supremely sensible pairing for roast turkey, which – without being rude – isn't the most complex of meats. The most interesting fact I know about cranberries is that when they're ripe and ready, the fields of bushes are flooded with masses of water so that the berries float to the surface and the farmers can harvest them with massive nets. Way cool.

Makes a decent bowlful

50g caster or granulated sugar,
    plus a little more to taste, if
    necessary
350g cranberries, either fresh or
    frozen (defrosted if frozen)
zest and juice of 1 orange
couple of pieces (about 30g)
    stem ginger, finely chopped
S & P

Put 3–4 tablespoons of water in a small, heavy-bottomed pan with the sugar and let it bubble away for 3–4 minutes, until it is starting to thicken and the bubbles have got a bit smaller.

Add the cranberries, orange zest and juice, and ginger. Once it comes back to the boil turn the heat down to low and stir on and off for the 15ish minutes it takes the cranberries to pop and break down, though I think it's nicer if they don't lose their shape entirely and turn to jam.

Taste: it should be quite sharp, but if it makes you wince, add a teaspoon more sugar.

'Festival of Light' Latkes לאַטקעס
with Sweet Cheese & Apple Sauce

When we were young, my sister and I always went to church on Sundays with our mum, who was a firm but not overly effusive Anglican. We served in church from the age of six, and one of my earliest memories is one of intense pride as I stared down at my new yellow wellies peeking out from under my long black cassock as we processed up the aisle behind Father Ian.

Small Daughter and I still go to the same church: she runs me ragged through the service, innocently bypassing the finer nuances of respect and piety ... giggling inappropriately in just the same way I remember doing with our mum some 35 years ago as my sister and I jostled in the pew. Mama would seem to tell us off with lots of hushing and nudging, but even at my young age I could sense that she was party to her daughters' sense of naughtiness. So, annoying as it is to everyone else in the congregation, I can't help smiling wryly as Delilah exhibits the same affable but naughty streak, and wondering how my dearest Ma might be enjoying the scene playing out below her.

Despite this early grounding in Christianity, as a teenager I became strongly attracted to Judaism, choosing to attend Jewish Assembly at school, rather than the main secular one. I liked the sound of Hebrew, the exoticness, and of course the fabulous food at my friends' Bar and Bat Mitzvahs. And then, after I had taken the path to chefdom, our family friend and my first great cookery idol, Claudia Roden, published a book on Jewish cookery that made me want to stride straight down to the nearest synagogue and sign up immediately.

What I particularly love about Jewish food is how everything has historic significance, and while the exact reason why latkes, these special potato fritter things of wonder, are specific to Hanukkah has been lost in the mists of time, what's for sure is that everybody looks forward to eating them.

Makes 10 biggies or 20 smalls (not that 'small' really exists in the Jewish Lexicon of Food)

1kg potatoes, peeled
3 eggs, beaten
4–5 spring onions, thinly sliced
big handful of parsley (about
    30g), finely chopped
about 1½ tsp sea salt and a good
    crack of pepper
veg/sunflower/rapeseed oil, for
    frying

Grate the peeled spuds on the largest holes of your grater and drop them into a big mixing bowl filled with cold water. Leave to soak to get rid of unwanted starch.

Now get your apple sauce going. Once the apples are on their way to being sauced (and for this you want more of a soft purée than chunky), mix the ricotta with the honey in a small bowl and leave to one side.

Back to the latkes: put the beaten eggs, spring onions, parsley and seasoning into another bowl or anything big enough to give

To serve:

1 batch of Apple Sauce (see page 269), rosemary replaced with ¼ tsp ground cinnamon

400g ricotta

2 tbsp clear honey

it all a good stir. Dredge up a handful of grated spuds from the water, let it drain through your fingers while still over the bowl, then squeeze the life out of it before dropping it into the eggy-herby mix. Do the same with the rest of the spuds, then give it all a good mix so the potato strands are all eggy-coated.

Check your apples and give them a gentle stir – the time they take to break down varies a lot, so as long as they're not catching on the bottom, keep the lid on and let them do their thing.

Put your best large frying pan on a medium–high heat and pour in oil to a depth of 2mm. It's not a bad idea to turn your oven/grill on to a low–medium heat (about 150°C/fan 130°C/Gas 2) as you'll be frying the latkes in batches so you'll need a place to keep them warm. Once the oil in the pan is hot but not smoking, use a serving spoon to dollop in biggies of the eggy spud mix, or a dessertspoon for smaller ones. You should get 4–6 in there, depending on your preferred size and the width of your pan. The mix should fizzle as it goes into the hot oil; use the back of the spoon to gently press them into flattish ovals.

To cook through, they'll take 5–6 minutes per side for big ones and 3–4 minutes per side for smaller ones. If they're colouring too quickly, turn it down. They may also need a 180° swivel if one half is darkening while the other remains totally blonde – what we're looking for is an all-over colour that is through golden brown to dark and crispy.

If you haven't turned off your apple sauce yet, now's probably a good time, and leave the lid off so it can cool a bit. Lift your latkes out of the frying pan, rest on some kitchen roll and give them a light season with sea salt. They really are best eaten immediately, but if you're going for family-style noshing, pop them in the warm oven while you get the next lot going.

Serve up with the apple sauce and the sweet ricotta cheese, and in your moment of bliss don't forget to spark up the menorah.

בתאבון!

Two for the Tree (& for Eating)

Stained Glass Window Biscuits

These were a part of my wonderful ex-wife's childhood, not mine, but I wish they had been! They're super beautiful, fun to make and look fab on the tree, but best of all was our daughter's face when she first bit into one and realised it looked like a biscuit but tasted like a sweetie. What surprise! What joy! Needless to say after that we had to move them all a bit higher up the tree ...

Makes about 30 biscuits

100g butter, at room temp, plus extra for greasing
100g caster sugar
1 egg, beaten
½ tsp vanilla extract
200g plain flour, plus extra for rolling out
½ tsp baking powder
pinch of salt
a packet of clear boiled fruit sweets (like Fox's Glacier Fruits or Robinsons Classic Fruit Sweets)

Either in a food processor, upright mixer or by hand, cream the butter with the sugar until pale, then pour in the egg and vanilla and beat a little more, until incorporated. Tip in the dry ingredients and fold until well combined, then scrape into some cling film and put in the fridge for 30 minutes.

Keeping all the colours separate, bash the sweets up into little pieces, either with a rolling pin or in a pestle and mortar – a good, noisy, child-friendly activity.

Preheat the oven to 180°C/fan 160°C/Gas 4. On a surface very lightly dusted with flour, roll out the biscuit dough as thinly as possible – about 3mm ideally. Cut out the biscuits into long, church window shapes and lay them on a non-stick, buttered baking tray (you might need a couple).

Either using festive cookie cutters or just freestyling, cut out Christmassy shapes from the middle of each biscuit and fill the holes with crushed up sweets; but don't mix colours – that would be psychedelic, man.

Make another little hole at the top of each biscuit for the string to go through. Bake the bickies in batches for about 8 minutes – they should be fairly pale rather than brown, so keep an eye on them. Leave to cool on the tray a little before lifting off with a palette knife. Thread with ribbon and hang on the tree: sweet treats for all till Twelfth Night!

Glittery Popcorn Tinsel

This is bonkers but beautiful and makes for a fun festive snack while you're decorating the tree.

popping corn, or ready-made,
    though it's not quite the same
    (50g popping corn makes
    about 3m of tinsel popcorn)
splash of oil
1 can of edible gold spray
edible glitter

You'll also need a needle
    and thread

Make the popcorn according to the packet instructions, then spread out on a tray and leave to cool for a little bit.

Use a needle and thread to string the pieces together, then spray with edible gold spray and sprinkle with edible glitter.

Drape all over the tree and admire your handiwork. It looks even better after a couple of drinks ...

Full-on Christmas Dinner
A festive feast for family & friends

Roast Goose

Flavourwise, goose smashes it over turkey, for me. But it has its drawbacks too, namely that there's not really a whole lot of good meat on there for a bird of its size. However, what you do get is jars and jars of yummy fat, which is a sound flavour investment for the year to come*, but that's not a lot of help when you've more than eight people to feed on Christmas Day. One option I've done when I've already turkeyed at Thanksgiving is to do a goose *and* a ham for Christmas. The contrasting meats work well together, and where the goose lets us down, the pig can provide (see over the page).

*It literally lasts a year in the back of the fridge, so is useful in the upcoming months for roasties, etc.

To feed about 6 grown-ups plus a couple of kids

1 x batch of The Other Must-know Stuffing (see page 319; optional but recommended) OR couple of handfuls of thyme and/or rosemary
1 goose, about 6kg (weight without giblets, which you do also need), at room temp
1 garlic bulb, halved through the equator
sea salt

First get your stuffing going, if so inclined. Weigh your bird, remove the giblets if still inside, and preheat the oven to 220°C/fan 200°C/Gas 7. Find a roasting tray that's big enough to hold the bird and sit a trivet or wire rack in it (so the bird isn't swimming in the fat it releases), then put in the oven to get hot.

Spoon the stuffing evenly around the bottom of the cavity, or just put the herbs and garlic in there. Season the outside of the bird well with sea salt, double up a piece of foil and pat that on to the breasts but not the legs. Once the oven is up to speed, take the tray out, pop the bird on the trivet or rack and stick it all back in the oven. Cook for 25 minutes, then turn the heat down to 190°C/fan 170°C/Gas 5 and roast for another 18 minutes per kilo, basting every half hour.

When the time's up, you can check if your goose is cooked by inserting a thin knife at the point where thigh meets breast and following 'McEvedy's Lip Service' on page 125. Then take the foil off and leave to rest uncovered for 20 minutes while you get on with the gravy (see page 273).

TURN FOR MORE FULL-ON CHRISTMAS FEASTING

That Festive Ham

This is a gift that just keeps on giving: the spicy smell that emanates from the oven as the ham's glaze caramelises simply epitomises Christmas, and she's good to go for suppers and sarnies all the way to Twelfth Night. Most rewarding.

Makes 12 days of leftovers (see photo, previous page)

5kg smoked gammon joint on the bone (from the knuckle end)
1–2 onions, halved
2 large carrots, peeled and halved
3 celery sticks
1 garlic bulb
1 tbsp peppercorns
3 bay leaves
handful of parsley stalks (if you have them – no biggie if not)
handful of whole cloves

For the glaze:
3 tbsp clear honey
2 tbsp English mustard
3 tbsp brown sugar

Find a pot big enough to hold the ham and pop it in. Cover with cold water then put a lid on and bring to a simmer on the stove. Now strain off all that water and start again with fresh, this time adding the veg, garlic, peppercorns, bay leaves and parsley stalks. Bring back to a simmer, covered, and cook for 2¾–3 hours, checking the water level every now and then, and topping up with boiling water to keep as much of the ham submerged as possible.

To check it's done, stick a skewer into the thickest part, leave it there for 5 seconds then feel the tip – you want it to be hot but not scalding. Lift the joint out and put aside. (When strained, the cooking liquor makes tasty stock for most piggy flavoured soups. Reduce by up to half but don't let it get too salty – hams differ in salt levels and reducing can make it too concentrated.)

Preheat the oven to 200°C/fan 180°C/Gas 6. In a small bowl, make the glaze by vigorously mixing together the honey, mustard and brown sugar until smooth and a bit loosened.

Once the ham is cool enough to handle, but not cold, use a long sharp knife to shave off all the skin and most of the fat underneath, leaving roughly 5mm of fat. It doesn't matter if it goes down to the meat in some places. Score a wide cross-hatch through the fat and just into the meat, and brush it all over with half the glaze. Stud each intersection of the cross-hatch with a whole clove, then double line the bottom of a roasting tray with foil and sit the ham in it.

Bake for 20–30 minutes, brushing on the other half of the glaze midway through – it's perfect when the glaze is golden, the ham is just beginning to brown around the slashes and it all smells like Christmas! Superb hot, cold or at room temperature.

Christmas Root Purée

The participants in this purée can change, but the one I feel is unchangeable is the swede. And maybe the carrots. And I guess I like the celeriac in there too. The Jerusalem artichokes are pure joy and well worth it. Just no spuds please; and pumpkin is a bit watery for this.

I always do something like this at Christmas – the orangey colour goes perfectly with all that brown, though it's really good at any wintery Sunday lunch or anytime that game comes to town.

For 8+ (see photo, page 315)

2kg root veg (swede, carrots, celeriac, Jerusalem artichokes, parsnips, butternut squash), peeled and cut into rough 5cm chunks
30g butter
200g double cream
S & P

Put all the veg in a wide pan, cover with cold water and add a heavy pinch of salt. Stick a lid on, bring to a simmer and keep it going until the veg is well and truly soft – this could take as long as an hour.

Once everybody is cooked but not dying in there, drain and leave for a good 10 minutes to steam-dry until there is no more steam but the veg is still warm.

Whizz in a food processor in a couple of loads, dividing the butter and cream between the batches. It should be silky smooth and like very superior baby food when you take it out. Season well and serve hot.

A Couple of Seasonal Stuffings

To stuff or not to stuff, that is my constant question. Serving some kind of stuffing at Christmas or Thanksgiving is totally obligatory, the question being do you put it – as the name implies – inside the bird, or bake it separately in a dish? There are benefits to each, so it's your call...

PRO BIRD

1. The meatalicious and fatty flavours of the bird permeate the stuffing. Yum.
2. Really, this is how it's supposed to be done.

PRO BAKE

1. If your stuffing is meat-free, veggies can eat it.
2. If it has sausage meat in it, it's easier to tell when it's cooked and thus less chance of killing those we love.
3. Baking gives a nice crispy top and makes it a lighter eat due to lack of animal fat.

Golden Breadcrumb & Herb Stuffing

I've made all kinds of fancy stuffings at Christmas and Thanksgiving over the years, but when sitting at a table laden with goodies, I've noticed this simple recipe always keeps people coming back. Good one for the vegetarians at Christmas, too.

Good for 8, but there won't be any leftovers (see photo, page 315)

2 tbsp olive oil
1 onion, finely chopped
3 garlic cloves, finely chopped
3 tbsp rosemary, finely chopped
2 tbsp thyme leaves, chopped
few sprigs of sage, leaves finely
    chopped
200g breadcrumbs, made from
    slightly stale, day-old bread
handful of flat-leaf parsley, finely
    chopped
zest of a lemon
good knob of butter
S & P

Preheat the oven to 180°C/fan 160°C/Gas 4. Put the oil in a biggish frying pan and sweat the onion, garlic, rosemary, thyme and sage over a medium heat for 5–7 minutes until the onion has softened and the herbs aromatised.

Meanwhile, put the breadcrumbs, parsley and lemon zest in a bowl, and once the oniony herbs have done their thing, tip them in too. Season with salt and pepper, stir well and mix in just a few tablespoons of water, enough to make a moist stuffing.

If it's going inside a bird then you know what to do, but if you prefer to keep it veggie, then choose an ovenproof dish that will hold it all (about 15 x 20 x 5cm) and rub with a knob of butter. Spoon in the stuffing, give it a bit of a pack down, then cover with foil and cook for 20 minutes, before whipping off the foil and baking for a last 10 minutes, until golden and gorgeous.

The Other Must-know Stuffing

This one is particularly good with goose. It's a classic, with almost medieval British Christmassy flavours: dried fruit, spice, brandy, shallots, sage. Oh, and animal fat.

About right for 8ish adults & kids

300g chunk of bread, ideally not pre-sliced, crusts cut off
2 banana or 4 regular shallots, chopped
1 tbsp oil or butter
few sprigs of sage, leaves roughly chopped
pinch of allspice
few scrapings nutmeg or ¼ tsp ground nutmeg
1 eating apple, peeled, quartered, cored and diced small
150g dried apricots, roughly chopped
70ml brandy
about 250ml hot chicken stock, depending on what kind of bread you're using
3 tbsp animal fat: it's usually duck or goose at Christmas but dripping (beef) or lard (pig) are also good, melted
S & P

Preheat the oven to 190°C/fan 170°C/Gas 5 and as it's heating up, tear the bread into roughly golf-ball-sized pieces. Put them on a baking tray and toast in the oven for 8–10 minutes until golden but not desiccated.

Meanwhile, in a saucepan sweat the shallots in the oil or butter until soft but not browning. Stir in the sage and spices and cook for another couple of minutes. Tip the whole lot into a mixing bowl along with the apple, dried apricots, brandy and toasted bread. Mix well and a little roughly to break down the bread chunks a bit, then pour on just enough hot stock to make it all come together – it should be a pleasantly soft mess, tacky to touch, but not mushy.

If you're going to stuff a bird with it, then just stir in the animal fat (unless it's a goose, in which case ditch the fat as the goose will make enough of its own), give it a final bit of seasoning and load it in.

But if your plan is to cook it separately, grease your chosen dish heavily with half the melted animal fat. Then fill it up with the stuffing without packing it down too much and drizzle the remaining fat on top.

Cover with foil and cook for 20 minutes, then take the foil off and bake for the same amount of time again, until golden and slightly crunchy.

Raised Game Pie for Boxing Day & Beyond

This impressive fellow emanates pride: it is one almighty pie ... something Henry VIII would happily have got his chops around. The making of it is nothing short of a declaration of love for your family and friends as well as for the art of cooking, because this is not one to rush. Enjoy it, and for every ounce of care you put in, I promise you the rewards will be manifold.

Makes 12–14 very handsome slices

1 x 400g piece of cooked ham
250g pork back fat, minced
500g venison, diced in 3cm chunks
2 duck breasts, skinned and cut into 6–8 largish chunks
150g unsmoked streaky bacon, sliced
8 partridge breasts, skinned
6 banana shallots or 12 regular ones, chopped small
5 garlic cloves, chopped
15g sage leaves, finely chopped
½ tsp allspice
30g butter
splash of extra virgin olive oil
60ml brandy
60ml port
S & P

For the pastry:
375g lard
1kg plain flour, plus extra for tin
2 tsp salt
2½ tbsp icing sugar
1 egg beaten with 1 tbsp milk

For the jelly:
750ml fresh chicken stock
2 tbsp port
4–5 gelatine leaves

On the morning of pie-making day, take the meat out of the fridge to come to room temperature. Butter a 26cm springform tin about 7cm deep. Lightly flour the tin, turn upside down and tap a couple of times to get rid of the excess.

In a wide pan, sweat the shallots, garlic, sage and allspice in the butter and a splash of olive oil for 15ish minutes until soft, golden and sweet; you don't want them to colour, so pop a lid on halfway through and turn the heat down low. Once done, turn the heat right up and immediately pour in both the boozes. Let the liquid reduce completely to just a dark, sticky binding and leave to cool.

Meanwhile, roughly chop the ham into 3cm pieces and put in a large bowl with the rest of the meat, except the partridge. Tip in the boozy shallots, season well and give it a jolly good mix. Preheat the oven to 180°C/fan 160°C/Gas 4.

For the pastry, melt the lard into 500ml water in a small pan over a low heat. Bring to the boil then immediately turn the heat off. Tip the flour, salt and icing sugar into a big bowl and make a well in the middle. Pour the hot, fatty water into the hole and incorporate the flour to make a dough. Turn out on to a lightly floured surface and knead for a minute or two to work into a ball.

Cut off a quarter for the lid, and pull off a tennis-ball-sized lump for 'Pie Hospital', in case you need to go there later. Wrap both in cling film to keep them moist, and put aside. Lightly but thoroughly flour your surface and your rolling pin too. Roll out the pastry to a circle about 40cm across: big enough to line your tin with a bit of overhang, then roll it up around your pin and unroll it over the top of the tin.

CONTINUED 👉

CONTINUED FROM
PREVIOUS PAGE

Using the flats of your fingers to even it out, press the dough into the tin, making sure you have a couple of centimetres of overhang all around the top. Press your knuckle all around where the sides meet the base, so the pastry isn't too thick there.

Now lift in half of the mixed meat, not packing it too tightly, and leave a centimetre or two of space all round the edge for the jelly to fill. Then lay in the partridge breasts like spokes on a wheel, narrow ends in the middle and fatter ends pointing outwards. Top with the rest of the meat, shaping it like a dome, then make a hole bang in the middle by sticking your finger half-way in (this helps the jelly distribute freely later).

Roll out the pastry lid to a circle to fit snugly on top, and lay it on the meat. Brush with the egg wash, then fold the overhanging lip of pastry up and over to cover the join, and press to make sure you have a good seal (a little crimping never goes amiss).

Egg-wash the circumference crown, not letting it drip between the pastry and tin or it may stick when you get it out. Cut a hole in the middle for steam to escape, and if you still have the strength, make some pastry leaves, eggwashing them too. Put the pie on a baking tray and bake for 1 hour 15 minutes, turning it and re-egg-washing halfway through. Then take it out of the oven and turn the heat up to 200°C/fan 180°C/Gas 6.

Carefully run a palette knife around the sides of the tin, taking care not to pierce the pastry, and very gently pop the clasp to release the tin, checking it's not catching anywhere. Lift the ring off. If liquid seeps over your baking tray you'll immediately know you've sprung a leak. DON'T PANIC – it's Pie Hospital time. Just calmly use the bit of pastry saved exactly for this purpose to plug the hole(s), making sure you blend raw into cooked. Be a little over-generous with the plugging – you need this baby to be watertight for the jelly stage. I promise your pie will still be magnificent; the fix may look drastic but I guarantee nobody will know. (Yup, I've been to Pie Hospital a few times, and once spent a whole weekend there trying to perfect this recipe.)

Egg-wash the sides and put it back in the oven for 15–20 minutes until the pastry is a dark golden all over (if the top had a good colour before this, then drape a piece of foil over it – this last bit is just to make sure the sides are properly cooked). Leave to cool completely: it's a bit massive for the fridge and few of us have a larder or pantry, so I generally put it in the bathroom in the winter, with the window open and door closed.

Once your pie is properly cold, warm the chicken stock with the port, and soak the gelatine leaves in cold water (four if using home-made stock; five if using bought stock). When the stock is steaming, turn it off, lift out the floppy gelatine leaves one at a time and whisk into the stock. Season, tip into a jug with a good pouring spout and leave to cool to room temperature.

When the stock is cool, get ready to start pouring it into the pie. If you have a thin funnel, stick it into the steam hole, or make one from greaseproof paper rolled into a cone. Pour the stock into the pie in gentle bursts over 10–15 minutes, with a couple minutes' break between each load. Keep going until the pie won't accept any more, or you run out of stock, or you see it seeping out the sides, in which case check yourself in to Pie Hospital again: use any leftover raw pastry to dam the holes – it doesn't matter how it looks stuck to the cooked pie – when the jelly has set (i.e. a few hours or overnight) simply cut off these pastry plasters with a small, sharp knife, and no scars will show.

Put the pie back in its cold place and leave overnight for the jelly to set. At this point it can keep for days. When it's pie-eating time, preheat the oven to top whack and once it's up to speed flash your pride and joy in it for just a couple of minutes: enough to give the pastry a glorious gloss, but not enough for it even to think about melting the jelly inside.

Take a moment to gaze adoringly at your masterpiece, because undoubtedly as a cook, you'll feel you've truly raised your game.

NB: once the glory moment is done, keep any leftovers in the fridge – they're most definitely good for a week or so.

13

Grown–up Puds
& Small Sweet Treats

AS mentioned earlier in the Art of Entertaining, Part 1, our parents had regular dinner parties in the dining room when my sister and I were growing up. (The room doubled as Pa's study so usually you couldn't even see the table as it was covered in maps.) The posh glasses would come out and napkins would be ironed and folded. Though I'm roughly the age now that they were then, and, like them, I have a dining room (that doubles as a shooting room – photos not pheasants) with lots of glasses (that don't quite match) and proper napkins (that *sometimes* get ironed), for some reason I don't feel like I've ever thrown a dinner party, not in the way that they did. In a parallel universe where having people over involves changing for supper and putting on make-up and strings of beads, I can't imagine what I'd be wearing, but I know that *these* are the puddings I'd be serving.

So far in this book I've focused more on the cross-generational winners in terms of sweet stuff. However, I felt that an unprecedented third chapter of puddings was required, namely recipes that for one reason or another are geared towards a more mature audience. Some are plain and simply not for the under-aged: chilli and rum with grilled pineapple ain't going to fly with the little people; and the chocolate cake in this chapter is so rich it would have my daughter sky-rocketing with delight followed by a meteoric crash and burn, and neither of us would want that. And then the Armagnac truffles are *both* rich *and* boozy.

But it's not that all the recipes are for a more sophisticated palate – a madeleine is really just a groovy-shaped sponge after all, and children will wolf them down without a second thought. To them, though, they may as well be hoofing a slice of Victoria sponge, whereas giving a warm, home-made madeleine to an adult, particularly a Proust-loving one, will make their day, and maybe even their week.

This book has now run its course of a lifetime of eating – or the lion's share of it at least – and while it felt most appropriate to me to begin our story with baking for the little ones, so it feels only right to end it with some recipes that are more adult-focused. Thus, these are the treats for when the kids are asleep (or at least pretending to be). Goodnight.

Pear Tarte Tatin

After careful research, hand on heart I think pears 'tatin' better than apples do. Pears soak up gooey caramel so well that it becomes a part of their being. Apples do it sometimes, but not as consistently. However, if you fancy an appley one, don't use Bramleys as they break down too much. Go for a standard eating apple, like Cox's or Granny Smith. Peel, quarter and core, then cook halfway in the caramel before laying on the pastry. And as a dinner party tip, for apples or pears, you can make most of this way before guests arrive – it's only the pastry that needs to happen at the last minute.

For 6

4–5 firm but ripe pears (depending on the size of the pears and the pan), peeled, cored and halved
1 lemon
100g caster sugar, plus extra for sprinkling on the pears
1 vanilla pod, split in half, seeds scraped out
500g puff pastry
30g butter
vanilla ice cream or crème fraîche, to serve

Preheat the oven to 180°C/fan 160°C/Gas 4. In a bowl, roll the pear halves in the zest of half the lemon, all of its juice, a light sprinkling of sugar and the vanilla seeds (keep the pod for later).

This is a one-pan affair: choose an ovenproof, heavy-bottomed frying pan (a cast-iron skillet is ideal) about 25cm across. Roll the pastry out to 5mm thick (no thicker!) and cut out a circle about 2–3cm wider than the top of the pan. Put the pan over a medium–high heat and pour in half the sugar. Wait until it melts and goes clear, then add the other half, not stirring but swirling the pan, and let it all turn a coppery caramel. If you're feeling brave, turn the heat up high, but be super vigilant. Whatever the heat, don't wander off as it can all happen quite quickly.

When you're happy with the colour of your caramel, turn the heat off and swirl in the butter. Chuck the vanilla pod in there (for flavour and beauty), then lay in the pear halves, cut-side up, with the thicker ends on the outside, like spokes on a wheel. Drape the pastry over the pears, tucking it in all around the edge and prick a few small holes in it to let the steam out.

Bake for 25–30 minutes, until the puff is puffed and golden. Take it out and let sit for a minute before turning. To do this slightly hazardous operation, get yourself a completely flat serving dish and hold it tightly on top of the frying pan. Calmly flip them both over – with hot caramel involved it's worth taking a degree of care – then lift off the pan. Beauteous. Serve hot with vanilla ice cream, or crème fraîche if you're feeling grown up.

A Pavlova for All Seasons

There's something so fabulously seventies about a pav that it truly chimes with my childhood. Once you have your base nailed, the only other thing to think about is pretty and complementary fruit. Here are three of my all-time favourites for different times of the year.

Makes 1 x 25cm pavlova (good for 8–10 people)

The Veale Family Drunken Grape Pavlova

This version comes from my funny, smart and slightly complicated friend Helen (Veale) who says her mum always made the meringue and then handed it over to her dad to get OCD with the drunken grapes.

400g grapes (ideally half red, half green)
75ml cream sherry
1 batch of Mama's Meringues, made into a pavlova base (see page 260)
200ml double cream
25g icing sugar

The day before serving, prepare your grapes. Slice them in half lengthways then pour on the sherry to cover. Leave overnight to infuse. You can make your meringue a day ahead too.

The next day, whip the cream with the sugar to the glorious soft peak stage (firm but still floppy), then gently fold in a couple of tablespoons of the sherry that the grapes were soaking in.

Gently splodge the cream into the pavlova's crater and smooth out before getting obsessional with your drunken grapes.

British Summertime Berry Pavlova

1 batch of Mama's Meringues,
    made into a pavlova base
    (see page 260)
200ml double cream
2 tbsp icing sugar, plus extra for
    shaking
1 punnet of strawbs, hulled then
    quartered or halved
1 punnet of raspberries
1 punnet of redcurrants or
    blackcurrants, left on their
    branches

First whip the cream with the icing sugar in a bowl to the
soft peak stage (firm but still floppy), then smother the central
plateau of the pavlova with it.

After that it's just a case of pile it high with the fruit and, just
before serving, go nuts with the icing sugar.

Paradise Pavlova

1 batch of Mama's Meringues,
    made into a pavlova base
    (see page 260)
200ml double cream
2 tbsp icing sugar
1 mango, peeled and cut into
    thick shards
1 ripe papaya peeled, deseeded
    and cut into thick shards
3 passion fruit

Whip the cream with the icing sugar to the soft peak stage
(firm but still floppy), then fill up the middle of the pavlova with
it and load on the mango and papaya.

Cut the passion fruit in half and use a teaspoon to scoop out
the seeds so that they fall all over the fruit shards.

Grilled Pineapple with Chilli & Rum

Sweet, feisty, boozy, pretty and hot; reminds me of a girl I once knew.

For 4

1 pineapple
½ red chilli, deseeded and sliced
2 star anise
2 tbsp clear honey
2 tbsp dark rum
zest and juice of 1 lime
small handful of mint leaves,
    roughly chopped or torn

You'll also need 1 large
    ziplock bag

Top and tail the pineapple with a big knife and stand it on one end. Slice off the skin, then slice vertically around the core and cut those chunky pieces into wedges. Pop the wedges in a large ziplock bag with the chilli, star anise, honey, rum, lime zest and juice and chopped mint and give it all a good shake. Leave to marinate in the fridge for an hour or two.

When you're ready to go, heat a griddle over a high heat till good and hot (if you don't have one, a skillet or heavy-bottomed frying pan will also do).

Cook the pineapple pieces for about 3 minutes on each side – basically until they've picked up a bit of colour, then move them to your serving dish. Pour over the marinade, making sure some of the chilli is showing. One to eat warm – it's a tropical thing.

The Richest Chocolate Cake in the World

Taste memories are not as widely recognised as visual or even olfactory ones, and yet if we truly delve deep enough into our past and open up our senses, they can reappear, clear as daylight.

If meringues were Mama's trademark kiddy pud (which they were), then this homage to all things chocolatey was what her friends came to know her for, and I was damned if I was going to write this book and not include her signature dinner party pudding.

It had been years since I'd tasted hers – a quarter of a century in fact – but with determination, the annual export of a small country's worth of chocolate, good advice from better bakers than me and, most importantly, my taste memory, I went to work. It only took eight goes to get it right.

Makes a 26cm cake – easily enough for 10, it's *that* rich

300g dark chocolate (70% cocoa solids; preferably Fairtrade)
220g caster sugar
180ml boiling water
220g butter, cut into smallish pieces, softened
2 tsp vanilla extract
1 tsp instant coffee granules
6 eggs, separated

To serve:
whatever dairy you fancy: whipped cream, vanilla ice cream, crème fraîche, Greek yoghurt

Preheat the oven to 180°C/fan 160°C/Gas 4 and pop the kettle on. Grease a 26cm round springform tin and line the base with greaseproof paper.

Either by hand or in a food processor break down the chocolate into small pieces: if you're doing it by hand I'd opt for the big holes of the grater, and if you're going by machine just give it a rough chop first.

Tip the chocolate into a heatproof mixing bowl, then stir in all but a heaped tablespoon of the sugar and pour on the boiling water to melt the chocolate. If there's not enough heat for the chocolate to melt, then just sit it over a pan of gently steaming water for a minute or two (making sure the bottom of the bowl doesn't touch the water), but take it off again as soon as the last of the chockie has melted.

Stir well, then mix in the butter, vanilla and coffee granules, sitting it over the pan of steaming water again if the butter is not melting. Turn off the heat, then add the yolks one by one, stirring after each one.

CONTINUED

CONTINUED FROM
PREVIOUS PAGE

Put the whites in another, bigger bowl for whisking (or do it in a mixer) with the last heaped tablespoon of sugar. Once they are firm and starting to hold shape, fold them into the chockie mix in three loads, making sure each one is fully incorporated before adding the next. This mix needs to be light and airy to balance with the sheer weight of chocolate, so try to do the folding-in quickly, without overworking.

Pour the mix into the prepared tin and bake for 40–45 minutes until the cake is cracked and a little crusty on top, with a bit of a wobble still going on in the middle (but not liquid).

Leave to cool in the tin completely – 2 hours should do it – and don't worry if it collapses in the middle a bit … it's that kind of cake and all will be forgiven later.

Once it's cooled to room temp, stick in the fridge to chill down and firm up. When cool, run a little sharp knife around the edge and unbuckle the ring. Flip on to a plate, peel off the greaseproof, then flip it again on to your serving plate, so the nice crusty top is uppermost.

If you've opted for whipped cream, you can spread it all over the cake if you want, like my mum did – she finished it with grated chocolate too. Or just do the dairy on the side. It doesn't matter; nothing really matters once you've tasted it. Slightly transcendental.

Crème Caramel (for Pa)

My father never cooked. When he occasionally agreed to 'do' Sunday lunch, it involved walking to the fishmonger and buying lobsters – already boiled, of course. But he did like good food, and as his life went on it became more important to him, maybe influenced slightly by his chef daughter. Crème caramel was his absolute favourite: he wasn't that fussy about it, but I am because there are so many wretched versions out there. This recipe has taken a lot of tweaking, but I'm pretty sure it's spot on now: not too eggy, just a little creamy, and with a proper deep, burnt caramel oozing over. NB: It's worth buying taller moulds if you're a true devotee to CC, though ramekins are okay too.

Makes 6–8, depending on your moulds (see photo, overleaf)

160g caster sugar
250ml whole milk
250ml double cream
3 eggs, plus 2 yolks
2 tsp vanilla extract

Preheat the oven to 140°C/fan 120°C/Gas 1 and put 100g of the sugar in a heavy-bottomed pan with 1½ tablespoons of water. Stir with a finger until all the sugar is wet, then put on the stove over a high heat; the sugar will dissolve and begin to caramelise.

When it turns deep bronze, take it off – there will be enough heat in the pan to finish it off. You want a slightly burnt, dark caramel with a proper bitter edge. It's a fine, fast-moving line between perfect and buggered, so be vigilant. Pour the caramel into your moulds – it should look a little like ruby port – and set aside while you make the custard.

Heat the milk and cream gently in a pan until just steaming. Meanwhile, whisk together the whole eggs, yolks, vanilla extract and remaining 60g of sugar by hand in a bowl. Once the dairy is up to temperature, pour it on to the egg mix, whisking lightly to combine. Share this mix between the moulds, then put them in a roasting tray and pour hot, not boiling, water into the tray to come halfway up the outsides of the moulds.

Bake for 25–30 minutes until just set but still with a definite little wobble. Take the tray out, then lift the moulds out of the water and cool to room temperature before putting in the fridge to get properly cold. To get these beauties out, run a small sharp knife round the inside of the mould. Hold just above a plate, let the air in to release the suction and your perfect pudding will plop satisfyingly out, followed by a gush of dark, rich caramel.

15-minute Chocolate Mousse

Imagine Angel Delight for grown-ups, and you're just about there. Insanely rich, easy and quick.

Makes 4 small glasses or espresso cups, which is plenty ... they're rudely intense

80g dark chocolate (70% cocoa
    solids; preferably Fairtrade)
2 eggs, separated
2 tbsp caster sugar, plus 2 tsp
75ml double cream
1 tbsp Kahlúa or Tia Maria

Roughly chop the chocolate, setting aside a nugget for grating on top. Melt the rest either in a heatproof bowl set over a pan of steaming water (not letting the bottom of the bowl touch the water), or in the microwave.

In a separate bowl, whisk the egg yolks with 2 tablespoons of sugar, then fold in the melted chocolate.

Whisk the egg whites with a teaspoon of sugar until stiff peaks form, then mix them into the chocolate base in three loads: beat the first lot in fully, fold in the second then third lots gently until just incorporated and there are no trails of fluffy white.

Spoon carefully into your four receptacles. If you're going to eat them within the hour, then there's no need to refrigerate. If making in advance, pop in the fridge but take them out a good half hour before you tuck in – it's a chocolate textural thing.

Just before serving, whip the cream with the Kahlúa or Tia Maria and the last teaspoon of sugar. Spoon it on top of the mousses and finish with a grating of chocolate.

Shown with: Crème Caramel (for Pa)

Florentines

Once you know how easy and fun these are to make, you'll never be over-charged for them again. And what's even better for your bank balance is that they make excellent presents, all boxed up with a pretty bow.

Glacé cherries are essential for me, but in terms of the basic nut mix you can pretty much make it with whatever's lurking in your cupboard (just not too old please – the oils in nuts go rancid over time, which is a boring way to ruin a great Florentine).

Makes 20ish bickies

150g mixed peel
100g glacé cherries, halved
100g flaked almonds
50g pistachios, roughly chopped
50g hazelnuts, roughly chopped
50g butter
50g double cream
75g caster sugar
25g clear honey
60g plain flour
200g dark chocolate (70% cocoa
    solids; preferably Fairtrade)

Preheat the oven to 180°C/fan 160°C/Gas 4.

Mix the candied fruit, cherries and nuts in a bowl. Put the butter, cream, sugar and honey in a small pan and bring to the boil.

Once the sugary goo in the pan has been simmering for a couple of minutes it will turn slightly golden. At this point turn off the heat and whisk in the flour, followed by the fruit and nuts. Give it all a good roll and a coat and leave to cool and firm up.

Line a baking tray with a lightly oiled sheet of greaseproof paper. Once the mix is cool enough to handle, roll it into walnut-sized pieces and put them on the tray, with about 5cm between each one (and if the mix hardens too much to roll, then just re-heat it a little to soften it). Squash the balls down just a touch – they'll spread out a bit more in the oven, then bake for 10 minutes, until golden. Take out and leave on the side to cool.

Melt the chocolate in a heatproof bowl set over a saucepan of steaming water, not letting the bottom of the bowl touch the water. Lift the Florentines off the paper (which may take a bit of coaxing with a palette knife), then dip their bottoms in the chocolate and put them back on the greaseproof, chocolate-side down. Leave to cool again at room temperature, so that the chocolate can set, then they're good to go.

Top: Florentines
Bottom: Madeleines

Madeleines

I adore madeleines (proper ones, not like what you get from a supermarket with a month-long shelf life) and so did Proust. My mum loved Proust, which is why the wine bar she set up round the corner from us in Shepherd's Bush in the late seventies was called Albertine. I doubt they ever made madeleines there but in some wonky way, I associate them with her in my mind.

There's no way round it, you need a madeleine tray to make madeleines, and preferably a metal one at that – I just don't buy that silicon does the same job. The metal ones can be tricky to find, but after much searching, I got mine from the lovely chaps at Kitchen Ideas on Westbourne Grove in London, but you could try the internet or French flea markets.

Everyone's heart melts over a warm, home-made madeleine.

Makes 12–14 (see photo, previous page)

90g butter, plus a bit more for
    greasing
2 eggs
70g caster sugar
2 tsp clear honey
pinch of salt
90g plain flour, plus a little extra
    for the tin
½ tsp baking powder
1 tsp vanilla extract

Preheat the oven to 200°C/fan 180°C/Gas 6, then melt the butter and leave to cool.

This is a hand job; a mixer could easily overbeat, so put the eggs, sugar, honey and salt in a big bowl and whisk together until pale and smooth, which should take about 5 minutes of labour.

Sift the flour with the baking powder and fold it into the eggy mix. Next stir in the vanilla extract and butter, which must be cooled so it doesn't react with the baking powder, then put in the fridge for 10ish minutes to rest and firm up.

Grease your madeleine moulds with a little melted butter, then wipe off any excess with kitchen paper. Sprinkle a little flour into each one, tap it all around so all the butter is floured, then turn it upside down and tap again a couple of times so what's not needed falls away.

Each mould will take roughly 1 tablespoon of the mix. Fill them to just below the rim, then bake immediately for 8–10 minutes until risen and golden brown.

Pop them out with a small palette knife and eat now – with friends, with memories, or just on your own.

Unashamedly 70s Chocolate Roulade (& it's flourless too)

As when JFK/Elvis/Lennon/Cobain died (delete for appropriate generation), you never forget where you were when you made your first roulade. Mine was some time between the Lennon and Cobain eras; I was blind drunk and I rolled my dad's friends something more like a Camberwell carrot than a roulade. Apart from my rolling technique, the recipe came from the great Helge Rubinstein, who moved in my dad's circle of friends. Although I've adapted her recipe quite a bit, this version still captures the character traits of a roulade born, like me, in that epic decade.

Good for 8–10

For the cake:
6 eggs, separated
200g caster sugar
50g cocoa powder, plus plenty
    extra for dusting
a little icing sugar, for dusting

For the filling:
150g milk or dark chocolate
    (70 per cent cocoa solids;
    preferably Fairtrade), plus
    extra for squiggling
250ml double cream
2 tbsp brandy or water
50g icing sugar

Preheat the oven to 180°C/fan 160°C/Gas 4. Line a high-sided baking tray, measuring about 30 x 20 x 5cm, with greaseproof paper and butter the greaseproof.

Whisk the egg yolks and all but a tablespoon of the sugar until pale (this takes a few minutes), then sift in the cocoa powder. Whisk the whites separately and, once fluffy, add the last tablespoon of sugar and whisk again until firm.

Fold the whites into the cocoa base in three stages: the first will loosen up the chocolatey mix, the second will lighten it further and the third will make it airy, just be careful not to overwork the mix, or you will knock the air out of it.

Tip the mix evenly into the prepared tray and don't play with it too much. Bake for 20–22 minutes until cooked but still springy – if overbaked, it won't roll. Meanwhile, tear off a second sheet of greaseproof paper about 5cm bigger on all sides than the sponge and dust it lightly with cocoa powder and icing sugar.

Cool the cake in the tin for 6–8 minutes (no more), then turn out on to the dusted greaseproof paper. Peel the old greaseproof off the sponge. Position the cake with one of its long sides closest to you, fold the border of new greaseproof over this long side and use it to help you roll the cake up tightly like a Swiss roll or

CONTINUED

CONTINUED FROM
PREVIOUS PAGE

newspaper (rolling the paper into it too). Leave it rolled up while you make the filling.

Melt 130g chocolate with 50ml of double cream either in a heatproof bowl set over a pan of simmering water (don't let the bottom of the bowl touch the water), or in the microwave. Stir in the brandy or water, and if it seizes up a bit, warm it gently again to make it spreadable.

Whip the rest of the double cream with the icing sugar, until smooth but firm. Now unroll the sponge and spread it with the chocolate, leaving a gap of about 2cm at both short ends, which makes it easier to roll.

Once the chocolate layer is completely cool, cover it with the whipped cream, again leaving that 2cm gap, and you're ready to roll. Using the greaseproof paper again to guide you (though not rolling the paper inside it this time), roll her up as neatly, tightly and proficiently as you can – don't worry if she gets the odd crack as they'll get covered up in the final step.

Once done, dust the whole thing with copious amounts of cocoa powder, then melt the last of the chockie and squiggle it on top using a teaspoon and a limp wrist. A-mazing!

Easy Armagnac Truffles

Just when your guests are leaning back, replete and satisfied with all that you've given them, out you come with a little plate of home-made truffles and right then, just for a moment, they are all just a little bit in love with you. If only they knew how simple these are to make, they wouldn't be quite so quick to offer up their hearts.

Makes 25–30 balls of love

100ml double cream
350g dark chocolate (70% cocoa
    solids; preferably Fairtrade)
knob of soft butter
2 tbsp Armagnac
about 70g good-quality cocoa
    powder, for rolling

Heat the cream gently in a pan until it's steaming and, as it warms up, chop the chocolate into little pieces. Put the chocolate in a heatproof bowl set over a pan of simmering water, making sure the bowl is not touching the water. Stir as the chocolate melts, then pour in the hot cream in two loads, using a spatula to mix until smooth after each lot.

Gently stir in the butter, followed by the Armagnac, then pour into a shallow tray, cover it with cling film and stick it in the fridge to get properly cold – an hour or two.

Once it has set firm, tip the cocoa powder on to a plate or small baking tray. Using a teaspoon as a size-guide, start taking spoonfuls of the mix and rolling them into balls in your hands, then dropping them into the cocoa. When you have about 10 balls in the cocoa give the tray a shuffle so they get totally covered. Take them out and put them in the fridge, popping one in your gob on the way, just to check.

Repeat for the next lot. If during proceedings the chocolate mix becomes unmanageably soft, just put it in the fridge to firm up again. Keep the truffles in the fridge till you need them, and boy will you need them. They'll keep for 3–4 days.

Key Lime Pie

I conducted some fairly extensive research on this American classic to determine what actually defines a key lime pie, and came to the conclusion that really, it can be anything limey, which in any Yank's book, we most certainly are. Think of this version as a roughly non-cheesy cheesecake, with a top that's ballsy with lime zest and lighter than angel farts, anchored down by a ginger nutty base.

Will make 8–10 people very happy

120g digestive biscuits
120g ginger nuts
80g butter, melted
3 eggs, separated
zest and juice of 5 limes
1 x 400ml tin condensed milk
½ tsp cream of tartar
60g caster sugar

Preheat the oven to 160°C/fan 140°C/Gas 3 and butter a 20cm springform tin that's about 7cm deep.

Bust up your biscuits until fairly well ground, either in a food processor or the old-fashioned way (by bashing them in a bag with a rolling pin). Tip into a bowl and stir in the melted butter, then dump into the tin and use the backs of your curled-up fingers to press it down and make sure it's well compacted. Stick it in the fridge to firm up.

Meanwhile, put the egg yolks in a mixing bowl and whisk with the lime zest, lime juice and condensed milk to just combine.

Either in another bowl using an electric hand whisk, or in an upright mixer, or by hand, whisk the whites until they start to go frothy. Doing it the old fashioned way with muscle is weirdly satisfying and only takes (me) about 4 minutes. Stir the cream of tartar into the sugar, and gradually add to the whites while they're still moving until you have a bowlful of stiff meringue. Fold the whites into the limey mix in two batches, then pour this on to your base.

Pop the tin on a baking tray, put in the oven straightaway and bake for about 25–35 minutes, until it's just set – firm around the outside with the faintest of wobbles in the middle.

Leave to cool completely – the pie is best served totally chilled, so once it's cooled to room temperature, stick it in the fridge for an hour at least. The top will crack a little as it contracts, but that's never bothered me, or anyone else that's ever been wowed by it. The longer you leave it, the limier it gets.

Frangipane Fruit Tarts

Ever since my River Café days twenty years ago, when I had to make a pear and almond version daily throughout the season, I've had a fond love for tarts like these. Not only are they pretty and yummy, but once you've got the two basic recipes down pat (sweet pastry and frangipane), they can be thrown together with consummate ease, thus making them perfect dinner-party stand-bys.

For 8–10

1 batch of Sweet Pastry (see page 370 – use half the recipe and freeze the rest)
plain flour, for rolling
1 egg white, lightly beaten
icing sugar, for dusting
crème fraîche, Greek yoghurt or vanilla ice cream, to serve

For the frangipane:
180g butter, softened
180g sugar (caster or granulated)
180g ground almonds
3 eggs
1½ tsp vanilla extract
good splash of amaretto (optional but recommended)

Your choice of fruit filling (see ingredients overleaf):
Rhubarb & Pistachio
Raspberry, Straight Up
Fig & Flaked Almonds

Lightly grease a 24cm fluted tart tin.

Once you've made and rested your pastry, lightly dust your surface with flour and roll it out to 2–3mm thick. Roll it up around your rolling pin then drape it over the tart tin and use to line the tin, making sure that you get it into the corners. Cut off the excess with a small sharp knife and pop the lined tin in the fridge to rest for an hour, or the freezer for 30 minutes.

Preheat the oven to 180°C/fan 160°C/Gas 4.

Once rested, prick the base of the case lightly all over, then drape a piece of greaseproof over the tart case and fill it with baking beans (see page 370). Blind bake for 20 minutes then carefully lift out the greaseproof with the beans and bake the case for a further 10 minutes, giving it a quick brush with the beaten egg white halfway through. It's easy to see when it's properly cooked as the base will be golden and shiny. Take the tart case out and leave to cool for 15 minutes. Reduce the oven setting to 170°C/fan 150°C/Gas 3½.

Knock up the frangipane, either in an upright mixer, by hand, with an electric hand whisk, or even in a food processor. Cream together the butter and sugar until pale. Add the almonds and once they are all incorporated, add the eggs one by one. Lastly, slosh in the vanilla and booze if you fancy it.

Scrape the frangipane into the cooked and slightly cooled tart case and then fill it with one of the seasonal ideas on page 351, or invent your own.

CONTINUED

CONTINUED FROM
PREVIOUS PAGE

Once you've added your filling, bake the tart for 35–45 minutes, until a knife stuck into the centre comes out clean and the top is lightly golden. Serve warm, dusted with icing sugar and accompanied with crème fraîche, Greek yoghurt or vanilla ice cream and a bowlful of pride.

Fruity Tips

Once you've got the hang of the basic principles, you can go off-piste from some of my favourites (given opposite) and use almost any fruit that's in season. In summer, try cherries, apricots and even peaches instead of raspberries. Stone the fruit if necessary, cut in half and just press into the frangipane slightly so the pieces are half submerged.

Autumnal fruit, such as pears and plums, don't need to be pre-cooked, but just be sensitive to their condition. Choose juicy fruit, not the drier ones, to keep your tart an easy eat. With pears, peel, quarter and core them before using.

In winter I depend more on dried fruit, which should be simmered first, preferably in something boozy. They generally love anything from the brandy family like Cognac, Armagnac or Calvados. Prunes are a classic, though dates are also good. (all stones out first though please).

Three Seasonal Frangipane Fillings

Rhubarb & Pistachio (good for early spring through summer)

4 rhubarb sticks, about 250g, split in half lengthways at the root end if they're thick, then cut into 3–4cm batons

20g pistachios, shelled and roughly chopped or smashed a little with the side of a knife

Lay the rhubarb on top of the frangipane in whatever pattern pleases you and press it in a bit. Scatter on the pistachios and cook as per the directions on the opposite page.

Raspberry, Straight Up (summer all the way, baby)

2 punnets (300g) raspberries

Depending on your need for tidiness, either randomly scatter or place the rasps into the frangipane in concentric circles. Give them a little push down so they are at least half submerged and bake as per the method opposite.

NB: Depending on the time of year and the variety, the water content of raspberries varies, and I've found that this can take up to 15 minutes more than the usual cooking time to dry out and colour pleasingly.

Fig & Flaked Almonds (for autumn)

4–5 figs, split in half through the stalk

10g flaked almonds

Push the halved figs into the frangipane, cut-side up. This is one of those rare occasions where even I go for tidy over random patterns – figs are such pretty things that they just suit it. Scatter flaked almonds on top and bake away as described opposite.

Egg Appendix

A Simple Omelette

For 1
2 large or 3 regular eggs
knob of butter
S & P

Some favourite fillings:
chopped herbs (parsley, tarragon
   and chives are the traditional
   fines herbes combo)
ham/mushrooms/grated cheese/
   baked beans

Whisk the eggs with some seasoning. Melt the butter in a heavy-bottomed frying pan over a medium heat and arm yourself with a wide rubber spatula. Run the butter all the way round the pan and up the sides, and as it starts to fizzle tip in the eggs.

Don't fiddle, but as you see an area around the edge where the egg is whitening, draw it into the middle. As the omelette begins to form, continue to draw in the sides, tipping the pan so that the liquid egg in the middle runs into the space. Now is the time to add any fillings before you do the folding part.

You want to fold it once the egg is mostly set, which is usually about 2 minutes after you poured them into the pan – you want it to still be a bit runny inside.

Hold the spatula in your favoured hand, wriggle it under the closest half of the omelette and use the other hand to tip the pan towards the spatula. Fold one side over t'other, and immediately slide it out of the pan on to a warm plate. If it's all gone to plan, your omelette should be neither anaemic nor browned, and still be very slightly runny when you break into it with a fork (an omelette should never be eaten with a knife).

Soft-boiled/ Hard-boiled Eggs

Disclaimer: freshness, pan size, egg size, ferocity of heat, where eggs are stored, etc. are all factors here.

Egg goes into boiling water, then ...
Soft-boiled = 4½ minutes
Soft–hard = 7 minutes
Proper hard-boiled = 10 minutes
   and left to cool

Boiled Quail's Eggs:

Just for the hell of it.
Also from when egg meets
boiling water:
Soft-boiled = 1½–2 minutes
Soft–hard = 2½–3 minutes
Hard-boiled = 4 minutes
(See photo, page 136. And for a top tip on peeling them, see page 135.)

Poached Eggs

For 1
2 eggs
1 tbsp white wine vinegar
salt

Put water in a saucepan to a depth of 5cm, stick a lid on and bring to the boil. Once at a rolling boil, season with salt and add the vinegar.

Crack the eggs into the water and immediately put a lid on. When you can hear/see that it has come back to a rapid boil (a minute or less) take the lid off and turn the heat down a touch. Don't panic if the egg white is all quite spread out at this stage – the motion of the fast-rising bubbles in a busy boil will force it up and around the yolk.

Prepare a landing mat (kitchen paper or tea towel) and find your slotted spoon. After 2 minutes, carefully lift one of the eggies out and gently prod the area of white just next to the yolk – it's ready if it feels soft but holds together. If clear albumen pools out, it's not ready, in which case dunk it back in the water for another 30 seconds or a minute.

As soon as the eggs are holding together, quickly lift them out one at a time, and as you put them on the landing mat gently flip over so the underside is on top – when poaching by this method they look neater bottoms-up. After 30 seconds, move on to your plate(s).

NB: One in a hundred eggies will explode as you crack it into the water and turn the entire thing murky. There's nothing to be done, don't take it personally – just get over it, change the water and move on.

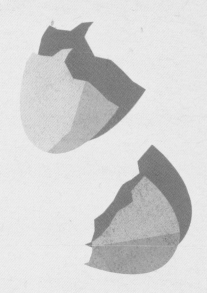

Scrambled Eggs
For 1
2 eggs
½ tsp Dijon mustard
1 tbsp double cream
1 tbsp butter
S & P

Whisk together the eggs, mustard, cream and seasoning. Have your plate/toast/receptacle ready as this is all over very quickly, and you don't want your eggs to overset as you scrabble for crockery.

Melt the butter in a frying pan over a medium heat until fizzling, and tip it all round the pan before pouring in the eggs. As the egg sets and whitens round the outside, use a rubber spatula to bring it into the centre of the pan, breaking it up on the way with a fast stirring motion. When the eggs are halfway to your idea of scrambled perfection, turn the heat off. They will continue to cook in the residual heat in the pan but are a lot less likely to overcook this way.

As they approach the finish line, do some fast-action stirring all round the pan to break up any remaining big pieces of egg (the texture you're looking for is in the title). Now get them out of there asap – every second counts at this point; in total they should be in and out of the pan in no more than 2 minutes.

Jam-jar Coddled Eggs
Coddling is an old English way of baking eggs in individually sealed containers. For reasons of energy-saving and, quite frankly, a better end result, I prefer these done on the stove top rather than the more conventional oven method. And just seeing as we're already breaking the rules, a coddler is a tough thing to come by, and it seems a shame to let a little thing like not having the right equipment prevent you from a small pot of egg heaven, so I use jam jars instead.

It really does make a very sublime, not to mention cute, brekkie – just don't go expecting a totally runny yolk; this is all about harmony between bedfellows: white, yolk, butter and seasoning.

For 1
1 egg
knob of butter
S & P

Find a small jam jar with a lid that fits and pierce 3–5 holes in the lid to let the steam out. Put a small pan of water on the hob and bring to the boil.

Butter the inside of the jar, crack the egg into it and season a little with salt and pepper. Slip a saucer into the bottom of the pan, then lower the jam jar on to it (the water should come two-thirds of the way up the jar).

Put a lid on the pan and simmer for 5½ minutes for small eggs or 6½ minutes for large, then using a tea towel carefully lift out the jar and leave to sit for a minute. Whip the lid off and give it a gentle stir to mix everything together before tucking in.

Spud Appendix

Best Jackets

For 2

2 big baking potatoes (usually 400–500g each)
sea salt

To serve:

butter
sour cream or crème fraîche
spring onions or chives
S & P

Preheat the oven to 200°C/fan 180°C/Gas 6.

Wash the spuds and while they are still wet sprinkle on a decent amount of sea salt. Put directly on the oven rack and bake for 1 hour, then turn the oven down to 180°C/fan 160°C/Gas 4 and cook for a further 1–1½hours, depending on the size of the spuds – a knife should go easily through the central flesh once through the skin.

In our house we split them open, mash each half with a knob of butter AND sour cream as well as spring onions and plenty of salt and pepper.

Pommes Boulangère

An old-school classic bit of Frenchery; essentially a dairy-free dauphinois, that cooks the slices of spuds in chicken stock instead of cream; not as naughty but just as yummy and much better for you!

For 8 (see photo, page 267)

good splash of olive oil
50g butter, plus a little extra for frying the potatoes and greasing
2 large onions, sliced
4 garlic cloves, chopped
3 sprigs of rosemary, 1 with leaves picked and chopped, plus a couple for the top
2 tsp thyme leaves
1.2kg (6ish) red-skinned spuds, skin on but well washed
500–750ml fresh chicken stock (either home-made, see page 373, or bought: the amount depends on the size of the dish)
handful of flat-leaf parsley, chopped
S & P

Preheat the oven to 180°C/fan 160°C/Gas 4. Put the oil and half of the butter in a wide pan over a high heat and as soon as the butter has melted, fry the onions and garlic. Once they have collapsed turn the heat down to medium and keep stirring regularly until golden and soft. Add the chopped rosemary, 1 teaspoon of the thyme leaves and some seasoning and let them cook for a few more minutes before turning the heat off.

Meanwhile get slicing your spuds – this is most easily done on a mandolin, but your best thin slicing with a knife is also good – just choose a good, very sharp knife and aim for 3mm-thick slices.

Put the stock in a pan and heat until it's steaming. Grease a wide ovenproof dish with a knob of butter – shallow-ish works best, about 7cm deep. Make a layer of spuds on the bottom, overlapping them in a concentric pattern, then season and scatter on a layer of onions. You should end up with 5–6 layers of spuds, so divide the amount of onions accordingly. Keep going until you have no more onions and finish with a layer of spuds, then stir the parsley into the hot stock before ladling it on – you want to just see the liquid appearing in and around the top layer, but the spuds shouldn't be swimming. Dot the top with the remaining butter in 6–8 knobs, give it a final crown of seasoning, scatter over the remaining rosemary and thyme and finish with the rosemary sprigs.

Cover the dish with foil and bake in the oven for 2 hours – the knife should go through with zero tolerance. Whip the foil off and crisp the top either by turning the oven up to top whack or by putting it under the grill for about 10 minutes.

Bubble & Squeak

Makes about 8 little ones (grown-ups will want 2 each), though you can use any quantities you want as long as half the weight is spud, which is needed to bind it

4 tbsp vegetable oil or light olive oil
1 large onion, sliced
200g cooked Savoy cabbage, shredded
250g mashed potato, preferably having hung around the fridge for a day or two to dry out, or cold if made fresh
knob of butter
plain flour, for dusting
S & P

Heat a tablespoon of the oil in a wide pan and fry the onion over a medium–high heat until good and golden – about 5 minutes with the odd stir. In a big bowl, mix the cabbage with the spud and a fair whack of both salt and pepper.

When the onions are done, tip them in too and give the pan a quick wipe with kitchen paper. Mix well and split into eight little patties.

Melt the butter in a tablespoon of oil over a medium heat and lightly dust the patties with flour on both sides. Fry them four at a time, turning after about 3 minutes once golden with crispy bits, and fry for another 3 minutes on the other side. Drain on kitchen paper and eat immediately or keep under foil on a warm plate until the next lot is done. Chuck in another knoblet of butter and splash of oil and let them start fizzling before getting started on the rest.

Killer Dauph / F**k me Dauphinois

*The method is the same for both versions, but F**k me (as featured on pages 99 and 102) is for two (otherwise it would be an orgy).*

*For 6–8 [2 for F**k me]*
550ml [100ml] milk, plus a bit more as needed
550ml [100ml] double cream
1 [half] small onion, sliced
2 [1] garlic cloves, unpeeled, smashed
3 [1] good sprigs of thyme
1–2 [1] sprigs of rosemary
2 [1] bay leaves
few peppercorns
couple of [1] scrapings of nutmeg
1.5kg [350g] spuds, peeled
80g [20g] grated cheese for the top (a mix of Parmesan and Gruyère works well)
knob [knoblet] of butter
S & P

Preheat the oven to 200°C/fan 180°C/Gas 6.

Put the milk, cream, onion, garlic, herbs, peppercorns and nutmeg in an appropriately sized saucepan, bring to steaming point and keep it there for 5–10 minutes to infuse.

Meanwhile, slice the spuds pretty thinly, about 5mm – a sharp knife is good, but a mandolin is better.

Generously butter an ovenproof dish around 30 x 20cm [about 10 x 8cm for F**k me] – anything that will fit your spud slices snugly – and start layering them, seasoning between each layer. Once you've laid on half, pour over half the infused dairy through a sieve. Do the same with the other half of the spuds then pour on the rest of the liquid, again through a sieve. The spuds need to bask in a

sea of dairy – they should neither be submerged nor protruding, so add a splash more milk if necessary.

Sprinkle the cheese on top, then cover the dish with foil and put on a tray in the oven (just in case she spills over) for about 1 hour [45 minutes for the little guy] – depending on your spuds, so check it after an hour by sticking a knife in: it should push through without resistance. Don't take the foil off until your spuds are properly tender though, which may take up to another 30 minutes. Once you're happy that they're cooked, whip the foil off and pop the dish back in to fulfil its bubbling, golden-topped potential, which will take about 15 [or in the little guy's case 8ish] more minutes.

Roasties

For 6 (see photo, page 315)
2kg spuds (nothing too waxy: King Edwards or Maris Piper work well)
8 tbsp fat (goose is fashionable; duck does the job just as well and there's something appealingly old-school about lard [pig] and dripping [beef]. For veggies, go for rapeseed oil)
sea salt

Preheat the oven to full pelt: 240°C/ fan 220°C/Gas 9, with your roasting tin inside; it needs to be a big 'un.

Peel and cut the spuds: whoppers into quarters, big ones into three, medium in half. If your spuds are small, you've bought the wrong kind. Put them in a saucepan with cold water to cover and 2 teaspoons of salt. Stick a lid on and bring to the boil. Once at a rapid boil take the lid off but keep it bubbling busily for

another 5–10 minutes until the potato edges are beginning to break up but the insides are still hard. Drain in a colander and let them have a good 5 minutes sitting in the colander steam-drying.

Pick up the colander and give it a shake to distress the outside of the spuds – this is what makes the yummy crunchy bits. The enthusiasm with which you shake them is all down to how far cooked they are: if they're softer than you intended or thought at this stage (which happens quite often, even to an old pro), then just give them a soft shake and don't play with them or else they'll fall apart.

Pull the heated tray out of the oven and put it on the hob – I usually do mine across two burners on a medium–high heat. Spoon in 5 tablespoons of your fat and as it melts and starts to smoke, use tongs or a gentle action with a big spoon to gently lift the spuds one by one

from the colander into the tray. You don't want them to be touching, and position any softer ones towards the middle where the heat doesn't penetrate quite as fiercely.

Once you get to the bottom of the colander transfer any smaller pieces that still have shape and form, but abandon anything that looks like mash. Share the last 3 tablespoons of fat between the spuds, making sure that each one gets a little hit on top and then sprinkle over a good amount of sea salt. DON'T touch them, not even a little bit. Just put them in the oven on the top shelf and after around 45 minutes they should look all good and roastie-ish. Use tongs to turn them and pop them back in the oven for another 15–25 minutes until crispy crunchy all over.

NB: If they're cooking a bit erratically, then just take out the ones that are done, keep them in a bowl somewhere warm and put the others back in the oven until they're ready.

Rosemary Oven Crunchies

For 4–6 (see photo, page 121)

1kg spuds (of the red-skinned variety), peeled and cut into 1–2cm dice
3 big sprigs of rosemary, washed and finely chopped
4 tbsp olive oil
S & P

Preheat the oven to 220°C/fan 200°C/Gas 7, and pop two large baking trays in the oven to get hot.

Toss the diced spuds with the rosemary, olive oil and plenty of seasoning. Once the oven is hot take the trays out and share the spuds between them. It's crucial they are spread out in one layer, not too closely packed, else they won't crunch.

Pop the trays in the oven, one above the other. After 10 minutes, take them out and give them a shuffle using a fish slice to make sure you don't leave the crunchy bottoms stuck to the tray. Put them back in the oven, swapping shelves. The top tray should be nicely golden and crisp after 20–25 minutes, so swap the trays round again and the other one won't take long to get to the same place.

Spot-on Mash

For 4 (see photo, page 307)

1.5kg mashing spuds, all of one variety please
1 tsp salt
200ml whole milk, plus a little more if necessary
60g butter
S & P

Peel and cut the spuds according to size: big ones into quarters, medium in half and small stay whole. Put in a pan with the salt, cover with cold water plus about 2cm and pop a lid on. Bring to the boil, then turn down to a simmer for 15–20 minutes until done, which you test by sticking a knife in and lifting the impaled spud above the water level. If it falls off, they're ready. Drain in a colander for a good few minutes to steam-dry and put the spud pan back on a low heat.

Pour the milk into the pan and melt the butter into it. When the spuds have had a good drain, tip them into the dairy and get busy with the masher.

Add more milk in splashes if necessary, working with the masher until a perfectly creamy, smooth mash is achieved. Check the seasoning: salt and pepper are both to be heartily embraced here, and it'll happily take up to 100g of butter, but that's your call – yummier, but approaching artery pile-up.

Home-made Chips
For 3–4 (see photo, page 121)
4 large all-purpose spuds (about
    1kg), like Maris Piper or good
    old King Edwards, scrubbed
    but skin on
2 litres vegetable or sunflower oil
salt (and vinegar)

Slice the spuds into long thin chips, about 1–2cm wide and as long as the spud is.

Heat the oil in a big, wide, deep pan, leaving plenty of space to bubble up when it gets hot. When you think it's up to temperature (at least 5 minutes) drop one chip in – it should sink and fizzle a bit, then float.

Preheat the oven to 140°C/fan 120°C/Gas 1 to keep the done ones warm, and prepare a tray with some kitchen paper for draining the chips.

Carefully lower about half of the chips into the hot oil and cook for 5–7 minutes, stirring occasionally, until golden and crispy. When you're happy with the colour lift them out with a slotted spoon on to the kitchen paper. Immediately season well with salt, then put the tray in the oven, and get on with the next batch.

Malt vinegar is optional but encouraged.

And one random friendly co-carb: How to Cook Rice
A simple, fail-proof way to cook lovely, fluffy long-grain rice.

70g long-grain rice per person
salt

Bring a pan of slightly salted water to the boil – you want plenty of water for the rice to cook in, so scale up your pan size accordingly.

Tip the rice in, give it a good stir and pop a lid on. Cook for 12 minutes then drain into a sieve. Once it's well drained, sit the sieve over the empty pan and run a little cold water over the rice so that you have about 2cm in the bottom of the pan. Put the pan back on the hob over a very low heat, with the sieve sitting on top of it. Cover with a lid and leave on the lowest heat possible to steam gently for another 5 minutes minimum, or until you need it – it'll happily just hang like this for half an hour.

Veg Appendix

A Cabbage for all Seasons

Flash-fried Sesame Spring Greens

For 2–4 as a side, depending on how many other dishes you're doing (see photo, page 196)

1 tbsp groundnut oil
2 tbsp sesame seeds
1 garlic clove, finely sliced
½ red chilli, finely chopped
1 head of spring greens (about 500g), quartered, cored and shredded into ribbons 2–3cm wide
light soy sauce
1 tbsp sesame oil

Heat the groundnut oil in a wide frying pan or wok, and toast the sesame seeds until golden. Add the garlic and chilli, and fry for a minute or so until fragrant.

Scatter in the greens and toss and fry for a few minutes, until vibrant and crunchy. Finish with the soy sauce and sesame oil and tuck in immediately.

....

Summer Slaw

Makes a big bowlful; for 6–8 as a side

1 good-sized ruby grapefruit (or 2 small ones)
250g asparagus (about 8 large spears)
1 celery stick, sliced very thinly
1 head of chicory, shredded (use red chicory if you see it)
½ small head of Chinese leaf, finely shredded
small handful of flat-leaf parsley, roughly chopped
small handful of mint, roughly chopped, plus a few small leaves

2 tbsp extra virgin olive oil
1 tbsp white balsamic vinegar or white wine vinegar
50g pumpkin seeds, toasted
50g sunflower seeds, toasted
S & P

Cut the top and bottom off the grapefruit so that it sits flat, then in downward slices cut off the peel. Holding it over a mixing bowl, cut between the segments so that they fall, pith-free, into the bowl. Give what's left a good squeeze into a smaller bowl, and pour any juice from the segments in with the rest of the juice, leaving the segments behind.

Snap off and chuck away the woody ends of the asparagus, then use a peeler to shave the rest of the stalks into thin ribbons, letting them fall into the mixing bowl too – don't worry too much about the tip as that's pretty tender as is. Chuck the celery, chicory, Chinese leaf and herbs into the mixing bowl too.

Use a fork to lightly beat the olive oil and vinegar into the grapefruit juice along with some salt and pepper and lightly dress the salad – don't overdo it, you just need enough to coat everything. Scatter over the seeds and a few extra mint leaves, as mint is the definitive taste of summer.

....

Autumnal Savoy & Bacon

For 6 as a side (see photo, page 275)

knob of butter
slug of oil
120g lardons, preferably smoked
1 garlic clove, chopped
1 medium Savoy cabbage, quartered, cored, leaves roughly chopped
150ml water (or chicken stock if you happen to have it)
3–4 tbsp double cream or crème fraîche
2 tsp mustard, ideally half Dijon, half wholegrain
S & P

Heat the butter and oil in a large, wide pan and fry the lardons over a medium–high heat until really golden and crispy, before stirring in the chopped garlic. Only cook the garlic for a minute or so – you don't want it to pick up much colour – then lob in the cabbage. Give it all a good stir then pour in the water or stock, season and stick a lid on. Cook for 5ish minutes, giving it the odd shuffle, until the cabbage is just cooked, then take the lid off and stir in the cream or crème fraîche, mustard and more seasoning if necessary. Bring back to the boil before serving.

....

Spiced Winter Braised Red Cabbage

For 6–8 as a side (see photo, page 232)

knob of butter
2 tbsp light olive oil or vegetable oil
1 large onion, finely sliced
a thumb (about 20g) of fresh ginger, unpeeled, knobbly bits trimmed and grated using the large holes of a grater
1 red cabbage (about 1.5kg), cored and sliced 2cm thick

½ tsp ground allspice
4 tbsp red wine vinegar
4 tbsp soft light brown sugar
4–5 eating apples, peeled,
    cored and cut into wedges
    or chunks
S & P

Choose a big heavy-bottomed pan or casserole dish and stick it on a medium–high heat to warm up. Melt the butter in the oil and sweat the onion in it until soft – about 5 minutes.

Once the onion starts to turn golden, stir in the grated ginger along with the cabbage, allspice, vinegar, sugar and quite a lot of seasoning. Give it all a damn good stir, stick a lid on and once it's heated through, simmer over a low–medium heat for 30 minutes.

Now stir in the apple, put the lid back on and simmer for another 20 minutes. Turn the heat off, leave to sit for 5 minutes, lid on, then check the seasoning and serve.

....

Brassicatastic

Brussels & Chestnuts
For 6 (see photo, page 315)
30g flaked almonds
splash of extra virgin olive oil
knob of butter
1 small onion, sliced
2 garlic cloves, finely chopped
1 tbsp rosemary, finely chopped
500g Brussels sprouts, trimmed,
    any whoppers cut in half
120g vacuum-packed cooked
    chestnuts, roughly chopped
½ glass sweet sherry (the kind
    your granny drinks)
splash of sherry vinegar
S & P

Put a wide, shallow pan over a gentle heat and toast the flaked almonds until golden, then tip them out on to a saucer and stick the pan back on the hob.

Add a 3-second pour of olive oil (about 3 tablespoons) to the pan, melt the butter in it then lob in the onion. Cook over a medium heat until softened and just beginning to go golden, then stir though the garlic and rosemary for a few minutes so they get properly aromatic.

Chuck in the sprouts and turn the heat up to high so that they too pick up a little bit of goldenness. Add the chestnuts, give it a stir then pour in the sherry and sherry vinegar and let them both half evaporate before going in with 3 tablespoons (or thereabouts) of water. Give it a bit of a season, pop a lid on and cook over a medium heat for about 5 minutes, giving the pan the odd shake until the sprouts are cooked tenderly with a touch of bite. Whip the lid off. There should be almost no liquid left and if there is any, let it simmer away. Allow to cool for just a minute, then taste for seasoning and finish with the toasted almonds.

....

Cauliflower & Broccoli Cheese
For 2 as a main, or 4–6 as a side
(see photo, page 267)
1 head of broccoli (not massive), cut
    into largish florets
1 small or ½ a large cauliflower, cut
    into largish florets
1 batch of Basic White Sauce
    (see page 369) but made
    with half the milk, i.e. 500ml
200–250g grated cheese (use any
    odd ends from your cheese
    box, but stick to cow's cheese)

big handful of dried breadcrumbs
big handful of grated Parmesan
½ tbsp thyme leaves (optional)

Preheat the oven to 180°C/fan 160°C/Gas 4. Butter a baking dish that's about the right size to hold the veg – you want it to be quite packed and piled, not spread out.

Bring a pan of salted water to a rolling boil. Blanch the broccoli and cauliflower together for about 5–7 minutes until cooked, but still with a bite (you may want to cook it all the way through for smaller folks), then drain thoroughly.

Knock up the white sauce, using only half the amount of milk as we want this to be a thick one. Melt the grated cheese into it, then stir in the veg. Spoon the whole lot into the buttered dish, tipping any sauce left in the pan over the top.

In a little bowl, mix the breadcrumbs with the grated Parmesan (and some fresh thyme leaves too if it's for grown-ups) and scatter all over the top. Bake in the oven for about 25ish minutes, until the top is golden and crispy and the whole thing is bloody irresistible.

....

Artichokes

Artichokes are one of my all-time favourite veg, but they're a bit of a bugger to handle. In their natural state they're prickly and look pretty impenetrable (smart evolutionary survival tactic), and when you do cut them back to their core they oxidise in seconds, turning a most unappealing brown, which is why prepped artichoke hearts need to be immediately immersed in lemon water, to prevent discolouration. For all that, their hearts (and leaves) remain close to mine.

Globe Artichokes Vinaigrette

For 2
2 big, beautiful globe artichokes, about 500g each
1 lemon
salt
House Dressing (see page 367)

Choose a massive pan (big enough to hold both of the artichokes), fill it with water and bring to the boil with a good grab of salt in it.

Squeeze half of the lemon into the water and the other half over your hands – prepping artichokes gives you mucky paws, the lemon helps to act as a barrier. As the water comes to the boil, trim the artichoke stalks at the base so they sit flat on a plate. At the first restaurant I worked at we used to prepare a lot of these, and the chef liked the tips of the base leaves to be squared off with a pair of scissors – he just thought it looked nice and tidy, and I tend to agree.

When the water is boiling, gently drop the artichokes in and rest a plate on top so they are weighted down. Simmer them for 30 minutes then check, though they

usually take about 35–40: they're ready when you tug at one of the leaves at the very bottom and it comes out without much of a struggle. Drain and leave to cool upside down on the draining board until you can comfortably handle them.

To finish preparing them, gently prise open the leaves at the top and keep opening them up until you can see a purple-ish point deep inside. Firmly grab it, give it a wiggle and tug it up – the whole thing should come away as one, revealing the hairy choke below; the final barrier between you and the heart.

Using a teaspoon and firm but sensitive strokes, dig out the hairy choke, which is embedded a little into the heart, so it does take some encouragement. Chuck it away – the only thing it's good for is reminding us that artichokes are closely related to thistles (the other clue being that fantastic purple); you really do want to make sure that there's absolutely none left attached to the heart, as that spoils the sublime experience of heart-eating.

Serve them at room temp, rather than cold, with little bowls or ramekins of dressing on the side and a massive bowl in which to chuck the leaves that have had the goodness sucked out of them.

Artichoke Crisps

I can think of no better nibble to go with a martini – this is definitely one for cocktail hour, though they're also excellent with the Poached Trout on pages 146–7. Once you've made them, they'll last an hour before going soggy.

Makes a bowlful – good for 4
1 lemon, halved
2–3 medium-large globe artichokes
about 500ml plain oil (vegetable or sunflower), for deep-frying
sea salt

First prep your artichoke: prepare a big bowl of cold water and rub half the lemon all over your hands before dropping it into the water; squeeze the juice of the other half straight in. One by one pull off the bottom third of the artichoke leaves, tearing them off toward the stem. A waist will appear about a third of the way up the bulbous bit – use a serrated knife to slice through it. Chuck the top in the bin and now use a small, sharp knife to cut away all of the dark green leaf stubs, as well as the tough outside of the stem, leaving the lighter coloured central core, which is the only bit of the stem that's tender enough to eat.

Once your heart is trimmed down so that all you can see is light green and yellow, the only thing left to do is to remove the choke, i.e. the furry bit in the middle, which is easiest done with a teaspoon. Scrape away at it gently but firmly – you'll know when you've hit the heart underneath it as it's much harder and more solid. Get rid of all the furry stuff, then put your naked heart into the lemony water and do the other ones.

Once your artichokes are prepped, heat the oil in a wide, deep pan set over a medium–high heat.

Slice the artichokes vertically as thinly as you can (a couple of millimetres thick), taking care when it comes to slicing through the stems as they can snap off (and if they do, just slice them up anyway). Pat the pieces in kitchen roll – you needed to have kept them in the water so they didn't oxidise and go black, but oil and water are not friends so give them a quick dry while you wait for the oil to come up to temperature.

Test the oil by dropping in one artichoke slice – it should sink, fizzle and then float. When you're good to go, carefully scatter in half the slices at once and turn the heat down to a solid medium – they'll take about 7 minutes to cook through and go golden brown. Lift out on to kitchen roll with a slotted spoon, season with sea salt, then get the next batch going.

Jewish Garlicky Hearts
aka Carciofi alla giudia
This is a traditional, classic Roman Jewish dish.

Makes 4, which is a starter for 2 on its own, or enough for 4 as part of an antipasti (just add some mozzarella and Parma ham)
4 globe artichokes
5 small garlic cloves
80ml extra virgin olive oil, plus a bit extra for drizzling
4 slices of sourdough bread
lemon pieces
S & P

Prep the artichokes down to the heart as per the method for the artichoke crisps (previous page), but stop before the slicing.

Find yourself a saucepan with a lid and test it can hold the artichokes quite snugly when they are all standing up, stalks in the air – if necessary trim the stalks a bit so that the lid sits properly flat.

Once you're happy with your equipment, season the insides of the artichokes. Peel and smash four of the garlic cloves and press one into each of their hearts. Now carefully put them back in the pan, stalks upwards, and pour in cold water to a depth of 2–3cm. Bring to the boil, then turn the heat down low, pour in the olive oil and stick the lid on, making sure it's sitting flat.

Simmer for 8–10 minutes, until a small sharp knife can be poked into the thickest part of the heart with little resistance, then take the lid off and turn the heat up. Let all the water evaporate and you'll be left with the artichokes frying in the olive oil. By now they will be a bit malleable, so press them down so that there is more of the heart in contact with the bottom of the pan. Continue to keep a watchful eye on them as they fry on both sides, making wonderful crispy bits, for about 4 or 5 minutes.

Meanwhile, attend to the bruschetta. Either on a griddle (ideal) or toaster, toast the bread. When ready, rub it lightly with half a cut garlic clove and drizzle with your best extra virgin.

Lift the artichokes out of the pan when they are beginning to get sticky and the outer leaves are crunchy and golden. Serve them slightly smashed on the bruschetta, with a sprinkling of sea salt and lemon on the side.

Rooty-toot-toot... How to Cook Beetroot (or not)

Steam-roasting Beetroot
Side or starter for 4
500g beetroot, raw and unpeeled
2 tbsp extra virgin olive oil
salt

Preheat the oven to 200°C/fan 180°C/ Gas 6. Give the beetroot a brief scrub under the tap and fit tightly into a roasting tray or ovenproof frying pan. Pour in water to a depth of about 2cm, then pour on the olive oil and a good sprinkling of salt.

Cover the dish tightly with foil and put in the oven on the middle shelf. Small-ish beets will take an hour or a bit less; big muthas up to 2 hours. Test them by sticking a thin knife in – it should go through to the centre with a bit of resistance.

Whip the foil off, lift the beets out and put aside to cool a bit - the trick to peeling them is to do so while they are still a bit warm – the skin just kind of rubs off with your thumbs.

Beetroot, Parsley & Sherry Vinegar Salad
Side or starter for 4
(see photo, page 236)
500g steam-roasted beetroot as above, cut into wedges
1 tbsp extra virgin olive oil
big handful of flat-leaf parsley, leaves picked

1 tbsp sherry vinegar (or try with white balsamic)
2 spring onions, chopped
S & P

Just toss it all together and concentrate when you season it. Sooooooo healthy and yummy.

Raw Beetroot & Walnut Mezze

Satisfying for 1 or as part of a group of mezze (see photo, page 198)
1 small raw beetroot, peeled and grated on big holes of a grater (wear latex/rubber gloves if you want to avoid finger staining)
80g Greek yoghurt
35g walnuts, chopped
squeeze of lemon juice, to taste
S & P

Mix the beetroot well with the yoghurt and nuts, then squeeze on lemon juice to taste, and a decent whack of both salt and pepper

Veg from the Med

Susi's Universal Slow-roast Tomatoes

These are great for brekkie, and they whip a salad into shape no end. They're an easy way to bring a bit of joy to shite tomatoes; slow-roasting intensifies sweetness and flavour, though you get out what you put in, so the better the quality ...
4 toms
pinch of chilli flakes
pinch of dried oregano
1 tbsp golden granulated sugar
1 tbsp red wine vinegar
extra virgin olive oil
S & P

Preheat the oven to 140°C/fan 120°C/Gas 1.

Cut the toms in half through the green bit and sit them on a small baking tray or frying pan, cut-side up. Sprinkle with the chilli, oregano, sugar, vinegar and seasoning and drizzle over some extra virgin. Bake for 1–2 hours, depending on the tomato, and its eventual home, like ...

Slow-roast Tomato & Goats' Cheese Salad

For 2 as a main, 4 as a side (see photo, page 87)
60g rocket
½ cucumber, cut into chunky cubes
1 batch of Susi's Universal Slow-roast Tomatoes (see left)
80g goats' cheese
few thin slices of red onion
couple of splashes of sherry vinegar
extra virgin olive oil, for dressing
S & P

Put the rocket and cucumber in a serving plate or bowl, stick the roasted toms on and around, crumble over the goats' cheese and scatter on the onions. Dress with a good shake of sherry vinegar and a light amount of extra virgin.Season with salt and pepper and the job's a good 'un.

Saracen Stuffed Peppers

For 4 as a main; 8 as a side (see photo, page 166)

3 tbsp extra virgin olive oil, plus extra for drizzling
1 large or 2 small onions, finely chopped
handful of pine nuts, about 25g
140g long-grain rice
½ tbsp dried mint
½ tsp allspice
¾ tsp ground cinnamon
500ml hot light chicken or veg stock
squeeze of lemon
handful of flat-leaf parsley, chopped
4 peppers (a mix of colours works well)
2 large tomatoes, quartered and deseeded
Greek yoghurt, to serve
S & P

Preheat the oven to 190°C/fan 170°C/Gas 5.

In a pan, heat the olive oil and fry the onions with the pine nuts over a medium–high heat for 5–7 minutes until the nuts are golden and the onion has softened.

Add the rice, mint and spices and fry for a minute as you stir, then pour on the hot stock. Put a lid on and bring to the boil before turning down to a steady simmer until the rice is just cooked and all the liquid is absorbed. This takes 12–15 minutes – take the lid off for the last couple of minutes if necessary so any excess can bubble away.

Turn the heat off, then stir in the lemon juice and parsley. Taste and season and taste again.

Slice the peppers in half, straight through the stalks. Scrape out the seeds, leaving the stalks intact, and fill them with the rice. Lay a tomato piece on top of each stuffed pepper, skin-side up.

Sit the peppers in a roasting tray, drizzle them generously with olive oil, cover the tray with foil, and roast for 25 minutes. Whip the foil off and cook for a further 10–12 minutes, until they are nicely browned. Serve with a last splash of good extra virgin olive oil and a blob of yoghurt.

Alternative Roast Med Veg

Ideal with chicken, fish or pork, or just on its own. Med veg usually means the standard triumvirate of courgettes, peppers and aubergines. This version is all the more interesting for branching out a bit.

Serves 6–8 (see photo, page 280)
½ butternut squash (about 500g), unpeeled, washed, seeds scraped out and cut into 3cm cubes
2 red onions, cut into very large dice
1 fennel bulb, trimmed and cut into 8–10 wedges through the root
1 large or 2 small courgettes, sliced into batons about 3cm long
50ml extra virgin olive oil
2 garlic cloves, chopped
2 tbsp rosemary, chopped
150g cherry tomatoes on the vine, cut with scissors into clusters of 3
S & P

Preheat the oven to 200°C/fan 180°C/Gas 6. Put all the veg except the tomatoes into a roasting tray big enough to hold them in one layer, not all piled up. Whack on the olive oil, garlic, rosemary and plenty of salt and pepper and use your hands to give it a damn good roll around so that all of it is well coated in the oil and aromatics.

When the oven is hot, put the tray in and after 30 minutes use a fish slice to upturn the veg and give it all a good shuffle around. Pop the tomato triplets on there too now, and hit them with a scant drizzling of extra virgin olive oil and seasoning, then cook for a further 15 minutes.

Gratin Provençal

Serves 4–6 (see photo, page 297)
3 nice sized, vine-ripened tomatoes
3 peppers
extra virgin olive oil
2 garlic cloves
2 courgettes, sliced 1cm thick and slightly on the bias so you make ovals, not circles
2 banana shallots or 4 regular, sliced into thin rings on a slight bias
1 tbsp thyme leaves, chopped
handful of finely grated Parmesan
S & P

Preheat the oven to 180°C/fan 160°C/Gas 4. Put a small pan of water on the stove, pop a lid on and bring to a rolling boil.

Cut the green spigot out of the tomatoes and lightly slash its bottom with an 'X'. Put a bowl of cold water (iced is ideal) next to the stove. Drop the toms into the boiling water, then after a count of 10 lift them out with a slotted spoon and drop them directly into their cold bath. Once they've cooled down, after just a minute or two, their skins should come away easily. Cut them into quarters, then scoop out and chuck away the seeds so you are left with 12 lovely, naked tomato petals.

Now, do the best job you can to cut the peppers into similar-sized pieces as the tomato petals. Choose an ovenproof dish, about 24 x 18cm, that looks like it will hold all the veg slices snugly. Grease the dish lightly with olive oil, then rub it with a cut garlic clove, before slicing both cloves of garlic thinly.

Put all the veg into a big bowl and free-pour a handsome glug of olive oil in there. Chuck in about three-quarters of the chopped thyme, season with enthusiasm, then toss so that everything is well coated.

Now start making the veg pattern: using one hand as a kind of bookmark to lean the slices against, use the other to pick up alternate pieces of each of the veg (except the garlic, which just gets slotted in now and then) until your dish is tightly packed and you're all out of ingredients – have a look at the photo on page 297; the process is a little bit slow at the get-go but you'll pick up speed soon enough.

Sprinkle on the rest of the thyme, cover the dish with foil and bake in the oven for 1 hour, then whip off the foil, turn up the oven to 220°C/fan 200°C/Gas 7, scatter the Parmesan all over and bake until golden and glorious – anywhere between another 5 and 15 minutes depending on your veg and your oven.

When you serve it up, make sure you hit each serving with a bit of the delicious veg juice that's accumulated at the bottom.

Going Underground

Carrot 'Soufflé'

This recipe came to me via my friend Tash's American mum. It was a way to get her third husband to eat some veg with his dinner. Hilariously, the original recipe had six times the amount of butter and four times the sugar than this, so I'm not really sure how much good it would have done the old boy anyway. It's a soufflé in the loosest possible way: puffed up and eggy, but unsophisticated in its moreishness.

For 6 as a side
8 or 9 biggish carrots (to make 750g once mashed), peeled and cut into chunks
100g butter, melted
35g plain flour
1½ tsp baking powder
1 tsp ground coriander
handful of fresh coriander, finely chopped
2 tbsp sugar (optional but could be the reason it's quite so moreish)
4 eggs, beaten
S & P

Put the carrot chunks in a saucepan and cover with cold water. Bring to the boil with a good pinch of salt, then simmer with a lid on for 30–40 minutes until properly soft. Drain and leave to steam-dry for a few minutes, then tip back into the pan and gently cook out any remaining moisture for 5ish minutes.

Preheat the oven to 190°C/fan 170°C/Gas 5. Move the cooked carrots to a food processor and whizz to a purée. Add the melted butter, flour, baking powder, ground and fresh coriander, sugar and some seasoning and pulse briefly to combine. Now pour in the beaten eggs and give it a final blast to incorporate.

Butter a high-sided baking dish that will hold your mix and allow it to rise by 3–4cm without going over the top. Tip in the carrot mush and bake for 35–40 minutes. Have a look at the top after 25 minutes and if it's going a bit dark, then cover loosely with foil.

It's done when the top has formed a nice crust, is slightly springy to touch, and when a skewer stuck into the centre comes out mostly clean, but not entirely. Weirdly yummy.

Orange & Caraway Roast Parsnips

Perfect side for 4
(see photo, page 270)
800g parsnips, peeled
3 tbsp olive oil
zest of 1 orange
½ tsp caraway seeds
1 tbsp clear honey
S & P

Preheat the oven to 200°C/fan 180°C/Gas 6. Take care how you cut the parsnips: you want to end up with equal-sized pieces roughly the size of your index finger. Essentially, and it does of course depend on your parsnip, cut the bottom third off as a stand-alone. Half what's left on both axes, and cut into wedges so they are roughly the size of the bottom third.

Put the parsnips into a roasting tray big enough so that they won't be too crowded. Pour on the olive oil, scatter over the orange zest and caraway seeds, drizzle with honey and season well. Give it all a good roll around then roast for 20 minutes. Use a fish slice to flip them over before popping them back in and cooking for another 10–15 minutes. They should be soft and squidgy with enticing crunchy bits at the edges.

How to Blanch Green Veg

There's a basic rule that applies to cooking veg in water: anything that grows below the ground you start in cold, and anything that grows above you start from boiling. Green veg grow above ground level almost without exception (I can't think of one, but some clever clogs out there will). It's about the plant photosynthesising to make chlorophyll, which is what makes them green. For this it needs sun, so no earth-dwellers apply.

What I really am talking about here is the art of cooking your chosen veg to the point to which it's cooked but still retaining bite, colour, flavour and, most importantly, nutrients. This applies to veg like mangetout, French beans, broad beans, runner beans, sugar snap peas, asparagus, as well as some of the cabbages like Hispi (aka sweetheart), spring greens, Savoy and white cabbage and broccoli.

Veg that blanching does not apply to are courgettes (they're 90% water anyway, so you'd rarely want to boil them), kale (wonderful, but intrinsically tough so needs more than just a quick blanch) and spinach, which can be blanched but then requires cooling and then squeezing out the water.

The method for blanching is simple but frequently ignored, leading to off-colour, overcooked, sad examples of the species:

- Choose your saucepan – it needs to be big enough so that the veg will not be over-crowded, which skews the cooking time.
- Over the highest heat, bring the water to a rolling boil with a lid on (to save energy).
- Season with a 5-finger pinch of salt if you're using a medium saucepan (scale up accordingly).
- Drop the veg in (no lid) and put a colander in the sink.
- As soon as the water has come back to the boil, drain immediately.
- Run cold water over the veg for a few seconds, directing it all over them with your hand – the aim here isn't to cool it down but just to remove a portion of the heat so that it doesn't keep cooking; it also helps to retain colour.
- Turn the tap off and leave to drain for a minute or two.
- Seasoning (salt and pepper) is encouraged but not obligatory; extra virgin olive oil or butter are to be considered on a case-by-case basis.

Garlic Sautéed Spinach
For 2 (see photo, page 99)
1 tbsp olive oil
300g spinach, baby or whole leaf
1 garlic clove, chopped
squeeze of lemon juice
S & P

Heat a wide pan with the tablespoon of olive oil until it's bloody hot. Have your spinach on hand and fry the garlic for less than a minute until golden. Throw the spinach in, a handful at a time and in quick succession, stirring all the time with tongs or a spoon. The whole lot should wilt down in a minute or two – the heat of the pan causes the water in the leaves to evaporate away almost instantly. Season with salt, pepper and a squeeze of lemon juice then lift out of the pan using tongs no more than 3 minutes after it arrived there.

Appendix 4
The Final Few

Dressings & Sauces

House Dressing

It's always seemed odd to me that restaurants have 'house wines', as they're not really houses and nobody lives there. This, therefore, is a true 'house dressing', as I make it at home, which is where we sleep and therefore qualifies as a house. Mustardy, garlicky and zingy – it's everything a dressing should be.

Makes a small jam jar
4 tbsp red wine vinegar
½ tsp clear honey
2 tsp Dijon mustard
1 garlic clove, finely chopped
good squeeze of lemon juice
80ml extra virgin olive oil
S & P (plenty of)

Pour the vinegar into a jam jar, add the honey, mustard, garlic, lemon juice and seasoning. Put the lid on and shake well for a minute before pouring on the olive oil. Shake again, taste for seasoning and leave at room temperature to settle down in flavour. It's better after an hour or overnight and will keep for a week or two.

Caesar Dressing
(plus a bonus recipe for Caesar salad)
Amazingly good with chips. And steak. And cos lettuce. All together please.

Makes 1 regular jam jar, or enough for about 8 main course portions of salad; the salad is enough for 2 (see photo, page 121)

For the dressing:
2 egg yolks
2 tbsp lemon juice
1 garlic clove, finely chopped
20g anchovy fillets (if they're salted, rinse before using)
15g Parmesan, chopped into smallish pieces
175ml sunflower oil
75ml extra virgin olive oil
handful of basil leaves
S & P

For the salad:
2 slices stale white bread, cut into bite-sized pieces
olive oil
1 large cos lettuce or 2 heads of Romaine or 4 Little Gem, cut into wide ribbons
20g Parmesan, finely grated
6 anchovy fillets

To make the dressing, whizz the egg yolks in a food processor with the lemon juice, garlic, anchovy fillets and Parmesan for a couple of minutes. Slowly drizzle in the sunflower oil, followed by 2 tablespoons of lukewarm water to loosen it up. Now go in with the extra virgin and once it's all

incorporated, chuck in the basil leaves and some seasoning and give it a final spin for just a couple of seconds.

Taste. More salt, pepper or lemon juice may be required according to personal preference, but the punch of the big guns (garlic, anchovy and Parmesan) will take a while to deliver so leave it a bit before going in too heavy with the seasoning. The dressing is good for a week in the fridge.

And to make the Caesar salad:
Preheat the oven to 180°C/fan 160°C/Gas 4. Spread the bread chunks out on a baking tray, season, drizzle on a little olive oil and bake in the oven for 12–15 minutes until golden.

Toss the croutons in a big bowl with your lettuce of choice and a quarter of the dressing, making sure that the dressing is properly coating the leaves – hands are the best tool for this.

Move the lettuce to plates or a serving bowl, scatter the dressed croutons on top, then the grated Parmesan. Finally, lay a few anchovy fillets on there too – some people prefer the white, escabeche ones for the top, but personally I'd go with good-quality brown.

Pan-Asian Dressing
Makes a small but potent amount
juice of 3 limes
1 tbsp caster sugar
1 tbsp fish sauce
1 tbsp light soy sauce
½ chilli, deseeded and finely chopped

Chuck it all in a jam jar and give it a good shake. Best used in a day or two.

Pesto

Makes a small jam jar

30g pine nuts
30g Parmesan, cut into rough
    chunks
1 smallish garlic clove, finely
    chopped
45g basil, leaves only
3 tbsp good extra virgin olive oil,
    plus more to cover (if storing)
S & P

Preheat the oven on to 180°C/fan
160°C/Gas 4. Chuck the pine nuts
on to an ovenproof frying pan or
small baking tray, pop it in the oven,
and keep checking on them, giving
them a shuffle every 5 minutes or
so until they are golden brown.

Drop the Parmesan, garlic
and toasted pine nuts into a food
processor and pulse for a few
seconds to roughly combine. Now
chuck in the basil and pulse again
until all the leaves are chopped up
quite small, but it's nothing like a
purée. Use a spatula to scrape it
into a little bowl, stir in the extra
virgin olive oil so that all the bits are
coated and then season with a bit of
salt and quite a lot of pepper. Taste,
and once you're happy, you've got
two options: eat now or save for later.

To use it straight away, stir in
another 2 tablespoons of extra virgin
to make it a little more liquidy. If you
want to store it, spoon it all quite
carefully into a small jam jar, trying
to avoid dribbling bits down the
inside. Give the bottom of the jar
a brief but firm bang on the table
to knock out any air bubbles, then
pour on a little more extra virgin
to make a thin layer between the
solids and the air. This will help
preserve it in the fridge for a
couple of weeks.

Salsa Verde

*Makes a small bowl or jam jar –
enough for 4 with a starter
or 2 greedies with a main
(see photo, page 114)*

1 garlic clove
2 anchovy fillets
1 tbsp capers, well rinsed if salted
    (which I think are the best)
3 cornichons
big handful of flat-leaf parsley, leaves
    picked
big handful of basil, leaves picked
big handful of mint, leaves picked
1 tsp Dijon mustard
juice of ½ lemon
1 tbsp red wine vinegar
3 tbsp extra virgin olive oil
S & P

Put the garlic clove on the middle of
your board and chop it pretty finely
with a big knife (you'll be appreciative
of its size later). Don't be tempted by
the food processor – it just is no good
for this one. Next, lay the anchovy
fillets, capers and cornichons on top
of the garlic and chop those down to
small pieces too. The third layer is all
the picked herbs: go at them until they
too are finely chopped.

Scoop everything into a bowl then
stir in the mustard, lemon juice and
vinegar so that it's all well combined.
Finally pour on the extra virgin:
you don't want it to emulsify, so do
this gently – it should be a beautiful
thing with pools of green oil. Season
heavily with pepper but go lighter
on the salt because of the anchovies
and capers.

Mayonnaise

*Your mayo is only as good as
the oil you use.*

Makes 1 regular jam jar

2 egg yolks
1 tsp Dijon mustard
1 handsome garlic clove, chopped
    tiny or grated on a microplane
juice of ½ lemon
300ml oil (for grown-ups I'd do
    150ml extra virgin and 150ml
    plain sunflower or vegetable; for
    kids go for pretty much all plain
    oil, with just a splash of extra
    virgin olive oil to finish)
S & P

Put the egg yolks, mustard, garlic
and lemon juice into a food
processor and whizz for a couple
of minutes until pale and frothy –
I find tipping it up does a better job
of mixing this quite small volume.
As it's all spinning round, very
slowly drizzle in all of the plain
oil (half if you're making the kids'
version), then sit it back down flat
and add a tablespoon of warm water
to loosen it up a little. Now, oh-so-
gently, go in with the extra virgin
(or remaining half of plain) and
once it's all incorporated turn it
off. Season with thought before
giving it a final whizz for a second
to get it all mixed in, then taste again
– it could need more salt or lemon
juice depending on your taste.
As this is made with fresh eggs
I'd give it no more than a week
in the fridge.

Basic White Sauce/ Béchamel/Cheese Sauce

Béchamel is the French version of white sauce, made with infused milk, which undoubtedly makes it more tasty. But the reality is it's not necessary to infuse the milk for quite a lot of dishes where a simple white sauce is called for. Béchamel is worth it for Bread Sauce and any occasion where the gentle flavours in the milk won't be trodden on, but in dishes like lasagne or cauliflower cheese, the mild back-note of infused shallot, bay leaf and peppercorns will undoubtedly be overpowered by the more robust players, so just leave it out. Then there's béchamel with cheese, also known as cheese sauce!

Makes just over 1 litre

For a basic white sauce:
75g butter
75g plain flour
1 litre whole milk
S & P

To make it into a proper béchamel:
1 garlic clove, peeled and smashed
    with the side of a knife
2 bay laves
1 shallot or small onion, roughly sliced
1 tbsp peppercorns
1 clove (optional)

To make the quantum leap to a cheese sauce:
around 300g grated cheese – amount
    varies depending on type of
    cheese. This weight is based
    on a decent but not mega-strong
    Cheddar, Gruyère or mozzarella,
    but for drier, saltier cheeses, like
    Parmesan, aged pecorino and
    mimolette, you'll need about
    100g and a lot less salt

If you're going for béchamel, as opposed to white sauce, then get your milk infusing first: pour it into an upright (as opposed to wide) saucepan and drop in the garlic, bay leaves, onion, peppercorns and clove, if you dig it. Bring slowly up to a steaming point and keep it there for 5 minutes to properly infuse.

The base for all three of these sibling sauces is a roux. In a second pan, melt the butter and once fizzling (but not browning), stir in the flour using a wooden spoon. Lower the heat right down and keep stirring the roux so that the floury taste is cooked out before the milk goes in – it takes just a couple of minutes.

Now, if you're going for the basic white sauce, pour about a quarter of the cold milk on to the roux (if you're going for the béchamel, pour the infused milk through a sieve), turn up the heat to medium–high and beat well with your spoon until it becomes a smooth, thick white paste. Switch your instrument of choice to a whisk and go in with another quarter of the milk. Whisk thoroughly and once all is smooth again in pan-land, turn the heat right up and repeat with the third and then final batches of milk, whisking continuously. Bring the

sauce to a gentle simmer for about 3–5 minutes, stirring regularly as it thickens, then turn off the heat and season with salt and pepper.

If you're making the cheese sauce, the cheese gets stirred in now, in which case hold back on the salt a bit. Any kind of white sauce is pretty robust, and will last for a good few days in the fridge, taking on a consistency akin to wallpaper paste.

15-minute Tomato Sauce

Makes about 500g
1 red onion, peeled
2 garlic cloves
3 tbsp olive oil
½ tsp chilli flakes
1 tbsp tomato purée
1 x 400g tin chopped plum tomatoes
2 bay leaves
½ tsp dried oregano
squirt of ketchup
S & P

If you have a food processor, quarter the onion and chuck that in along with the garlic. If you don't, roughly chop them by hand (and this may become a 20-minute sauce).

Heat a wide pan with the oil and fry the onion and garlic over a high heat for a few minutes, until going golden. Sprinkle in the chilli flakes and stir for a couple of minutes before adding the tomato purée. Coat the onions well in the purée as you carry on cooking for a couple of minutes. Pour in the tin of toms, chucking in the bay leaves and oregano too, along with a slug of ketchup and some seasoning. Bring up to a simmer and let it bubble away for about 5 minutes if it's for pasta, a little longer if it's pizza-bound so it can thicken up.

Houmous

Makes a jam jar or little bowlful

1 x 400g tin chickpeas
1 large or 2 small garlic cloves,
    finely chopped
2 tbsp tahini
2 tbsp lemon juice, plus more to taste
50ml olive oil, plus a bit of extra
    virgin to finish
S & P

Tip the chickpeas plus their liquid into a small saucepan and bring to the boil, then turn down the heat and simmer gently for 5–7 minutes, until they are warmed through. Turn the heat off and leave to cool for a few minutes.

Put the garlic, tahini and half the lemon juice into a food processor, along with a good pinch of salt and some pepper. Use a slotted spoon to lift in the chickpeas and half their water and blitz till smooth (you may need to add more of the liquid to get it to a lovely consistency – it depends on the chickpeas). As she's still spinning, drizzle in the olive oil and remaining lemon juice, then scrape it all into a bowl and taste for seasoning: salt, pepper and lemon juice, as you like. Finish by half stirring in a good splash of extra virgin, leaving a little to pool on top.

Pastries

Shortcrust Pastry
(and how to blind bake a tart case)

Makes enough for three 22cm fluted tart tins or two biggies (28–30cm) – and freezable for up to 3 months

600g plain flour, plus extra for
    rolling out

2 tsp salt
2 tsp caster sugar
300g butter, cold and cubed
3 eggs, plus 1 egg white, for glazing

In a food processor, whizz together the flour, salt and sugar for just a minute to aerate it before dropping the butter down the chute, piece by piece.

Beat the eggs with 2 tablespoons of water and slowly pour this down the chute as the machine's spinning, but stop as soon as a dough has formed. Scrape it on to a floured surface and just bring it together – you don't really want to work it at all. Cut it in half or into thirds, depending on the size of your tart tin, wrap each piece in cling film and put in the fridge or freezer to rest and firm up – an hour in the fridge or a swift half hour in the freezer (or just leave in the freezer for next time).

When you're ready to go, lightly dust your surface with flour and roll out the pastry to about 2–3mm thick. Roll it up around your rolling pin then drape it over the tart case to line it, making sure that you get into the corners.

Cut off the excess with a small sharp knife and pop the tin back in the fridge or freezer for another rest.

The last stage is the blind baking. Preheat the oven to 180°C/fan 160°C/Gas 4. Prick the pastry base all over with a fork. Scrunch up a big piece of greaseproof paper and cover the pastry with it. Fill it with baking beans to weigh it down (if you don't have ceramic ones, these can be any dried pulse) and bake for 20 minutes, then carefully lift out the greaseproof paper and beans and bake the case for a further 5 minutes, until golden brown.

Finally, lightly whisk the egg white until it's just frothy, brush that all over the pastry and pop it back in the oven for a final 3–5 minutes – just long enough for the white to go hard and shiny, which will stop your pastry from going soggy once it's loaded up with filling.

Sweet Pastry

Makes enough for two 24cm tart rings

350g plain flour, plus extra for
    rolling out
120g icing sugar
250g butter, cold and cubed
1 egg, plus 1 egg white, for glazing

In a food processor, whizz together the flour and sugar for a few seconds to aerate, then drop the butter down the chute piece by piece.

As soon as the butter is all incorporated, crack in the egg, and spin for just a moment more. Scrape it into a piece of cling film, then once it's all wrapped up, stick it in the fridge or freezer to have a bit of a rest and firm up – an hour in the fridge or a swift half hour in the freezer.

After resting it'll be in a good state to work with. Depending on your preference, you can either roll it out on a lightly floured surface, or grate it on the large holes of the grater and press it into the tart ring with your fingertips (I do either, depending on my mood – they work just as well).

Once your tart case is beautifully lined, pop it back in the fridge to firm up again, about half an hour (or in the freezer for 10 minutes). Finally, follow the blind baking instructions for shortcrust pastry (see opposite).

Preserves

Raspberry Jam

This recipe makes perfectly delicious raspberry jam. In my recipe I reduce the jam quite a lot, which helps it set (other recipes use the addition of pectin to help with the setting but I find I get a great result without it).

Makes 1 litre, so 3–4 jars
1kg caster sugar
1kg raspberries

Preheat the oven on to 110°C/fan 90°C/Gas ¼. Find yourself 3–4 standard-sized (250ml) jam jars (with lids that fit, obviously), and stick a couple of saucers in the freezer for testing later.

Put the sugar in a bowl in the oven to warm up and put the jars and lids in the oven on a baking tray to sterilise.

Tip the raspberries into a very large pan over a medium heat and run a masher over them. Let them come to a busy boil before adding the hot sugar, then bring back to the boil. Hold at a busy simmer for 10–12 minutes, skimming regularly and stirring often as it darkens and thickens.

When you feel it's getting sticky and jammy there are a couple of tests to check it's at the right consistency to set. Firstly, drop some off the end of a teaspoon on to one of the chilled saucers: if it falls in a steady stream, cook it down more; if it falls off in blobs, that's a 'good-to-go'. Once you have blobs, give them a bit of a gentle push with your finger – what you're looking for is a formed skin that wrinkles as it's shoved. If it's not there, let it bubble down a bit more, then try again on the other chilled saucer. When you've scored on both counts don't hang around, get it straight into the hot jars and seal with the lids immediately.

Plum Jam

And here's the theory for stoned fruit.

Makes about 1 litre, so 4ish jars
700g caster sugar
1kg plums, halved and stoned

Preheat the oven on to 110°C/fan 90°C/Gas ¼. Find yourself 4 standard-sized jars (with lids that fit, obviously), and stick a couple of saucers in the freezer for testing your jam later.

Put the sugar in a bowl in the oven to warm up and put the jars and lids in the oven on a baking tray to sterilise. Cook the plums in 200ml of water for about 15–20 minutes, uncovered, until their skins are loosening and the plums are starting to break down, before adding the heated sugar.

Bring back to the boil, then let it simmer busily for 10–12 minutes, skimming regularly and stirring often as it darkens and thickens. Test in the same way as described for the raspberry jam, left.

Granny Annie's Dark Chunky Marmalade

There's a small window for buying Seville oranges. Look out for them just after Christmas until early February. Granny Annie says don't upscale the recipe as it never works as well – just make a second batch if you really need that much marmalade in your life. Annie isn't actually my granny, but a cousin of some sort on my mum's side. That doesn't reflect how close we are, and what with small daughter being distinctively lacking in grandparents on my side, we both feel it's an appropriate title. I'm sure my mum would wholeheartedly approve – she was Annie's godmother and loved her dearly.

Makes about 3 litres (7–9 jars)
1.5kg Seville oranges
2 lemons
2.7kg granulated sugar
1 tbsp black treacle
You will also need:
1 piece of muslin, about 50cm square (doubled over if it's the very flimsy kind)
waxed paper or greaseproof paper, cut into circles to fit inside the jars

Scrub the oranges and lemons under warm water and pick off the green stalk at the top.

Choose your marmalade-making saucepan. It needs to be pretty big, about a 7–8-litre capacity to allow for bubbling up, then drape the piece of muslin over the top of it.

Cut the oranges and lemons in half around the equator, as you would for juicing, and squeeze them into the pan through the muslin.

Now find yourself a shallow-bowled dessert spoon – you're going to use it for digging, so preferably one with a slightly pointy end. Holding a half orange in one hand and the spoon in the other, dig out all the pith, pulp and membrane until the inside of the fruit is smooth and white, and let this fall into the muslin. Do the same with the other oranges and lemons.

Twist up the muslin so that all of the gubbins is inside it and tie it to the pan handle – loosely enough that it sits on the bottom of the pan but tightly enough that it won't unravel.

Then use a really sharp knife to slice the rind of the oranges and lemons into thin-ish matchsticks and tip them into the pan.

Pour in 3.4 litres of cold water, then Annie always leaves it for an overnight soak and soften at this stage (though when prodded she admitted that it was wasn't obligatory, it was just to spread the work over two days).

Whenever you're ready, pop a couple of saucers in the fridge for testing later, and bring the contents of the pan to the boil, then turn down to a busy simmer. You need it to reduce by around a third over about 2 hours, so if it's happening either too fast or too slowly, just adjust the heat. Don't rush this step as once you add the sugar the skins will toughen, so it's crucial that they are tender

enough before moving on.

Still working on the heat, lift the muslin bag out of the liquid, then use a slotted spoon to squeeze the life out of it against the side of the pan, scraping the jelly-like goo off the muslin with a spoon and dropping it back into the pan. This step is vital as it's where most of the pectin comes from that will set your

marmalade, so don't skimp on the muscle – it may take a good 5 minutes (it's surprisingly satisfying, not to mention beautiful, watching it ooze through the pores of the fabric). Once you've ditched the contents you can give the muslin a good rinse, wash it in the machine and use again next year.

Pour the sugar and treacle into the pan and stir until it's all dissolved – feel the bottom of the pan with your spoon for any granular bits and don't go on to the next step until you are sure that ALL of the sugar has melted. Now turn the heat up and bring to an impressive rolling boil – be careful as it will rise up the pan in a Vesuvian way, and the contents will be about as hot too! From when it's at the ferociously bubbling molten lava stage give it 20 minutes with no skimming, but stir occasionally so the pieces of orange don't catch on the bottom. During this time it will rise right up the pan, doubling in size,

and if you've got a sugar thermometer you want it to hit the 'jam' mark, which is 105°C.

Meanwhile, heat the oven to 140°C/fan 120°C/Gas 1. Put your jam jars and lids in the oven (bottom oven on the Aga says Annie) for 15 minutes or so – you need them to be a bit too hot to handle when the marmalade goes in.

Get a saucer out of the fridge and drip half a teaspoon of marmalade on to it. Let it cool for less than a minute then push your finger into the little pool and lift it up about a centimetre: this is all about checking that it's at the right viscosity for setting. What you're looking for is a wrinkling on the surface as you push your finger into it then lift your finger up a centimetre – the marmalade should stay in contact with your finger.

From the point when it's had the 20 minutes of hard boiling, check it for these signs every couple of minutes on a new bit of cold saucer – it will happen pretty quickly, but can take up to half an hour of boiling.

Once you're happy, take it off the heat, and leave to cool for about 20 minutes, using this time to give it a good careful skim. The marmalade needs to firm up a bit before you put it in the jars so that the pieces of orange will be suspended, as opposed to sinking to the bottom.

Give it a quick stir and then ladle the marmalade into a jug – much easier for tidy pouring. I suggest doing one jar first and leaving for a minute or two to see how she settles. When you're happy with your orange dispersion, fill the jars right up to the top so there's minimal space for air in there. Immediately pop the wax paper circles right on to the surface of the marmalade to prevent contact with the outside world (air = bugs = mouldy marmalade). Leave to cool completely with the lids off, preferably overnight, and then screw the lids on tight. The marmalade's good to go straight away, but hide those for later in a cool, dark place.

Stocks: Chicken, Fish & Veg

These are all designed to make about double what you need right now, so that you can freeze half for next time.

Chicken Stock

Makes 1.5–2 litres, depending on how far you choose to reduce it
1kg chicken bones/wings/carcass
2 medium onions (or 1 and a leek), 2 large carrots and 2 celery sticks, unpeeled and halved (all 3 is ideal but any 2 will do)
1 garlic bulb, halved through the equator
2 bay leaves
a few peppercorns if you have them to hand
handful of parsley stalks (which is why you should always keep them once you've used the leaves – they last for ages in the fridge till the next stock-making day)
250ml white wine (only for the brown stock version)

There are essentially two different ways to make chicken stock: blonde or brown. To make the simpler version, the blonde one (haha), just put the chicken bones/wings (either raw or from a roast dinner) straight into a big saucepan with all the other bits (except for the wine, which is for the brown version only) and cover with cold water.

Bring to the boil with a lid on (it uses less energy), then skim, if necessary, to get rid of any surface scum. Take the lid off and turn down until it's just steaming (no bubbles). Hold it like this for 1 hour or so, then strain and reduce, skimming regularly as the scum comes to the surface. For soup or risotto, I'd reduce it by a third; for gravy more like two-thirds.

To make the brown version, which has a deeper flavour, put the bones and all the vegetables except the parsley stalks into a roasting tray and roast for about 30 minutes, turning them a couple of times until smelling yummy and browning at the edges. Tip everything into a big saucepan and cover with water. Put the roasting tray on the hob on a high heat and pour in the wine. Stir so that the tasty, sticky stuff on the tray is picked up. Once reduced by half, tip the wine and all the tray gubbins into the saucepan. Chuck the parsley stalks in now, and carry on as with the blonde recipe.

Fish Stock

Makes about 2 litres
1kg fish bones (generally avoiding heads, though salmon are good, and definitely no guts or gills)
2 medium onions (or 1 medium onion and 1 leek)
1 large carrot (optional but good)
2 celery sticks (or 1 celery end)
1 garlic bulb, halved horizontally
fennel, if you have any, or a few seeds
2 bay leaves
handful of parsley stalks
few sprigs of thyme
few peppercorns
mushroom stalks, if you have any
...and I tend to float a tomato in there, and sometimes a chilli too if I know the end game, such as a fish stew with a bit of bite to it

Put everything in a big pot and cover with cold water. Bring to the boil with a lid on (it uses less energy), then skim if necessary to take off any surface scum. Take the lid off and turn down until it's just steaming (no bubbles). Keep it like this for 15 minutes, then strain it, being careful not to pour in the small pieces of detritus that are always lurking at the bottom of the pan. Reduce over a high heat by a third, skimming the scuzz off regularly, and your fish stock is now ready for use.

Veg Stock

Makes 2 litres
2 onions
2 carrots
2 celery sticks or one celery end
1 leek
1 garlic bulb, halved through the equator
handful of mushrooms (fresh or

dried)
1 tomato
handful of parsley stalks
2 bay leaves
2 sprigs of rosemary
small bunch of thyme
aromatics: peppercorns, fennel
    seeds (not many), chilli if you
    fancy, coriander seeds

Put everything in a big pot and cover
with cold water. Bring to a boil with
a lid on (it uses less energy), then
skim, if necessary. Take the lid off
and turn down until it's just steaming
(no bubbles). Keep it like this for
30 minutes, then strain and you're
ready for action.

And finally...

Dried Bananas
(an excellent snack)
*This is not the prettiest snack
(possibly the ugliest) but it's very
yummy. And apart from banana
bread it's a good use for bananas
that are turning brown. They keep
very well and curiously, are even
better after a couple of days ... if
they last that long! Delilah's fave,
and I remember loving them too
as a little 'un.*

soft, browning/blackening bananas
    (they need to be pretty near
    the end of their lives), peeled
plain oil (vegetable or sunflower),
    for greasing

Preheat the oven to 120°C/100°C/
Gas ½.
    Cut the bananas in half
crossways, then split each half down
its central axis, and finally cut each
quarter lengthways again so you end
up with eight fingers.
    Lay some greaseproof paper on
a small baking tray and grease very
lightly with oil. Bake for 1–1½ hours
(the riper/blacker the bananas were,
the shorter the cooking time), until
they have firmed up but still give a bit
when you squeeze them. Eat warm or
cool – a truly excellent snack.

A Decent Cuppa

Bag: boil the kettle with no more
water than you need. Choose a
favourite cup and chuck a bag in.
As soon as the kettle boils, pour on
to the bag, but don't overfill – leave a
good half-thumb of space at the top
(an overfilled cup is just annoying).
    Leave for 3 minutes then give
the tea plus bag a quick stir before
lifting the bag out, and once it's
above the water level give it a firm
squeeze against the side to get a last
push out (which I often think is the
one that makes the cuppa).
    Stir in milk, if desired, (always
after brewing, never before) and
lastly check the colour, which should
be rich, not insipid. That really is all
it takes.

Pot: boil the kettle with about half a
cup more water in it than you need,
then, as the kettle is approaching
boiling, tip that amount into the
teapot to warm it through. Swirl it
around gently as the kettle begins
to boil, then empty out the water
and go in with the tea: 2 bags for
2 people, 2–3 bags for 3, and 3 bags
for 4. Or loose leaf as you like it
(and if you're the kind of person
who prefers loose leaf, you don't
need me to tell you how much to
put in).
    Cosy on and leave for 4–5
minutes to infuse, gently giving it
the odd swirl from time.
    With a pot of tea, milk
and sugar should always be
served on the side, but the
same rules of fill level and
colour-checking apply.
    NB: in winter, a dash
of whisky really is
excellent in tea, especially
when accompanied by
a little sugar. This is
almost too nice, so should
be reserved for when you
really need and deserve
it, i.e. after returning
from a long bracing
walk or sitting through
a freezing footie game ...
particularly if you lost
(Go on you Rs!).

INDEX

A

Aga Khan lamb, 278
Ali's authentic aubergine curry, 219
all-day Spanish tortilla, 86
alternative roast med veg, 364
American pancakes, 37
apples
    apple snow, 13
    baked with oats & stem ginger, 248
    blackberry & apple crumble, 246
    rosemary apple sauce, 269
Armagnac truffles, 345
artichokes, globe
    crisps, 361–362
    Jewish garlicky hearts, 362
    vinaigrette, 361
Asian dressing, 367
asparagus
    steamy asparagus, loving Hollandaise, 92–93
    summer slaw, 359
aubergines
    Ali's authentic aubergine curry, 219
    melanzane parmigiana, 52
Auntie Jam's lemony lattice treacle tart, 242
autumnal savoy & bacon, 359
avocados
    avocado & black bean salsa tortillas, 137
    avocado and mint dressing, 200
    ceviche cocktail, 138
    prawn & avocado wrap, 71
    swine topping, 62

B

bacon
    autumnal savoy & bacon, 359
    bacon & egg tart, 154
    black bean & bacon soup, 163
    cardiac carbonara, 128
    chicken BLT sub, 71
    flat-pack cooking the Mexican way, 64
    green/brown lentil & bacon soup, 58
    pimped-up beans, 63
    ribollita, 183
    soup additions, 188
baking, 11
baking powder, 42
banana bread, 19
bananas, dried, 374
beans
    avocado & black bean salsa tortillas, 137
    black bean & bacon soup, 163
    bonfire chilli con carne, 303
    burgers, coleslaw, corn & smoky beans, 228–231
    chicken, chorizo & butterbean stew, 206
    flat-pack cooking the Mexican way, 64
    pimped-up beans, 63
    ribollita, 183
    smoky beans, 230
    white bean & rosemary soup, 165
Béarnaise sauce, 93
béchamel sauce, 369
beef
    beefed-up French onion soup, 178
    bonfire chilli con carne, 303
    burgers, coleslaw, corn & smoky beans, 228–231
    chateaubriand with red wine sauce, 123
    forerib, Yorkies & proper horseradish, 271–272
    pan-seared onglet, 120
    rendang, 197
    sirloin, griddled, 120
    steak preparation, 118–119
    stew with caraway dumplings, 285–286
    testing for doneness, 124–125
    Wellington for Waterloo, 298–300
beefed-up French onion soup, 178
beetroot
    beetroot, parsley & sherry vinegar salad, 362–363
    beetroot, salmon & couscous salad, 80
    beetroot & walnut mezze, 363
    mackerel with raw beetroot & walnut mezze, 199
    steam-roasting, 362
beetroot, parsley & sherry vinegar salad, 362–363
beetroot, salmon & couscous salad, 80
beetroot & walnut mezze, 363
better-than-Bird's custard, 249
bicarbonate of soda, 42
biscuits
    gingerbread families, 22
    stained glass window biscuits, 312
bistro salad, 126
black bean & bacon soup, 163
blackberry & apple crumble, 246
blanching green vegetables, 366
blind baking, 370
bloody big bol, 211
bolognese sauce, 211
bonfire chilli con carne, 303
Bootsie's chicken noodle soup, 187
'Brass-up-your-manners-for-Granny' trifle, 251
bread
    bread sauce, 276
    brioche bread & butter pudding, 245
    bun-in-the-oven buns, 192
    croutons, 188
    flat-pack cooking the Mexican way, 64
    golden breadcrumb & herb stuffing, 318
    Irish Kate's oaty soda bread, 34
    Mrs Johnson's cheese pudding, 235
    toast toppers, 60–63
    see also sandwiches
bread & butter pudding, 245
bread sauce, 276
breadcrumb & herb stuffing, 318
bream, steamed in the bag, 108
breast-feeding porridge, 207
brioche bread & butter pudding, 245
British pancakes, 38
British summertime berry pavlova, 329
broccoli: cauliflower & broccoli cheese, 360
Brussels & chestnuts, 360
bubble & squeak, 355–356
bun-in-the-oven buns, 192
burgers, coleslaw, corn & smoky beans, 228–231
burnt Camp rice pudding, 258
butter chicken, 195
butterbeans: chicken, chorizo & butterbean stew, 206
buttercream, vanilla, 32
butterfly cakes, 26
butternut squash
    alternative roast med veg, 364
    tart with red onion & goats' cheese, 151–152

C

cabbage
    autumnal savoy & bacon, 359
    bubble & squeak, 355–356
    Danny's coleslaw, 228
    flash-fried sesame spring greens, 359
    ribollita, 183
    spiced winter braised red cabbage,
      359–360
Caesar dressing, 367
Caesar salad, 367
cakes and bakes
    bun-in-the-oven buns, 192
    butterfly cakes, 26
    Cornish saffron cake, 252
    crunch-topped banana bread, 19
    Florentines, 338
    madeleines, 340
    Mama's meringues, 260
    marshmallow crispies, 20
    never-fail Victoria sponge, 26
    peanutty millionaire's shortbread, 40
    richest chocolate cake in the world,
      332–334
    Samson & Delilah flapjacks, 21
    squashed fly scones, 27
canapes
    avocado & black bean salsa
      tortillas, 137
    chorizo with quail's eggs, 135
    crab on cuke, 137
caraway dumplings, 285–286
carciofi alla giudia, 362
cardiac carbonara, 128
carrots
    Danny's coleslaw, 228
    'soufflé,' 365
cashew nuts, stir fry with pork and sugar
    snaps, 226
cauliflower & broccoli cheese, 360
ceviche cocktail, 138
chateaubriand with red wine sauce, 123
cheese
    barbecue corn on the cob, 231
    butternut, red onion & goats' cheese
      tart, 151–152
    cauliflower & broccoli cheese, 360
    cheese columns, 17
    cheese sauce, 369
    cheesy lucky dip, 239
    Chicago chilli tuna melt, 62

    contemporary nut roast, 281
    macaroni cheese, 223
    melanzane parmigiana, 52
    Mrs Johnson's cheese pudding, 235
    pear, Parma ham & pecorino salad, 140
    pig melba, 62
    salad with integrity & value, 200
    slow-roast tomato & goats' cheese
      salad, 363
    soup additions, 188
    swine topping, 62
cheesy lucky dip, 239
chestnuts
    with Brussels sprouts, 360
    contemporary nut roast, 281
Chicago chilli tuna melt, 62
chicken
    Bootsie's chicken noodle soup, 187
    butter chicken, 195
    chicken, chorizo & butterbean stew,
      206
    chicken BLT sub, 71
    chicken breast with chickpea pilaf, 74
    chicken dinner (the simple way), 274
    chilli chicken kebab, 70
    Chinesey wings, 48
    Lebanese chicken salad, 75
    the lighter side of chicken pie, 215
    not Pot Noodle, 55
    perfect chicken breast, 75
    spatchcock poussins with sweet chilli
      & yoghurt marinade, 131
    testing for doneness, 125
chicken livers, pink parfait and port jelly,
    143
chicken stock, 372–373
chickpeas
    pilaf, 74
    salad with integrity & value, 200
chicory
    steamed bream in the bag, 108
    summer slaw, 359
chilli con carne, 303
chillies
    bonfire chilli con carne, 303
    ceviche cocktail, 138
    Chicago chilli tuna melt, 62
    chicken kebab, 70
    crab & chilli risotto, 149
    grilled pineapple with chilli & rum, 331
    horny chocolate & chilli martinis, 96

    spaghetti with chilli, parsley & garlic,
      129
    spatchcock poussins with sweet chilli
      & yoghurt marinade, 131
    spring prawn dumplings and chilli
      dipping sauce, 145
Chinese sausage rolls, 29
Chinesey chicken wings, 48
chips, 358
chocolate
    15-minute mousse, 337
    Armagnac truffles, 345
    cake, 332–334
    chocolate & chilli martinis, 96
    fudge icing, 30
    peanutty millionaire's shortbread, 40
    tips, 30
    types, 43
    unashamedly 70s chocolate roulade,
      343–344
chocolate & chilli martinis, 96
chorizo
    chicken, chorizo & butterbean stew,
      206
    with quail's eggs, 135
chow-down clam chowder, 168
Christmas dinner, 314–319
Christmas root purée, 317
cidery onions, 220–222
citrus drizzle, 33
clam chowder, 168
cocoa powder, 43
coddled eggs, 354
coleslaw, 228
contemporary nut roast, 281
corn on the cob, 231
Cornish saffron cake, 252
coronation kedgeree, 216
courgettes
    alternative roast med veg, 364
    gratin Provençal, 364–365
    grilled salmon with couscous &
      courgettes, 79
couscous
    beetroot, salmon & couscous salad,
      80
    grilled salmon with couscous &
      courgettes, 79
crab & chilli risotto, 149
crab on cuke, 137
cranberry sauce, 309

cream cheese
    icing, 32
    summer snack, 63
cream of tartar, 42
crème caramel, 335
croquembouche, 295
crumbles, 246
cumin lamb kebab, 70
curry
    Ali's authentic aubergine, 219
    beef rendang, 197
    butter chicken, 195
    pumpkin & coconut, 304
    red lentil dhal, 56
    Thai seafood, 94–95
custard, 249

D

Danny's coleslaw, 228
dauphinois, 102, 356
a decent cuppa, 374
desserts
    see puddings
Doctor's orders stracciatella, 186
dressings
    Caesar, 367
    house, 367
    pan-Asian, 367
dried bananas, 374
drinks
    chocolate & chilli martinis, 96
    a decent cuppa, 374
drunken grape pavlova, 328
dual citizenship pancakes, 37–38
duck: raised game pie, 321–323

E

eggs
    all-day Spanish tortilla, 86
    better-than-Bird's custard, 249
    boiled quail's, 353
    Caesar dressing, 367
    cardiac carbonara, 128
    carrot 'soufflé,' 365
    cheesy lucky dip, 239
    chorizo with quail's eggs, 135
    coddled, 354
    crème caramel, 335
    egg-fried rice with 'everlasting' veg, 46
    hangover eggs, 51
    hard-boiled, 353

    mayonnaise, 368
    Mrs Johnson's cheese pudding, 235
    omelette, 353
    passionate soufflés, 105
    poached, 353
    scrambled, 354
    soft-boiled, 353
    soup additions, 188

F

fennel
    alternative roast med veg, 364
    fennelly sausage pasta, 157
    soup, 172
    steamed bream in the bag, 108
fennelly sausage pasta, 157
'Festival of Light' latkes, 310–311
festive ham, 316
fig and flaked almonds frangipane tart,
    348–351
fish
    beetroot, salmon & couscous salad,
      80
    ceviche cocktail, 138
    Chicago chilli tuna melt, 62
    coronation kedgeree, 216
    kedgeree, 216
    mackerel with raw beetroot & walnut
      mezze, 199
    poached trout with warm potato salad
      & artichoke crisps, 146
    salmon & leek fishcakes, 237–238
    salmon with couscous & courgettes,
      79
    sea bass baked in herbs and salt, 296
    sea bass, lentils & salsa verde, 115
    spicy tuna salad, 81
    steamed bream in the bag, 108
    summer snack, 63
    testing for doneness, 125
    Thai seafood curry, 94–95
    tuna niçoise, 81
    tuna salad, spicy, 81
fish stock, 373
flapjacks, 21
flat-pack cooking the Mexican way, 64
Florentines, 338
flour, 42
frangipane fruit tart, 348–351
French onion soup, 178
frosting, nougat-marshmallow, 33

full-on Christmas dinner, 314–319
full-on veggie noodle stir-fry, 76

G

game pie, 321–323
garlic sautéed spinach, 366
gingerbread families, 22
glittery popcorn tinsel, 313
globe artichoke vinaigrette, 361
goats' cheese
    butternut, red onion & goats' cheese
      tart, 151–152
    slow-roast tomato & goats' cheese
      salad, 363
goose, roast, 314
Granny Annie's dark chunky marmalade,
    371–372
grapefruit: summer slaw, 359
grapes: drunken grape pavlova, 328
gratin Provençal, 364–365
gravy, 273
green veg, blanching, 366
green/brown lentil & bacon soup, 58

H

ham
    cheesy lucky dip, 239
    festive ham, 316
    pear, Parma ham & pecorino salad,
      140
    raised game pie, 321–323
The Hand Game, 124
hangover eggs, 51
hangovers, 49, 51
hard-boiled eggs, 353
harissa
    fennelly sausage pasta, 157
    seared squid, 116
hazelnut-crusted rack of lamb & f**k me
    dauphinois, 102
herbs
    golden breadcrumb & herb stuffing,
      318
    Puy lentil & herb salad, 59
    salsa verde, 368
    sea bass baked in herbs and salt, 296
    soup additions, 188
Hollandaise sauce, 92–93
horny chocolate & chilli martinis, 96
horseradish sauce, 271
house dressing, 367

I

icings
  chocolate fudge icing, 30
  citrus drizzle, 33
  cream cheese icing, 32
  nougat-marshmallow frosting, 33
  vanilla buttercream, 32
Irish Kate's oaty soda bread, 34

J

jacket potatoes, 355
jam
  plum, 371
  raspberry, 370–371
  tarts, 24
jam-jar coddled eggs, 354
jelly
  mango, 257
  port, 143
Jerusalem artichoke soup, 177
Jewish garlicky hearts, 362
juice, for hangovers, 51

K

kebabs
  chilli chicken, 70
  cumin lamb, 70
  lemongrass prawn, 70
kedgeree, 216
key lime pie, 346

L

lamb
  Aga Khan lamb, 278
  cumin lamb kebab, 70
  hazelnut-crusted rack of lamb & f**k
    me dauphinois, 102
  lamb, prune & pearl barley casserole,
    205
  lamb, yoghurt & herb pitta, 71
  shepherd's pie, 233–234
  testing for doneness, 125
lambs gamboling in fields of barley, 205
lasagne as you like it, 212
latkes, 310–311
leaf-free grilled tuna niçoise, 81
Lebanese chicken salad, 75
leeks
  leek & potato soup, 176
  salmon & leek fishcakes, 237–238
  Vichyssoise, 176

lemon curd tarts, 24
lemongrass prawn kebab, 70
lemons
  citrus drizzle, 33
  Sussex pond pudding, 255–256
lentils
  Ali's authentic aubergine curry, 219
  green/brown lentil & bacon soup, 58
  lentil herb salad, 84
  pork chop with lentils, pears & ginger,
    82–84
  Puy lentil & herb salad, 59
  red lentil dhal, 56
  sea bass with lentils & salsa verde, 115
lettuce
  Caesar salad, 367
  see also salads
the lighter side of chicken pie, 215
limes
  citrus drizzle, 33
  key lime pie, 346
  pan-Asian dressing, 367
lucky dip, cheesy, 239

M

macaroni cheese, 223
mackerel
  with raw beetroot & walnut mezze, 199
  summer snack, 63
madeleines, 340
Mama's meringues, 260
mango
  ceviche cocktail, 138
  jelly, 257
  paradise pavlova, 329
marinade for steak, 118
marmalade, 371–372
marshmallow crispies, 20
martinis, chocolate & chilli, 96
mashed potatoes, 357–358
mayonnaise, 368
McEvedy's Lip Service, 125
meat, testing for doneness, 124–125
melanzane parmigiana, 52
meringues, 260
millionaire's shortbread, 40
minestrone, 180
miso soup, 199
moules marinière, 100–101
mousse, 15-minute chocolate, 337
Mrs Johnson's cheese pudding, 235

mushrooms
  soup additions, 188
  soup with meaning, 171
  Tabernacle mushrooms, 60
mussels
  moules marinière, 100–101
  mussel soup, 101
  Thai seafood curry, 94–95

N

never-fail Victoria sponge, 26
noodles
  Bootsie's chicken noodle soup, 187
  not Pot Noodle, 55
  pea & peanut noodle salad, 76
  veggie noodle stir-fry, 76
nougat-marshmallow frosting, 33
nut roast, 281

O

oats
  apples baked with oats & stem ginger,
    248
  Irish Kate's oaty soda bread, 34
  Samson & Delilah flapjacks, 21
oaty soda bread, 34
omelette, 353
onglet, pan-seared, 120
onions
  alternative roast med veg, 364
  beefed-up French onion soup, 178
  butternut, red onion & goats' cheese
    tart, 151–152
  toad-in-the-hole with cidery onions,
    220–222
orange & caraway roast parsnips, 365
oranges
  citrus drizzle, 33
  Granny Annie's dark chunky
    marmalade, 371–372
other must-know stuffing, 319

P

panacea for the poorly, 184
pan-Asian dressing, 367
pancakes, 37–38
pancetta
  bacon & egg tart, 154
  black bean & bacon soup, 163
  cardiac carbonara, 128
  ribollita, 183

soup additions, 188
pan-seared onglet, 120
papaya: paradise pavlova, 329
parsnips: orange & caraway roast parsnips, 365
partridge: raised game pie, 321–323
passionate soufflés, 105
passion fruit
    paradise pavlova, 329
    passionate soufflés, 105
pasta
    bolognese sauce, 211
    Bootsie's chicken noodle soup, 187
    cardiac carbonara, 128
    lasagne as you like it, 212
    macaroni cheese, 223
    minestrone, 180
    penne with potatoes & pesto, 202
    spaghetti & meatballs, 225
    spaghetti with chilli, parsley & garlic, 129
    Susi's fennelly sausage, 157
    see also noodles
pastry
    choux, 293–294
    hot-water pastry for raised pies, 321
    shortcrust, 370
    sweet, 370
pâté: pink parfait and port jelly, 143
pavlova for all seasons, 328–329
pea & peanut noodle salad, 76
peanutty millionaire's shortbread, 40
pearl barley: lamb, prune & pearl barley casserole, 205
pears
    pear, Parma ham & pecorino salad, 140
    pork chop with lentils, pears & ginger, 82–84
    tarte tatin, 326
peas
    pork, cashew & sugar snap stir-fry, 226
    very green spinach & pea soup, 175
penne with potatoes & pesto, 202
peppermint creams, 14
peppers
    gratin Provençal, 364–365
    Saracen stuffed, 363–364
pesto, 368
    penne with potatoes & pesto, 202
pies
    key lime, 346

the lighter side of chicken, 215
    raised game, 321–323
    shepherd's, 233–234
    sweet potato & marshmallow, 308
pig Holstein, 111–112
pig melba, 62
pimped-up beans, 63
pineapple with chilli & rum, 331
pink parfait and port jelly, 143
pizza dough, 39
plum jam, 371
poached eggs, 353
pommes boulangère, 355
popcorn tinsel, 313
pork
    cashew & sugar snap stir-fry, 226
    chop with lentils, pears & ginger, 82–84
    pig Holstein, 111–112
    roast with crackling, 266–269
    slightly porky lentil herb salad, 84
    testing for cooking level, 125
    Vietnamese pot-bellied pig with pickled veg, 282–284
porridge, 207
port jelly, 143
potatoes
    all-day Spanish tortilla, 86
    best jackets, 355
    bubble & squeak, 355–356
    cheesy lucky dip, 239
    chips, 358
    chow-down clam chowder, 168
    dauphinois, 356
    'Festival of Light' Latkes, 310–311
    hangover eggs, 51
    leaf-free grilled tuna niçoise, 81
    leek & potato soup, 176
    penne with potatoes & pesto, 202
    poached trout with warm potato salad & artichoke crisps, 146
    pommes boulangère, 355
    roasties, 356–357
    rosemary oven crunchies, 357
    salmon & leek fishcakes, 237–238
    shepherd's pie, 233–234
    spot-on mash, 357–358
    Vichyssoise, 176
poussins, spatchcock with sweet chilli & yoghurt marinade, 131
prawns
    lemongrass prawn kebab, 70

prawn & avocado wrap, 71
spring prawn dumplings and chilli dipping sauce, 145
Thai seafood curry, 94–95
profiteroles for the people, 293–294
prunes, lamb, prune & pearl barley casserole, 205
puddings
    15-minute chocolate mousse, 337
    apple snow, 13
    apples, baked with oats & stem ginger, 248
    Auntie Jam's lemony lattice treacle tart, 242
    blackberry & apple crumble, 246
    brioche bread & butter pudding, 245
    burnt Camp rice pudding, 258
    crème caramel, 335
    croquembouche, 295
    crumbles, 246
    frangipane fruit tarts, 348–351
    grilled pineapple with chilli & rum, 331
    key lime pie, 346
    passionate soufflés, 105
    pavlova for all seasons, 328–329
    pear tarte tatin, 326
    profiteroles for the people, 293–294
    Sussex pond pudding, 255–256
    unashamedly 70s chocolate roulade, 343–344
pumpkin & coconut curry, 304
Puy lentil & herb salad, 59

Q
quail's eggs
    boiled, 353
    chorizo with quail's eggs, 135
quesadillas, 64

R
raised game pie, 321–323
raspberries
    British summertime berry pavlova, 329
    frangipane tarts, 348–351
    jam, 370–371
red cabbage, spiced winter braised, 359–360
red lentil dhal, 56
rhubarb and pistachio frangipane tarts, 348–351
ribollita, 183

rice
    chickpea pilaf, 74
    cooking method, 358
    crab & chilli risotto, 149
    egg-fried rice with 'everlasting' veg, 46
    kedgeree, 216
    risotto primavera, 150
    Saracen stuffed peppers, 363–364
    Turkish yoghurt soup, 167
Rice Krispies, marshmallow crispies, 20
rice pudding, 258
richest chocolate cake in the world,
    332–334
risotto
    crab & chilli, 149
    primavera, 150
roast tomato soup with salsa picante, 174
roasties, 356–357
rosemary apple sauce, 269
rosemary oven crunchies, 357

S

saffron cake, 252
salads
    beetroot, parsley & sherry vinegar,
      362–363
    beetroot, salmon & couscous, 80
    bistro, 126
    Caesar, 367
    Lebanese chicken, 75
    lentil herb, 84
    pea & peanut noodle, 76
    pear, Parma ham & pecorino, 140
    Puy lentil & herb, 59
    salad with integrity & value, 200
    slow-roast tomato & goats' cheese, 363
    spicy tuna, 81
    summer slaw, 359
    tuna niçoise, 81
    warm potato salad with poached trout,
      146
salmon
    beetroot, salmon & couscous salad, 80
    with couscous & courgettes, 79
    salmon & leek fishcakes, 237–238
salsa picante, 174
salsa verde, 368
Samson & Delilah Flapjacks, 21
sandwiches
    chicken BLT sub, 71
    lamb, yoghurt & herb pitta, 71

    prawn & avocado wrap, 71
Saracen stuffed peppers, 363–364
sauces
    15-minute tomato, 369
    basic white, 369
    Béarnaise, 93
    béchamel, 369
    bread, 276
    cheese, 369
    chilli dipping sauce, 145
    cranberry, 309
    gravy, 273
    Hollandaise, 92–93
    horseradish, 271
    mayonnaise, 368
    pesto, 368
    rosemary apple sauce, 269
    salsa picante, 174
    salsa verde, 368
sausages
    Chinese sausage rolls, 29
    Susi's fennelly sausage pasta, 157
    toad-in-the-hole with cidery onions,
      220–222
scallops
    ceviche cocktail, 138
    Thai seafood curry, 94–95
scones, 27
scrambled eggs, 354
sea bass
    baked in herbs and salt, 296
    ceviche cocktail, 138
    with lentils & salsa verde, 115
    Thai seafood curry, 94–95
seafood
    ceviche cocktail, 138
    chow-down clam chowder, 168
    crab & chilli risotto, 149
    hangovers, 51
    lemongrass prawn kebab, 70
    moules marinière, 100–101
    prawn & avocado wrap, 71
    seared squid with harissa, 116
    spring prawn dumplings and chilli
      dipping sauce, 145
    Thai curry, 94–95
sesame spring greens, 359
shepherd's pie, 233–234
shortbread, peanutty millionaire's, 40
shortcrust pastry, 370
sirloin, griddled, 120

slow-roast tomatoes, 363
smoked haddock, coronation kedgeree, 216
smoky beans, 230
snacks
    cheese columns, 17
    chorizo with quail's eggs, 135
    dried bananas, 374
    glittery popcorn tinsel, 313
soda bread, 34
soft-boiled eggs, 353
soufflés, passion fruit, 105
soups
    beefed-up french onion, 178
    black bean & bacon, 163
    chicken noodle, 187
    chow-down clam chowder, 168
    Doctor's orders stracciatella, 186
    extra additions, 188
    fennel, 172
    green/brown lentil & bacon, 58
    Jerusalem artichoke, 177
    leek & potato, 176
    minestrone, 180
    more than miso soup, 199
    mushroom with meaning, 171
    mussel, 101
    panacea for the poorly, 184
    ribollita, 183
    roast tomato with salsa picante, 174
    Sunday lunch soup (from a roast
      dinner), 277
    Thai dragon juice, 184
    Turkish yoghurt, 167
    very green spinach & pea soup, 175
    white bean & rosemary, 165
spaghetti
    with chilli, parsley & garlic, 129
    and meatballs, 225
Spanish tortilla, 86
spatchcock poussins with sweet chilli &
    yoghurt marinade, 131
spinach
    garlic sautéed, 366
    very green spinach & pea soup, 175
spot-on mash, 357–358
spring greens, flash-fried with sesame, 359
spring prawn dumplings and chilli dipping
    sauce, 145
squashed fly scones, 27
squid
    seared with harissa, 116

Thai seafood curry, 94–95
stained glass window biscuits, 312
Stateside our Side, 305–309
steak
  chateaubriand with red wine sauce, 123
  marinade, 118
  pan-seared onglet, 120
  preparation tips, 118–119
  sirloin, griddled, 120
  testing, 124–125
steamed bream, 108
steamy asparagus, loving Hollandaise,
  92–93
stock
  chicken, 372–373
  fish, 373
  veg, 373
stracciatella, 186
strawberries: British summertime berry
  pavlova, 329
stuffings
  golden breadcrumb & herb stuffing, 318
  the other must-know stuffing, 319
summer slaw, 359
summer snack, 63
Sunday lunch soup (from a roast dinner),
  277
Susi's fennelly sausage pasta, 157
Susi's universal slow-roast tomatoes, 363
Sussex pond pudding, 255–256
sweet pastry, 370
sweet potato & marshmallow pie, 308
sweetcorn, cheesy barbecue corn on the
  cob, 231
sweets
  Armagnac truffles, 345
  gingerbread families, 22
  peppermint creams, 14
  stained glass window biscuits, 312

T

Tabernacle mushrooms, 60
tarts
  Auntie Jam's lemony lattice treacle,
    242
  bacon & egg, 154
  butternut, red onion & goats' cheese,
    151–152
  frangipane fruit, 348–351
  jam, 24
  lemon curd, 24

pear tarte tatin, 326
tea, a decent cuppa, 374
Thai dragon juice, 184
Thai seafood curry, 94–95
Thanksgiving Dinner, 305–309
toad-in-the-hole with cidery onions,
  220–222
toast toppers, 60–63
tomatoes
  15-minute sauce, 369
  cheesy lucky dip, 239
  chicken BLT sub, 71
  gratin Provençal, 364–365
  roast tomato soup with salsa picante,
    174
  slow-roast tomato & goats' cheese
    salad, 363
  Susi's universal slow-roast tomatoes,
    363
tortillas (bread)
  flat-pack cooking the Mexican way, 64
  prawn & avocado wrap, 71
tortillas (crisps), avocado & black bean
  salsa, 137
tortillas (eggs), All-day Spanish tortilla, 86
treacle tart, 242
trifle, 251
trout, poached, with warm potato salad &
  artichoke crisps, 146
tuna
  Chicago chilli tuna melt, 62
  niçoise, 81
  spicy tuna salad, 81
turkey, roast, 305–306
Turkish yoghurt soup, 167

U

unashamedly 70s chocolate roulade,
  343–344

V

vanilla, 43
vanilla buttercream, 32
veal Holstein, 111–112
Veale family drunken grape pavlova, 328
veg stock, 373
vegetables
  alternative roast med veg, 364
  blanching, 366
  Christmas root purée, 317
  gratin Provençal, 364–365

more than miso soup, 199
  panacea for the poorly, 184
  risotto primavera, 150
  veggie noodle stir-fry, 76
  Vietnamese pickled veg, 282
  see also salads; specific vegetables
venison: raised game pie, 321–323
very green spinach & pea soup, 175
Vichyssoise, 176
Victoria sponge, 26
Vietnamese pot-bellied pig with pickled
  veg, 282–284
vinaigrette, globe artichokes, 361
vodka, chocolate & chilli martinis, 96

W

walnuts: beetroot & walnut mezze, 363
Wellington for Waterloo, 298–300
white bean & rosemary soup, 165
white sauce, 369
winter braised red cabbage, 359–360

Y

yeast, 43
yoghurt soup, 167
Yorkshire pudding, 271–272
  toad-in-the-hole with cidery onions,
    220–222

Allegra McEvedy

Described by the *Independent* as 'a caterer with a conscience', Allegra McEvedy lives and works by the philosophy that there are more ways for a chef to make a difference than by winning Michelin stars, and that good food should be available to everybody.

Allegra has been cooking professionally for 20 years, working her way through a clutch of London's best restaurants including the River Café and The Groucho Club, as well as spending eighteen months cooking for several iconic American restaurants. Her US adventures included running the kitchen at Robert De Niro's New York restaurant, *Tribeca Grill*, and catering for an exclusive Democratic Party fundraiser, which involved personally cooking for President Clinton.

In 2004, Allegra co-founded LEON, the award-winning, healthy, fast food restaurant group.

She has many TV and radio credits to her name, including co-presenting BBC's *Economy Gastronomy* and fronting *Allegra's Turkish Delights* for the Good Food Channel.

Allegra is a patron of the Fairtrade Foundation, a Fellow of the RSA (The Royal Society for the encouragement of Arts, Manufactures and Commerce) and is a spokesperson for Compassion in World Farming. She is also patron of The Food Chain (a charity that delivers hot meals to people with HIV and AIDS), as well as the Notting Hill Farmers' Market and the London Gay Symphony Orchestra. In 2008, she was awarded an MBE for services to the hospitality industry, with the citation of promoting healthier eating and ethical sourcing in the UK.

Allegra lives in West London with her daughter. This is her sixth (and biggest) book.

Acknowledgements

This was a book I not only wanted to write, but needed to, in order to put right the great wrongness of my mum's lost recipe book and set Delilah up for life. There are some folks to whom I'm eternally grateful, and indeed couldn't have done it without:

To my friend and agent, Rosemary Scoular, who believed in this book from its embryonic stage, as well as understanding its importance to me.

To Jenny Heller, a surprising soulmate, for getting it, getting me, and truly making it happen in the most generous of ways.

To my amazing co-cooks, Kate and Deniz: from the cheese straw Parthenon in September and the bird tree Christmas, right through the full-on shoot in February: you ladies stayed with me all the way. My thanks to you is just Too Big (and Kate, for the second time in two books, our food helped grow a beautiful baby ... welcome little Ciarán!)

Also to Dandan, our fourth musketeer in the kitchen, not only for the plate-propping but whose energy was priceless just as we were losing the will.

To Ione Walder at Quercus, for her calm navigation and cool collectiveness throughout: you brought this whole thing together.

To David Eldridge and Holly Giblin at Two Associates, who translated my messy thoughts into beautiful design with humour and soul.

To Chris Terry, lens-meister extraordinaire, who with his trusted Danny brought light and joy to the recipes, and most importantly made them real.

To Imogen, the gentlest, firmest of copy editors, for treading lightly on my sensitivities but firmly on my stubbornness.

To Emma Callery, for her excellent proofreading and for seemingly enjoying it too.

Also at Quercus, thanks to Bethan and Caroline for their incessant puppy-like positivity about my rather poor social media skills, and to Nick Clark, Paul Oakley, Ben Brock, Barry Baker, and everyone in Sales, Marketing and Publicity.

Supplier-wise, I'm lucky to have Veronica and Miles at Chef's Connection – not only do they kindly keep serving me great produce, but they field my random questions too.

Tony at The Fishmonger's Kitchen is a chef's dream: knowledgeable, helpful and so smiley you always feel happier after he's delivered his wares.

Finally the team at Macken Brothers, led by Rodney, who always come up with the goods, whether birds, beef or butchery. They never fail to deliver, no matter how tricky my request.

On the home front, as ever my first thoughts are for my Ma & Pa. It's been a long time but you are still strong in my mind, and I love seeing you in my dreams. Holding you tight.

To Susi & Grammy, for the more tangible love and support.

To Floss and the kids (Alfie, Gracie, Ursie & Hal) for helping eat the vast amount of food we produced whilst testing the recipes – especially the rice pudding mistake.

To Tess, for doing the most important job of all – looking after D while I was putting this baby to bed.

To Nat, who made a late entrance into the timeline of the book, but has been so thoughtful and helpful in my life.

To Janine, for meeting me for a drink that night, and for all that is to come.

And lastly to Delilah: my focus, my life, my light ... and my constant distraction. Lub you.

Quercus Editions Ltd
55 Baker Street
7th Floor, South Block
London
W1U 8EW

First published in 2013

A catalogue record of this book is available from the
British Library

ISBN 978 1 78206 287 5

Printed and bound in China

10 9 8 7 6 5 4 3 2 1

Publishing Director: Jenny Heller
Editor: Ione Walder
Design and illustration: Two Associates
Food styling: Allegra McEvedy, Kate McCullough
and Deniz Safa
Copy-editing: Imogen Fortes

Note on ingredients:
All recipes were tested using medium eggs.
Use free-range wherever possible, and ideally free-range
chicken too. Apart from poultry, pigs are the only other
animal that are intensively farmed in this country, and
we love pigs, so please try and buy higher welfare pork.
All sugar, coffee, tea, chocolate, bananas, nuts, spices etc.
should be Fairtrade where possible.